EUROPE

ca. 1,800,000 B.C.E. *Homo erectus* appears

ca. 450,000–100,000 B.C.E. Lower Paleolithic Period, or Old Stone Age; stone tools appear in Europe

ca. 130,000 B.C.E. Neanderthal peoples reach Europe

ca. 100,000–40,000 B.C.E. Middle Paleolithic Period

ca. 40,000–35,000 B.C.E. Modern *Homo sapiens* (Cro-Magnon peoples) migrate into Europe from Africa; beginning of Upper Paleolithic Period

ca. 30,000–26,000 B.C.E. Last signs of Neanderthals in Europe

ca. 17,000 B.C.E. Cave paintings at Lascaux, France

ca. 13,000 B.C.E. Cave paintings at Altamira, Spain

ca. 12,000–8000 B.C.E. End of last Ice Age; glaciers over Scandinavia begin to melt

ca. 10,000 B.C.E. Bow and arrow appear

ca. 10,000–6000 B.C.E. Mesolithic Period, Middle Stone Age; agriculture introduced

ca. 6000–5000 B.C.E. Neolithic Period, or New Stone Age, begins for southern Europe with introduction of agriculture

ca. 4500 B.C.E. Agriculture spreads through central Europe

ca. 3300 B.C.E. "Iceman freezes in Italian Alps

ca. 3000 B.C.E. Bronze Age; Minoan civilization begin

ca. 3,000–2,000 B.C.E. Indo-European tribes settle throughout Europe

ca. 1900 B.C.E. Building begins on Stonehenge, England

ca. 1500 B.C.E. Volcano destroys island of Thera; end of Minoan civilization

ca. 1400 B.C.E. Mycenaens replace Minoans as major political force in Aegean

ca. 1100 B.C.E. Dorians topple Mycenaens

ca. 1000 B.C.E. Bronze Age ends

ca. 900–750 B.C.E. Homer composes Greek epics *Iliad* and *Odyssey*

ca. 753 B.C.E. Traditional founding of Rome by Romulus and Remus

ASIA AND THE PACIFIC

ca. 1,700,000 B.C.E. *Homo erectus* in Asia

ca. 500,000–250,000 B.C.E. Appearance of Beijing Man, *Homo erectus* specimen

ca. 70,000–20,000 B.C.E. Modern *Homo sapiens* appear in Asia

ca. 50,000–40,000 B.C.E. *Homo sapiens* migrate to Australia

ca. 30,000–20,000 B.C.E. Ancestors of the Australian aborigines emerge

ca. 20,000 B.C.E. Earliest evidence of agriculture in region

ca. 10,000 B.C.E. Land bridges disappear triggered by end of ice age

ca. 10,000–300 B.C.E. Joman hunting and gathering culture inhabits Japan

ca. 8500–6000 B.C.E. Millet farming in northern China; settlements in Korea, Vietnam, and Thailand

ca. 4500 B.C.E. Millet farming in India

ca. 1766–1122/1027 B.C.E. Beginning of recorded Chinese history and government

ca. 1800–1000 B.C.E. The *Rig, Sama,* and *Yajur Vedas* composed

ca. 1600–600 B.C.E. Aryan warriors invade India; Aryan and Indian cultures mix to produce foundations of Hindu religious beliefs and caste system

ca. 1122/1027–403 B.C.E. Zhou Dynasty established; Confucianism is spread

ca. 1000 B.C.E. Millet farming in Japan

ca. 1000–600 B.C.E. Irrigation in Vietnam

ca. 700 B.C.E. Linear Chinese script

ca. 600–200 B.C.E. *Upanishads,* religious epics, composed in India

ca. 500 B.C.E. Confucian philosophical tradition and Daoist religion evolve

ca. 444 B.C.E. Chinese develop accurate calendar based on 365.5-day year

ca. 400 B.C.E. Beginning of construction of Great Wall

ca. 400 B.C.E. The *Arthasastra,* book of advice for rulers, written in India

ca. 400–180 B.C.E. Mauryan clan rule India

AMERICAS

ca. 40,000–35,000 B.C.E. Possibly earliest settlement by humans in Americas

ca. 23,000–20,000 B.C.E. Earliest ice-free passage between glaciers

ca. 13,000 B.C.E. Paleo-Indians cross landmass from Asia into Alaska and south

ca. 10,000–8000 B.C.E. Clovis people arrive in Southwest; domestication of maize

ca. 8000–6000 B.C.E. Spread of agriculture

ca. 6000–5000 B.C.E. Start of first stage of Anasazi culture; domestication of potato

ca. 3114 B.C.E. Date Maya assigned to beginning of current cycle of creation

ca. 3000 B.C.E. People from coastal Peru dig first irrigation channels in Americas

ca. 2600 B.C.E. Earliest evidence of Mayan culture in central America

ca. 2000 B.C.E.–C.E. 250 Mayan Preclassic Period

ca. 1500 B.C.E. Olmec civilization flourishes in Mexico

ca. 1200 B.C.E. Olmec people develop first written language in Americas

ca. 700 B.C.E. Writing among Maya

ca. 600 B.C.E. Adena culture thrives

ca. 400 B.C.E. Earliest known carved stone calendar, by Maya; Olmec culture declines

ca. 300 B.C.E. Pioneer Period of Hohokam culture begins

ca. 250 B.C.E. Mayan script appears

ca. C.E. 250–900 Classic Period of Maya

ca. C.E. 550–900 Stable Colonial Period of Hohokam culture

ca. C.E. 600 Mayan city of Tikal is largest city in Mesoamerica

ca. C.E. 700–900 Pueblo I Period; Anasazi build multilevel houses and first kivas

ca. C.E. 899 City of Tikal abandoned

ca. C.E. 900 Mayan cities, except those in Yucatán Peninsula, abandoned; culture replaced by Toltecs by C.E. 1100

ca. C.E. 900–1200 Sedentary Period of Hohokam culture reaches peak; build hundreds of miles of irrigation canals

THE ANCIENT WORLD

CIVILIZATIONS OF

ASIA AND THE PACIFIC

Volume 5

Set Contents

The Ancient World

Civilizations of

Asia and the Pacific

Volume 5

GENERAL EDITOR
Sarolta Takács, Ph.D.
Rutgers University

CONSULTING EDITOR
Eric Cline, Ph.D.
The George Washington University

SHARPE REFERENCE
an imprint of M. E. Sharpe, Inc.

DEVELOPED, DESIGNED, AND PRODUCED BY DWJ BOOKS LLC
Principal Author: Kenneth R. Hall

SHARPE REFERENCE

Sharpe Reference is an imprint of M.E. Sharpe, Inc.

M.E. Sharpe, Inc.
80 Business Park Drive
Armonk, NY 10504

Library of Congress Cataloging-in-Publication Data
The ancient world / Sarolta Takács, general editor; Eric Cline, consulting editor.
    p.cm.
Includes bibliographical references and index.
ISBN 978-0-7656-8082-2 (set : alk. paper)
1. Civilization, Ancient--Encyclopedias. 2. History, Ancient--Encyclopedias.
I. Takács, Sarolta A. II. Cline, Eric H.
CB311.A535 2007
930.103--dc22   2006101384

Printed and bound in Malaysia
The paper used in this publication meets the minimum
requirements of American National Standard for Information Sciences—Permanence of Paper for
Printed Library Materials,
ANSI Z 39.48.1984

TI (c) 10 9 8 7 6 5 4 3 2 1

All images provided by Getty Images and the following:
background image: Colin Samuels/Photonica
inset images (left to right):Harvey Lloyd/Taxi/Getty Images; Dennie Cody/Taxi; Digital Vision; Demetrio
Carrasco/Dorling Kindersley; Sylvain Grandadam/Stone

Contents

List of Illustrations

Photos

Topic Finder

Preface

Studying the world's history is like being an explorer who travels across centuries to unfamiliar lands. The traveler encounters ancient cultures and civilizations and, above all, has countless opportunities to examine both what was thought to be familiar and what was completely unknown.

The history of the ancient world, much like that of the modern era, is a series of interactions played out by familiar and unfamiliar characters upon a stage of equally diverse geography. Knowing how these interactions occurred and evolved, and how, at times, they were obstructed, is crucial to both the study of the past and an understanding of the present, in terms of both progress and conflict. The five volumes of *The Ancient World: Civilizations of Africa, Europe, the Americas, the Near East and South-west Asia,* and *Asia and the Pacific* help readers step back in time, making familiar what was unknown.

The way we interact with others today—learning a world language and exploring another culture, for example—is not very different from how people in the ancient world interacted with each other. Geographical characteristics, however, played a much more dramatic role in governing the interactions among ancient peoples than they do in interactions among modern ones.

Humans have been on the move from the beginning. Paths they have taken and other peoples they have encountered have always been functions of the geographical opportunities or hindrances they have faced. From Africa, the first place where humans lived, populations began to migrate north into Europe and throughout Asia as the glaciers of the last Ice Age receded. In the South Pacific, people seeking fertile hunting and fishing grounds sailed from one island to another centuries before open sea travel was thought possible in the West. As a result of the Ice Age, a land bridge, known as Beringia, connected Eastern Siberia, Asia, and North America, a connection that the Bering Sea now covers. Beginning around 13,000 B.C.E. or even earlier, humans called Paleo-Indians, in search of food, crossed from Asia into what is now Alaska and from there moved farther south.

While populations spread across the globe at an early time, their growth was limited by a reliance on hunting and foraging for subsistence. In order for large civilizations to develop, humans had to learn how to manipulate their environment; the cultivation of crops became a necessity for survival. The earliest evidence of crop cultivation appeared in Jericho (an oasis in the Jordan Valley) around 8,000 years ago. From there, agriculture spread in all directions, giving rise to the greatest of the early civilizations, those of Egypt and Mesopotamia. These kingdoms rose along what is known as the Fertile Crescent, a region of rivers, oases, and arable coastland that stretches in a curve north from the Persian Gulf, across the northern reaches of modern-day Iraq, and south along the Levantine coast into the Nile Delta region of northern Egypt.

Although different civilizations have been, and continue to be, separated by distance and by variation in climate and topography, not to mention differences in languages, traditions, and belief systems, some elements of one culture's intellectual history closely resemble those elements in other cultures. The creation and flood narratives of the Old Testament, for example, exist alongside similar tales in the ancient cultures of the Middle East, the Mediterranean region, and Africa. Ancient stories about the creation of the world, genealogy, agricultural practices, and morality have been found to bear striking similarities all over the globe among groups of people who had little, if any, possibility of interacting.

With countless movements and human interactions obscured by time, distance, and varying perspectives, surveying the terrain of the ancient world may seem intimidating. As your guide, the volumes of this series provide a road map of the past. *The Ancient World* allows you to travel back in time to examine the origins of human history, how the environment shaped historical development, and how civilizations developed.

Articles are arranged alphabetically, and sidebar features expand the coverage: "Turning Points" discuss topics such as inventions that have propelled civilization forward; "Great Lives" reveal individuals whose extraordinary deeds shaped a people's history and culture; "Links in Time" connect the past to the present or one period to another; "Links to Place" draw some startling parallels in far-flung places; and "Ancient Weapons" reveal amazing early technology. May this journey offer you not only facts and data but also a deeper appreciation of the past and an understanding of its powerful connection to the present.

Sarolta A. Takács

Ancient Asia and the Pacific Basin: More Than the Sum of Its Parts

Early Asian civilizations developed through a combination of human migrations, local innovations, and the adaptation of customs and beliefs from more advanced societies. The initial spread of civilization in Asia and the Pacific Basin resulted from migrations of early humanoids from Asia to Southeast Asia to Australia in roughly 55,000 B.C.E., followed by another wave of aboriginal settlers from Asia some 35,000 years later. Maritime travelers, originally based in south China, the Philippines, and Taiwan, settled the eastern Indonesian archipelago about 10,000 B.C.E. By about 1500 B.C.E., they began to migrate farther east to the Pacific Islands.

Most ancient Asian and Pacific Island societies began as nomadic hunting-and-gathering and sojourning bands that eventually adopted a settled agricultural lifestyle. These early agricultural communities formed the foundations for more complex, centralized societies of Asia's major premodern powers, India and China. From India, Hindu and Buddhist civilization spread to Tang-era China (C.E. 618–907), where it blended with China's earlier Confucian tradition. This tradition in turn led to the development of imperial neo-Confucian traditions in neighboring Korea, Japan, and Vietnam.

PREHISTORY

The earliest evidence of human habitation in Asia is the remains of *Homo erectus,* a human ancestor who walked upright and used tools, including fire, dating to roughly one million years B.C.E. Discovered in China's southwestern Yunnan Province in the 1980s, these remains are some 100,000 years older than similar ones found on the Indonesian island of Java in 1891, which were dubbed "Java Man." By the time modern *Homo sapiens* appeared in Asia (between 70,000 and 20,000 B.C.E.), humans inhabited most of the continent.

In 70,000 B.C.E., Asia was joined to both North America and Australia by land bridges. By 40,000 B.C.E., early *Homo sapien* hunters and gatherers migrated from Southeast Asia to the Lake Mungo re-

gion in what is now southeastern Australia. Some 10,000 years later, the ancestors of Australia's aboriginal peoples migrated to the southern and eastern parts of the island continent. Ancestors of these early immigrants still inhabit the highlands of India, China, Taiwan, and Hokkaido Island in Japan. Between 15,000 and 10,000 B.C.E., northern Asian populations also traveled east to settle in what is now North America.

By 10,000 B.C.E., the land bridges had disappeared, covered by rising sea levels triggered by the end of the most recent Ice Age. Australia and the islands of the Pacific became isolated from the mainland and its surrounding islands, such as Japan, the Philippines, and Indonesia. As a result, the cultures of the two regions developed along significantly different lines. For example, while most mainland populations had adopted a settled agricultural lifestyle by 1000 B.C.E., Australian aborigines remained a hunting-and-gathering society until the arrival of European settlers in the late 1700s C.E.

THE LAND AND ITS PEOPLE

Asia is by far the world's largest continent, almost half again the size of Africa and larger than North and South America combined. Its great expanses consist of large swathes of fertile land broken by vast stretches of some of the world's most difficult and hostile terrain. China, for example, not only features productive coastal areas and the fertile valleys of the Yellow and Chang rivers but also the forbidding Gobi and Taklimakan deserts in the northern and western parts of the country.

Settled agricultural communities appeared in the river valleys of China and India before 4000 B.C.E., in Southeast Asia by 2000 B.C.E., and in Japan shortly after 1000 B.C.E. These early farming societies cultivated dry rice, or millet, as their staple grain. By around C.E. 1000, communities had switched to the cultivation of wet rice, originally developed in mainland Southeast Asia. These settled cultures eventually evolved into the continent's first centralized states: China's Shang dynasty (1766–

1122/1027 B.C.E.), the Mauryan kingdoms in India (ca. 400–180 B.C.E.), and the early Korean kingdoms sometimes referred to as "Old Choson" (late fourth century B.C.E.).

Nomadic and seminomadic peoples inhabited the peripheries of the settled civilizations, interacting with and often profoundly shaping those agricultural societies. Around 1600 B.C.E., seminomadic Aryan tribesmen from southern Russia's steppe grasslands entered India through the Hindu Kush mountain passes. The resulting mixture of Aryan and existing local Indian cultures produced both the Hindu faith, which predominates in India to this day, and India's caste system, a social hierarchy that separates classes by degrees of ritual purity. Social influence, however, traveled in both directions. In the thirteenth century C.E., the nomadic Mongols from the steppes of central Asia conquered virtually the entire continent except for India, Japan, and Southeast Asia. Mongol rulers, however, readily adapted to and often adopted the cultural and religious practices of the societies they conquered. Local culture changed the Mongols more than the Mongols changed local culture.

EARLY PEOPLES AND CIVILIZATIONS

Natural barriers such as seas and mountain ranges encouraged the evolution of distinct societies in the various regions of Asia and the Pacific. In time, many of these separate societies contacted one another, sharing beliefs and practices and creating elements of a common culture. The popularity of Buddhism in India, China, Japan, Korea, and Southeast Asia is one example of a local cultural practice that spread widely by social exchange. Other societies, such as the Australian aborigines and the Polynesians and Micronesians of the Pacific, developed unique cultures as a result of their isolation from mainland Asia.

China

In China, the Shang were the first in a series of imperial dynasties that oversaw the growth and consolidation of the Chinese state. The succeeding Zhou dynasty (1122/1027–221 B.C.E.) was a time of intellectual development. It was during this era that the philosopher Confucius spread his notions of the importance of orderly social behavior. Confucianism soon evolved into the guiding principle of Chinese secular political authority and administration.

Early Chinese history was marked by periods of stability broken by periods of disorder and chaos. In 403 B.C.E., the Zhou dynasty collapsed, leading to the so-called "Era of the Warring States," which ended in 222 B.C.E., when the Qin state emerged as the victor. Likewise, the fall of the Han dynasty (206 B.C.E.–C.E. 220) triggered 350 years of turmoil until the Sui dynasty (C.E. 581–618) reestablished imperial authority. Similar disruptions in central rule occurred again in the early 900s and in 1279, when the nomadic Mongols conquered China. The Ming restored ethnic Chinese rule in 1368, and China retained a traditional imperial structure until the early twentieth century.

India

Like China, India struggled with internal divisions and waves of invasion. By 600 B.C.E., several competing kingdoms had arisen in India, as had Buddhism, an alternative to the dominant Hindu religious tradition. The Mauryan kingdom, which emerged as north India's preeminent culture by 400 B.C.E., adopted Buddhism and its more inclusive social doctrines. The collapse of the Mauryan state about 180 B.C.E. was followed by a series of invasions from the northwest that continued until the early fourth century C.E. Among the attempted invaders was the Macedonian emperor Alexander III, the Great, who, in the 320s B.C.E., brought Greek culture to India's northwestern frontier but failed in his attempt to add India to his vast empire.

Alexander's death in 323 B.C.E. led to the collapse of his empire and a transitional period during which the Greek invaders competed for control over northwest India with the Asia-based Scythians and the Iran-based Parthians while numerous Indian rulers held authority over all the Gangetic plain. The Gupta Empire (ca. C.E. 320–550), claiming descent from earlier Mauryan rulers, finally restored central authority and reinstated Hindu social and religious practice in north India. The fall of the Gupta rulers was followed by a period of competition among small regional states in the north, which ended with the arrival of Islamic invaders in the second millennium C.E., leading to 500 years of Muslim rule over the north Indian heartland that was the home of Buddhism and Hinduism. South India was ruled by the Cera, Cola, Pandya, and Pallaum original Hindu dynasties from C.E. 600 and was never subject to Muslim rule.

Southeast Asia and Japan

Centralized kingdoms developed much later in Japan and Southeast Asia. In Japan, the Yamato emerged about C.E. 400 as the most powerful of a group of local clans and consolidated their power into imperial rule. Power shifted among competing clans until the late twelfth century, when imperial authority collapsed. After this time, a series of military leaders, known as *shoguns,* wielded power in Japan, exercising their authority over a network of regional clans. This system led to frequent struggles between competing clans for control of the shogunate. Although torn by internal rivalry and infighting, Japan avoided invasion despite several attempts by Chinese Mongol emperors in the thirteenth century. Nevertheless, Japan was receptive to outside cultural influences. Early Japanese society borrowed heavily from China, including the importation of Buddhist and Confucian ideas in the seventh century C.E.

In Southeast Asia, early regional Hindu kingdoms arose in what is now Cambodia in the mid-sixth century. Shortly after 800, King Jayavarman II began the process of assimilating these states into a Khmer Empire centered at Angkor. Thai armies conquered the Khmer Empire in 1431 after more than 100 years of periodic conflict. Vietnam was under periodic Chinese rule until 960, when the Ly state established the Buddhist-Confucian kingdom. This realm was the target of repeated Chinese annexation attempts thereafter.

Australia and the Pacific Islands

Because of their isolation, Australia and the Pacific islands developed along paths that were quite different from those in the remainder of Asia. The islands that comprised Micronesia and Polynesia developed a wide range of political organizations.

Some were ruled by a supreme chief; in others, a local chief shared power with heads of family clans; still others were ruled by a group of roughly equal confederated chiefs. In Australia, by contrast, no central government of any type emerged among the aboriginal population, which remained organized in small nomadic bands. Australia and the Pacific islands developed cultures unique from those of the mainland, remaining isolated from cultural influences such as Buddhism, Hinduism, and Confucianism.

ASIA IN TRANSITION

In the early fifteenth century C.E., the new Ming emperors, who had come to power in China in 1368, sent the admiral Zheng He and his fleet of Chinese battleships and troop transports to assert China's interests across the entire Indian Ocean (1405–1433). Zheng He eliminated pirates and promised military assistance, continuing Chinese support for local political regimes that guaranteed the regular flow of international products from the Middle East to China. Partly in response to the Ming initiatives, the fifteenth century in Asia witnessed substantial increases in trade volume, participants, and the diversity of traded commodities. Among these were Indian cotton and Chinese and Japanese silk; Chinese, Thai, and Vietnamese ceramics; and Indonesian spices. In this age, conversions to Islam increased, especially among the multiethnic populations who were based in a network of Indian Ocean ports and who became the most prominent among Indian Ocean traders. As Ming interest in being directly involved in Indian Ocean affairs diminished in the 1430s, the international trade re-centered in the Melaka international marketplace, which became the critical intermediary in East–West trade. There international traders exchanged Middle Eastern and Indian products for Southeast Asia's spices and China'a silks and porcelain. This prosperity attracted the attention of Europeans, who had previously had little direct contact with the Indian Ocean realm.

The European presence in Asia changed dramatically in the early sixteenth century, however. At that time, advances in shipbuilding and navigation (some, ironically, imported from Asia) enabled

European sailors to explore the open oceans, opening new routes to Asia. In 1498, Portuguese explorer Vasco de Gama became the first European to sail directly to India around the Cape of Good Hope at Africa's southern tip. Twelve years later, the Portuguese military established a trading port at Goa on India's southwestern coast.

Goa was only the first of many Asian regions to fall under European domination or outright control during the next 400 years. By 1900, all of India and most of Southeast Asia had become European colonial possessions. China, although nominally independent, was carved up into economic spheres of influence by leading European powers and the United States, and was politically powerless. Imperial Russia annexed large tracts of central Asia and Siberia, while Great Britain claimed the entire continent of Australia. The United States joined with European countries and Japan in gaining control over most of the Pacific islands as well. Japan and Siam (modern Thailand) remained the only independent states of note.

CONNECTIONS TO TODAY

Like many other former colonies around the world, most Asian nations regained their independence following World War II. However, these new states were shaped strongly by ideas of secularism and representative government, which had gained popularity in the West during the nineteenth and early twentieth centuries. Most of the new states shunned the close ties with religious orders that had characterized ancient Asian governments. In fact, in Communist states such as China, government was actively hostile not only to religious influence but also to traditional social organization. China's Communist rulers rejected the Confucian system that had been in place for more than 2,000 years and tried to replace it with nineteenth-century Marxist doctrines imported from Europe.

Despite these changes, ancient social and cultural beliefs and practices continue to influence the lives of many Asians today. For example, although India is a secular state, most Hindus still observe the caste system, which plays an important role in determining occupation and social status. Also, although Japan has embraced Western education, style, and technology more enthusiastically than any other Asian nation, its traditional customs are remarkably resistant to Western influence. For thousands of years, Asia's people have absorbed, adapted, and transformed outside influences—a process that continues throughout the region to this day.

FURTHER READING

Basham, A.L. *The Wonder That Was India.* New York: Grove Press, 1959.

Bellwood, Peter. *Conquest of the Pacific: The Prehistory of Southeast Asia and Oceana.* Oxford: Oxford University Press, 1979.

Ebrey, Patricia Buckley. *China: A Cultural, Social, and Political History.* Boston: Houghton Mifflin, 2006.

Lieberman, Victor. *Strange Parallels. Southeast Asia in a Global Context,* 800- 1830. Cambridge, UK: Cambridge University Press, 2003.

Roberts, J.M. *Prehistory and the First Civilizations.* New York: Oxford University Press, 2002.

Kenneth R. Hall

Map of Ancient Asia and the Pacific

The vast Central Asian plateau, centered on Mongolia, has served as a highway for commerce and conquest since ancient times. It formed the heart of the the famous Silk Road trade route that joined ancient Rome and Han China in the second century B.C.E. It was also home to nomadic warriors such as the Mongols, Aryans, and Huns, whose movements and invasions dramatically shaped the course of Asian history.

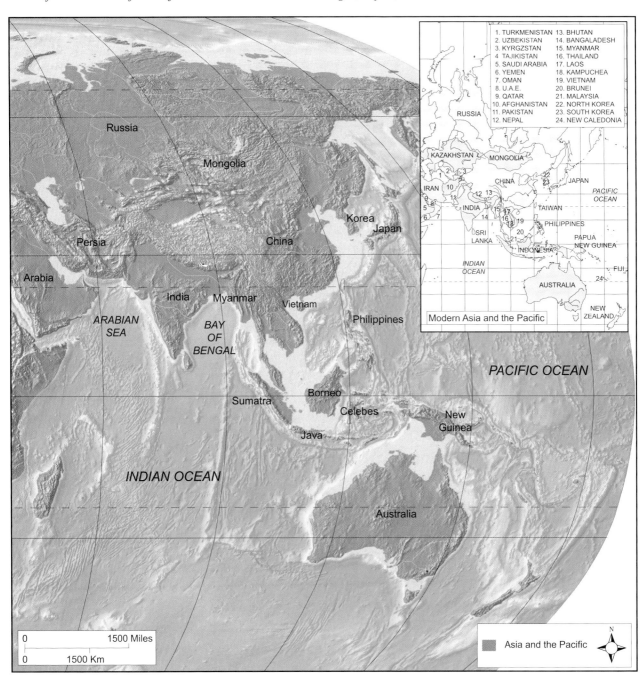

Modern Asia and the Pacific

1. TURKMENISTAN
2. UZBEKISTAN
3. KYRGZSTAN
4. TAJIKISTAN
5. SAUDI ARABIA
6. YEMEN
7. OMAN
8. U.A.E.
9. QATAR
10. AFGHANISTAN
11. PAKISTAN
12. NEPAL
13. BHUTAN
14. BANGALADESH
15. MYANMAR
16. THAILAND
17. LAOS
18. KAMPUCHEA
19. VIETNAM
20. BRUNEI
21. MALAYSIA
22. NORTH KOREA
23. SOUTH KOREA
24. NEW CALEDONIA

0   1500 Miles
0   1500 Km

Asia and the Pacific

Aboriginal Peoples

Hunting-and-gathering and simple agricultural cultures, which date back to 20,000 B.C.E. and whose modern descendants represent the last primitive inhabitants of the Indian Ocean and Asian Pacific basins. The origins of most aboriginal cultures are unclear, but those that have survived were pushed from fertile lands into less productive ones by migration and invasion. Small groups of these societies still live in rugged and less-accessible areas in a number of modern Asian and Pacific nations.

Original aboriginal societies were based on the family, usually in cooperation with other, neighboring families who together formed a tribal band. The group survived by a combination of small-scale agriculture, hunting, and gathering of wild grains and vegetables. Economic activity was seasonal, with hunting taking place around the schedule of planting and harvesting. Males typically were responsible for hunting and fishing, whereas females and children gathered fruits, grains, and vegetables from the surrounding countryside. The normal diet consisted of cultivated and wild grains (including rice), roots and tubers (tapioca and yams), beans, coconuts, fruits, and vegetables. The aboriginal peoples supplemented their diet with small game and domesticated animals including chicken and pigs.

Although they possessed a relatively simple material culture, aboriginal peoples did develop technology with which to exploit the environment. Agricultural implements used by aboriginal groups included digging tools made of deer horn, bone, wood, stone, and metals such as bronze, tin, and iron. Hunters often used spears or arrows coated with poison made from the roots and stalks of local plants. They also employed snake venom or the poisonous stingers or skin covering of fish such as the stingray. Many aboriginal shelters featured wood plank floors, some substantially elevated above the moist or frozen soil below, which offered protection against not only the elements but also predators such as snakes, insects, and wild animals.

Aboriginal religions were **animistic**, centered on the belief that spirit forces control the realm of nature and were the source of a society's well-being. Frequently, both men and women in aboriginal societies tattooed their bodies as a form of protection against possession by harmful natural spirits. Tattoos also served as marks of personal accomplishment and social status.

Today, aboriginal cultures still cling to a precarious existence in Asia. They include the inhabitants of Australia's interior desert region known as the Outback; Adavasi tribal populations in the mountainous regions of northeastern India such as Assam; the Ainu, who live in Japan's Hokkaido island frontier; the Xungen people of China's mountains and deserts; and assorted semi-isolated mountain and jungle dwellers scattered across Taiwan and Southeast Asia. These aboriginal communities remain distinct in many ways from the majority populations of their countries, such as in the use of languages that are not written but have rich oral traditions.

See also: Agriculture; Archeological Discoveries; Australia; Japan; Monsoons; Myths and Epics; Tools and Weapons.

FURTHER READING

Blusse, Leonard, and Natalie Everts, eds. *The Formosan Encounter: Notes on Formosa's Aboriginal Society.* 2 vols. Taipei: Shung Ye Museum of Formosan Aborigines, 2000.

Fitzhugh, W. *Ainu: Spirit of a Northern People.* Seattle: University of Washington Press, 2004.

Morrison, Kathleen D., and Laura L. Junker, eds. *Forager-Traders in South and Southeast Asia.* Cambridge, MA: Cambridge University Press, 2002.

Agriculture

The ready availability of productive land in premodern Asia, combined with the general underpopulation of the Asia-Pacific region before C.E. 1500, shaped the pattern of agricultural development there. As the result of natural catastrophes, climate change, or conflict with neighboring groups, Asians frequently moved from less fertile to more productive yet unoccupied areas.

The earliest evidence of settled agriculture in Asia dates to roughly 20,000 B.C.E. Millet, or dry rice, sorghum (grain-producing grasses), and other natural dry zone grains (wheat, barley, and rye) predate wet rice as the staple grains in the early densely settled river plains of northern India and China. Archeological evidence demonstrates the initial cultivation of millet in northern China around 8500 B.C.E. and its widespread cultivation by 5000 B.C.E.; people in India's Indus Valley were growing millet by 4500 B.C.E.; millet cultivation in Japan and Korea did not begin until 1000 B.C.E. Millet (dry rice) and *sawah* (wet rice) cultivation were incompatible. As sawah production spread from mainland Southeast Asia to southern China and then to other neighboring regions in the first millennium C.E., it replaced millet production wherever there was sufficient water and a favorable climate.

EARLY SHIFTING CULTIVATION

Humans initially cultivated millet in the Asian highlands in order to avoid the seasonal flooding in the lowland river basins. Asian farmers used what is commonly called "slash-and-burn," "shifting," or swidden ("burned field") cultivation. Swidden cultivation is a rotational system in which living vegetation is cut in early winter, dried during the dry months, and burned late in the dry season, and a crop of rice, corn, bananas, and a wide range of other vegetation is planted in the fertile ash. Early swidden farming used few agricultural tools. Planting usually involved making holes in the ground with pointed sticks and placing two or three seeds in each hole; the plow was not used. Crops often were harvested by hand, without the use of a blade. Although they did not need draft animals, most villagers kept dogs, chickens, and pigs. Nevertheless, most of their animal protein came from fish and wild game.

Swidden cultivation required shifting cultivation cycles because rain rapidly washed away the nutrients that were added to the soil in the initial burn off. After two harvests a field was allowed to lay fallow (unplanted) for at least 10 years in order to replenish the nutrients in the soil, after which the cycle was repeated. In about 50 years, declining soil productivity would force swidden cultivators to move elsewhere to clear and burn new highland forests. Then, perhaps after a 50- or 100-year interval, they might return to their original land, which by that time would be reforested and ready to clear once more.

The cultivation of dry rice, or millet, eventually gave way to wet-rice agriculture in the southern regions of ancient Asia that had plentiful seasonal rainfall. Wet rice was better suited to planting on hillside terraces, such as those shown in the photo above. (Keren Su/Lonely Planet Images/Getty Images)

Shifting cultivation of rice by small human bands was ideal for sloping highland areas with adequate drainage and little likelihood of flooding. It required little labor and produced a substantial food surplus relative to the size of the workforce. Slash-and-burn regions could usually produce a stable food supply, but local migration cycles, together with the relatively low yield per acre, limited highland population density to 20 to 30 persons per square mile (2.6 sq km) and made it difficult to pool significant surpluses.

The transition from upland shifting to lowland settled cultivation, which was well underway in India and China by 3000 B.C.E., may have been caused by population pressure. This move was supported by new technology such as improved tools, better water management, and a calendar, in use in China by 2637 B.C.E., which took advantage of seasonal

cultivation. In this initial phase of agricultural transformation, millet and other traditional grains were cultivated by settled and increasingly populous village societies, which were sustained by the rich alluvial, or sediment rich, soils on the plains of the Indus, Ganges, and Yellow rivers.

WET-RICE CULTIVATION

It is generally believed that wet-rice cultivation became common in Southeast Asia, central and southern China, coastal southern Asia, Sri Lanka, southern Japan, and southern Korea during the first millennium C.E. Initially, in Thailand, Cambodia, and Vietnam, wet-rice seeds were distributed at the beginning of the monsoon season on a ploughed floodplain that had been subdivided into small fields bordered and contained by elevated earth, a

Terraced Farming

Throughout the Asia-Pacific region, mountainous regions have been reshaped over the centuries into terraced pond fields, especially to grow wet rice. Terraced farming in upland regions of China, Southeast Asia, and elsewhere was a response to landscapes that had very little flat land for agriculture. It was also a practical response to Asia's heavy seasonal monsoon rains. Terraces protected naturally fertile lowlands from harsh flooding, stopped monsoon rainwater from running freely down the hillsides, and stored enough water to support successful wet-rice farming. Water from the upper terraces made its way, by the force of gravity, to each succeeding terrace level, in a carefully controlled flow from hilltops to the valleys below.

Regional rice-growing cycles created a regular cycle of planting and harvesting that shaped the calendar of human events. These annual cycles reinforced a conservative and group-oriented approach to social organization, marked by commitment to a central cultural authority, an emphasis on group welfare over the needs or desires of individuals, and a preference for cultural continuity over change.

Historians debate whether terraced agriculture, and irrigated wet-rice agriculture as a whole, required the efforts of a well-organized and hierarchical "hydraulic" society, and whether it contributed to the development of early centralized political systems. In a "hydraulic society," the great majority of individuals are subordinated politically and ritually to those who build and maintain the terraces, water canals, and storage tanks that comprise the water management system. In such a society, the needs of the individual are secondary to the welfare of the group. The social system reflects the natural hierarchical structure of terraced farming, with both water and power flowing from top to bottom.

practice called bunding. The rice matured after the annual flooding of monsoon-swelled rivers and lakes filled the terraced fields with water. The wet-rice crop grew quickly, needed little work, and was harvested after the floodwaters receded.

Other cultures of Asia adapted a more labor-intensive seeding method that was developed in the Champa regions of central and southern Vietnam in the first centuries C.E. In this method, farmers sowed seed in small flooded seedling beds before, rather than at the beginning of, the rainy season. While the seedlings took root, farmers and their families prepared nearby bunded fields, weeding and breaking up the soil with hoes until the monsoon rains came. Farmers then transplanted the seedlings by hand, leaving enough space between them for each plant to grow.

Both types of sawah cultivation systems depended on capturing the nutrient-rich dissolved matter in the annual floodwaters or irrigated water. Farmers therefore took special measures to minimize the loss of water through the soil. To the already rich layers of soil, farmers added fertilizer, such as water buffalo and duck excrement. They then used wooden and, later, metal-tipped plows to turn over the existing mulch, transforming the flooded soil into a creamy mud 12 to 20 inches (30.5 to 51 cm) deep. Using water buffaloes, they then ploughed the irrigated fields to make the land suitable for the reception of seeds and seedlings.

One limitation of sawah cultivation is that the soil becomes more acidic as it dries out. This reduces the soil's ability to retain nitrogen, which is vital to a maturing wet-rice crop. Farmers adapted to these conditions by developing a range of different rice varieties, from those with an 80-day growing period (for lands that were moist much of the year and allowed double and even triple harvests) to ones with a growing period as long as 270 days (for lands that had unpredictable annual rainfall).

Proper irrigation was another key to success in sawah cultivation. Bunded-field farmers generally made small canals to spread wet-season floodwater more evenly over their fields. In some areas, temporary channels and water wheels diverted water for gravity-fed irrigation. Farmers collected runoff water in large ponds for domestic use during the dry season; such ponds were especially associated with temples. In a few areas, such as China, Java, Cambodia, Vietnam, and Sri Lanka, ancient regional canal networks are still used today. Terracing, which involved the elaborate construction of level bunded fields on mountainsides, allowed productive wet-rice cultivation of otherwise marginally productive hills and mountains. Terrace farmers channeled rainy season water from highlands to lowlands by a network of dams and canals.

The seedling method gave higher yields per unit of land used but did not yield the highest amount of food based on the amount of work required. By either the broadcast or seedling method, a productive wet-rice farmer could normally expect an annual output of 20 to 25 bushels of grain per acre (20 to 25 bushels per 0.4 hectare). A field of two and one-half acres (one hectare) could support a household of approximately 10 to 20 people and still provide an additional surplus. In early times, one rice crop proved adequate to supply local needs. However, a second could be harvested with the available technology if the weather was good, irrigation and water storage facilities were available, and there were incentives to produce a surplus for external consumption.

To prevent cultivated fields from returning to the wild state, a grassland periphery was commonly maintained around cultivated fields. This served as a border against the forest as well as a buffer against enemies and wild animals. Settled agriculturalists also used fire to maintain the border between sawah and swidden zones of habitation. The old, taller grasses that burned were replaced by shorter, younger varieties that provided more nutritious grazing fodder for livestock.

AGRICULTURE AND EARLY CIVILIZATION

There were three food staples in the sawah regions of Asia: rice, fish, and coconut. Rice production was affected by periodic disease, rodents, and insects. Fish and coconut, however, were virtually free of pests and diseases. Properly prepared, rice and fish—the latter usually dried or fermented—could be stored for more than a year. Coconuts (the source of fruit, sugar, oil, and palm wine) could not be stored as long, but were available at three-month intervals.

Most people ate rice, whether dry or wet, in preference to other grains or starches. Reliance upon other staples was socially unacceptable, except during rice famines when sawah cultivators could normally turn to root crops (such as taro and tapioca, grown as supplemental crops in sawah areas) and yams (gathered from nearby forests or cultivated in rain-fed fields). Sago palms were another alternate source of starch. During the dry season, local populations grew a variety of vegetables, such as beans, tomatoes, and peppers, to supplement their normal rice diet. Early Asian rice cultivators also supplemented their diet by networking with highland hunters and gatherers, both to reduce the highlanders' inclination to raid their villages and to exchange their diverse agricultural produce for forest products (such as woods, bamboo, and lacquer) and meat.

Urbanization in the early sawah regions was the exception rather than the rule, despite its potential for high productivity. In part this was due to cultural preference, the geographical isolation of the productive regions, and the intensive labor demands of wet-rice cultivation.

Control or protection of access to water was an important issue, with social and political consequences. In regions where rainfall was plentiful, where there were multiple water sources useful for irrigation, or where there was no threat from outsiders (such as raids by hill populations and seminomads from the grassland steppes) there was little need or opportunity for a political elite to manage or dominate the water system. But, where there was a limited water source, or where there was a need to coordinate water management (such as building regional dike networks to contain and manage destructive seasonal flooding), political development was likely.

See also: Aboriginal Peoples; Angkor Wat; Archeological Discoveries; Australia; China; Culture and Traditions; India; Japan; Java; Korea; Micronesia; Monsoons; Myths and Epics; Society; Technology and Inventions; Tools and Weapons; Vietnam.

FURTHER READING

Bellwood, Peter S. *The First Farmers: The Origins of Agricultural Societies.* Malden, MA: Blackwell, 2005.

Lansing, J. Stephen. *Priests and Programmers: Technologies of Power in the Engineered Landscape of Bali.* Princeton, NJ: Princeton University Press, 1991.

Rawski, Evelyn S. *Agricultural Change and the Peasant Economy of South China.* Cambridge, MA: Harvard University Press, 1972.

Ancestor Worship *See* China; Culture and Traditions; Japan; Society.

Angkor Wat

Hindu temple complex that, along with the accompanying temples of Angkor, formed the ritual and political center of the Khmer kingdom of Angkor (c.e. 802–1432) in what is now Cambodia. These included a series of pyramidal commemoration temples (dating from the reign of Yasovarman I [r. 889–900], all of which recognize the royal patron deity Siva). The spectacular remains of these ancient temple complexes are located north of Cambodia's Tonle Sap, or Great Lake, and surrounded by the fertile wet-rice–producing heartland of the powerful Angkor realm.

Angkor Wat, the most renowned example of ancient Khmer architecture, honors Visnu, the Hindu deity of goodness and mercy. King Suryavarman II (r. 1113–ca. 1150) built the temple to commemorate his deified ancestors and proclaim his rule at the center of the universe. Angkor Wat was intended to be the earthly recreation of Mount Meru, the celestial home of the gods. Its five towers represent heavenly Mount Meru and the four surrounding mountain peaks.

Angkor Wat consists of five focal towers surrounded by a 660-foot-wide (200-m-wide) rectangular outer moat. The approach to the towers crosses a causeway over the moat and proceeds through two terraced courtyards, each framed by galleries covered in carved reliefs. The outer gallery wall carvings depict kings giving orders to their soldiers and courtiers, scenes from mythical Hindu epics and texts, and celestial women, or *apsaras.*

The Angkor Thom Bayon was a later Mahayana Buddhist ritual complex built by Jayavarman VII (r. 1181–ca. 1218), who restored the Angkor realm following a devastating 1177 invasion from the neighboring Champa kingdom in what is now central Vietnam. The Bayon Buddhist shrine was the sacred ritual center of Jayavarman's newly constructed Angkor Thom capital city that lay just to the north of the Angkor Wat ritual complex, which had been plundered and desecrated by the Chams several years before.

The entire Angkor Thom complex is surrounded by a high wall and is enclosed by a 330-foot-wide (100-m-wide) rectangular moat that is crossed by five causeways, each of which leads to a gate. The causeways are guarded by stone Cham and Khmer warriors who hold a snake, or *naga* (serpent spirit), rope. Together these represented the sacred connection between the secular world of humans and the celestial Angkor Thom temple complex: the warriors signify the world of humans and the snakes the world of the divine. Each of the gateways, as well as the three towers of the Bayon, bears four massive sculpted heads that face in each of the cardinal directions. The heads represent the realm's new patron deity, the *bodhisattva* (or saint) Avalokitesvara. According to local belief, this bodhisattva of compassion can plead humanity's case with the divine Lord Buddha or directly intervene on humankind's behalf.

North of the Bayon shrine, the Angkor Thom royal palace complex included older ancestral temples and royal residences, and a substantial parade

The ancient Hindu temple complex at Angkor Wat, in modern Cambodia, was built in the early twelfth century c.e. as the new ritual center. Angkor Wat was the ritual center of the powerful Khmer kingdom of Angkor (c.e. 802–1432).(Colin Samuels/Photonica/Getty Images)

ground that was framed on one side by the palace walls. One of the most impressive segments of these walls, at the base of the royal reviewing platform, is covered with life-sized reliefs of the royal elephant corps. Other segments contain larger-than-life depictions of mythical creatures, which, together with the Bayon's celestial Buddhist shrine, helped ensure the success of the renewed Angkor realm.

See also: Buddhism; Hinduism; Khmer Empire.

FURTHER READING

Coe, Michael D. *Angkor and the Khmer Civilization.* London: Thames and Hudson, 2005.

Ortner, Jon, Ian W. Mabbett, et al. *Angkor: Celestial Temples of the Khmer.* New York: Abbeville Press, 2002.

Archeological Discoveries

Archeological sites in Asia and the Pacific document the earliest appearance of human ancestors outside of Africa. They also shed light on the transition of hunting-and-gathering societies into settled agrarian communities and then their progression to becoming urban communities and temple centers.

HUMAN EVOLUTION

The earliest evidence of human habitation in Asia is the remains of *Homo erectus,* a human ancestor who walked upright and used tools including fire, dating to roughly one million years B.C.E. Discovered in China's southwestern Yunnan Province in the 1980s, these remains are some 100,000 years older than similar ones, dubbed "Java Man," that were found on the Indonesian island of Java in 1891. At that time this was the earliest find of *Homo erectus* remains beyond Africa.

Other discoveries during the twentieth century confirmed that the *Homo erectus* species was widespread in Asia by 500,000 B.C.E. This was the date of "Beijing Man," discovered near Beijing, China, in 1921, which was reconfirmed by a find near Xian, China, in the 1990s, dating to about 600,000 B.C.E. The major technological advance by *Homo erectus* over time was the fashioning of handheld axes that had a cutting edge rather than the earlier axes with a blunt edge, which were likely used for chopping, scraping, and digging.

Between approximately 70,000 and 20,000 B.C.E., Asia's *Homo erectus* inhabitants evolved into modern *Homo sapiens*. Most of what is known about Asia's early *Homo sapiens* comes from the study of remains discovered in China and Australia. The earliest preaboriginal populations of *Homo sapiens,* described as "robust heavy boned humans" are found in northwestern Australia and date to 50,000–40,000 B.C.E. By 40,000 B.C.E., there were settlements of early *Homo sapiens* hunters and gatherers in the Lake Mungo region of southeastern Australia. In 1968, an American archeologist, Jim Bowler, discovered evidence of a ritual cremation at Lake Mungo dating to about 23,000 B.C.E. Between 30,000 and 20,000 B.C.E., "Gracile" populations, the ancestors of Australian aborigines, inhabited a series of sites widely spread across southern and eastern Australia.

EARLY AGRICULTURE IN SOUTHEAST ASIA

The earliest evidence of fixed permanent settlements in Asia comes from the uplands of the Mekong and Red rivers in northern Vietnam and Thailand. Dating roughly from 8000 to 2000 B.C.E., the best-known sites are clustered around Ban Chiang in northeastern Thailand's Udon Thani Province plateau. First discovered in 1957, the sites feature remains of the earliest rice cultivation in Asia, although archeologists debate whether the rice was a wild or domesticated variety. Clay pots at the site contain food remains, and the bones of chickens and pigs reveal elements of the local diet. The site also yielded bronze tools and weapons, as well as clay and wooden "rollers" used to mark patterns on local bark cloth. Ritualized burials at the site include bronze tools, weapons, and pottery. One site contains a large cemetery, suggesting some degree of permanent settlement.

Archeologists speculate that the Thai sites represent the earliest evolution of Asian agriculture among a society that was displacing earlier hunters and gatherers. Remains at the sites indicate that dependence on root crops such as taro and yams, which grew easily in the tropical floodplains, was giving way to cultivation of millet rice (or dry rice), which grew wild in the uplands. Early upland populations adopted a mixture of hunting-and-gathering and slash-and-burn cultivation, still practiced among highland populations in Southeast Asia and southern China. Slash-and-burn, or swidden, cultivation involves the clearing of fields by cutting wild vegetation and burning off the residue.

Between 1000–600 B.C.E., regional archeological sites demonstrate that some swidden cultivators migrated from the highlands into Vietnam's Red River floodplain. They abandoned swidden practices, instead adopting a so-called "hydraulic" agriculture based on irrigation. By controlling and managing the annual Red River floodwaters, farmers in the region developed the earliest wet-rice agriculture. This initial wet-rice civilization developed into what an archeologist, R. Heine Gildern, dubbed the "Dongson" culture (500 B.C.E.–C.E. 43), named for the original site of the discovery, in the 1920s, of the civilization's large cast bronze ritual drums.

EARLY AGRICULTURE IN CHINA

The earliest settled agricultural sites in China appeared about 4000 B.C.E., the date of the **artifacts** uncovered at Banpo, a large village site discovered

ARCHEOLOGICAL DISCOVERIES

1891 Dutch anatomist Eugene Dubois unearths remains of "Java Man," first *Homo erectus* specimen found in Asia, dating to ca. 900,000 B.C.E.

1920s Local Vietnamese villagers discover monumental Dongson culture bronze drums dating to ca. 500 B.C.E.

1921 Archeologists discover remains of "Beijing Man," later identified as a *Homo erectus* specimen dating to ca. 600,000 B.C.E.

1921 Excavation of first Yangshao culture site in Henan, China, dating to ca. 4000–2000 B.C.E.

1928 Chinese archeologist Wu Jinding excavates first Longshan culture site in Shandong Province, China

1949 Discovery of first artifacts associated with early Japanese Jomon culture near Iwajiku, Japan

1954 Discovery of Banpo, most famous Yangshao culture site, near Xian, China

1957 Evidence of early human settlement in Southeast Asia first uncovered near Ban Chiang, Thailand

1968 American archeologist Jim Bowler discovers evidence of ritual cremation at Lake Mungo, Australia, dated ca. 23,000 B.C.E.

1975 Earliest excavation of Taosi, largest Longshan culture site in China

1976 Discovery of extensive grave goods in tomb of Chinese emperor Wu Ding's wife provides key insights into aristocratic life during Shang dynasty

1995 Chinese archeologists discover remains of Yangshao settlement surrounded by pounded earth walls dating to ca. 3000 B.C.E.

in 1954 near modern-day Xian in northern China. The culture to which the artifacts (dating from 4000 to 2900 B.C.E.) at the Banpo and other Yellow River basin archeological sites belonged has been named Yangshao, after the village in the Henan Province where the red painted pottery common to these sites first came to the attention of Western archeologists in 1921. Yangshao sites provide the earliest dated evidence of the transition from hunting and gathering to settled agriculture in China.

The Yangshao sites indicate that farmers in this region of northern China moved directly from hunting and gathering to settled intensive agriculture without ever adopting swidden as an intermediate step. Remains at Banpo show that the local population independently domesticated wild forms of wheat, barley, and millet, which was the most prominent crop. The prominence of pottery at the Yangshao sites suggests its use in storing the surpluses of crops that are associated with the development of early agriculture.

The consequences of this commitment to settled agriculture are demonstrated at a Yangshao site at Xishan in Henan Province, discovered by Chinese archeologists in 1995, which is surrounded by a defensive wall of pounded earth. Although this is typical of village sites from roughly 3000 B.C.E. in the adjacent upper Chang River basin to the south, Xishan is the only Yangshao site so guarded.

The earliest permanent settlements in the upper Chang River basin of western and southwestern central China date to as early as 4500 B.C.E. They are distinguished from the Yangshao villages to their north by the cultivation of swamp rice rather than millet, and by their kiln-fired, highly polished black pottery. This ware was named Longshan after the first excavated site of this culture (ca. 3000–2000 B.C.E.), which was unearthed by a Chinese archeologist, Wu Jinding, in 1928. Early Longshan archeological remains are associated with a region that was warmer and wetter than that of their neighbors in northern China, and had a longer growing season.

This image shows some of the more than 8,000 life-size terra-cotta soldiers found in the tomb of the Chinese emperor Shihuangdi (r. 221–210 B.C.E.). In addition to foot soldiers, the tomb includes figures of archers, warriors on horseback, and charioteers. (Digital Vision/Getty Images)

TURNING POINT

Terra-cotta Soldiers

In 1974, farmers digging a well near modern-day Xian in northern China discovered an "army" of more than 8,000 life-size sculpted and painted clay warriors. The figures stand in underground pits next to the tomb of the first Qin emperor Shihuangdi (r. 221–210 B.C.E.). The imperial tomb and its terra-cotta army celebrate the Qin emperor's unification of China in 221 B.C.E. but also proclaim his ability to maintain that empire in the afterlife.

In the first of the four pits, 6,000 warriors stand in rows four deep in squads of 70; in the second pit are 89 wooden chariots, 500 chariot and cavalry horses, and 1,000 infantry in a u-shaped battle formation. The third pit contains the command headquarters staffed by military officers. The fourth pit is empty, apparently because the emperor died before it could be filled with other figurines.

The pits provide a valuable picture of the Qin army's forces, use of weapons, and military tactics. In the second pit, 1,000 troopers are protected by 334 archers armed with crossbows, lined in eight clusters; 160, who are wearing heavy armor, are kneeling in a front line and others stand at the rear. The second pit contains 64 chariots, in eight clusters. Each chariot is commanded by an archer, and is guarded by a soldier on each side and another at its rear. In the center of this pit there are 19 war chariots and 100 warriors. In the rear are three clusters of six chariots, 124 vaulting horses, and warriors armed with bows. Each chariot carries two people—a charioteer and his scout. Each section can engage the enemy on its own or attack or defend as a whole.

MAJOR ARCHEOLOGICAL SITES OF ASIA AND THE PACIFIC

Treasured artifacts, such as pottery and tools, which have been unearthed and   *recovered in China, Japan, Korea, along the Indus Valley, and throughout*   *Southeast Asia, provide a glimpse of how ancient Asian societies lived and thrived.*

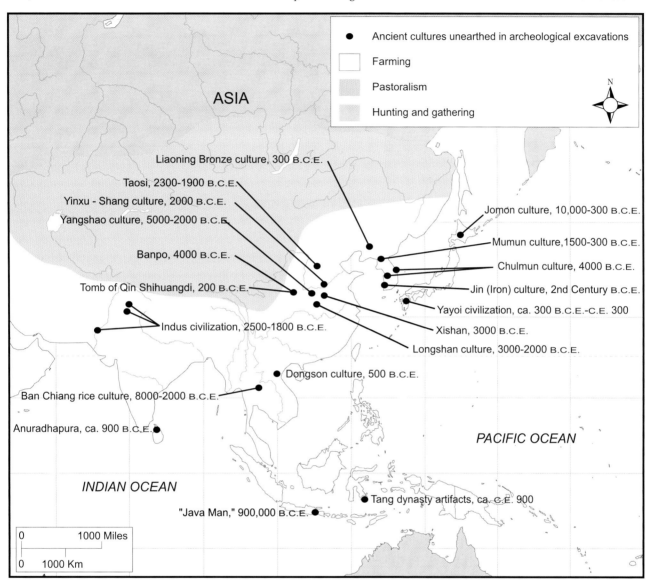

Thick walls made of successive layers of stamped earth commonly surround Longshan archeological sites. Chinese written accounts of this era, dating to the sixth century B.C.E., reported that these walled cities provided protection against the hunters and gatherers who lived in the highland frontiers to the south and west of the Longshan sites. These seminomadic populations, who had not made a similar commitment to settled agriculture, periodically raided the prosperous agricultural communities, especially in times of famine.

Taosi, in China's Shaanxi Province, which dates to about 2300 to 1900 B.C.E., is the largest Longshan archeological site, at almost 100,000 square feet (9,300 sq m). Excavated by Chinese archeologists from 1975 to the present day, Taosi yielded similar artifacts to those at other Longshan sites, but also contained the first known Chinese ritual solar observatory, a common feature in China's later imperial courts. The observatory opens to the east, allowing observation of the sunrise during solstices and equinoxes. Taosi residents likely enlisted these observations in their attempts to

LINK IN TIME

The Great Wall

The Great Wall of China is a massive defensive structure measuring roughly 4,000 miles (6,400 kilometers) long, cutting across northern China from Inner Mongolia in the east to the Yellow River and Gobi Desert in the west. It began as a series of disconnected sections built by competing factions during the Era of Warring States (403–222 B.C.E.) to protect ancient China from its seminomadic neighbors to the north and west. Emperor Qin Shihuangdi (221–210 B.C.E.) was responsible for connecting the previously constructed sections into a continuous defensive wall.

In contrast to the Great Wall visible today, which was improved by later dynasties, the Qin wall consisted of a mound of loose stone and wooden frames covered by packed earth. The eastern section was built on a wall constructed originally during the Zhao dynasty (ca. 1045–221 B.C.E.) and later rebuilt by the Yan regional state (475–222 B.C.E.), which contributed during both the Zhao dynasty and the Era of Warring States. The middle section represented mostly new construction, and included strategically placed beacon towers from which fires were lit to signal other sections of the wall in case of impending attacks. The third (western) section included new segments linking several walls built by earlier states as protection against their Chinese neighbors.

The Great Wall is perhaps history's greatest public works project. Chinese dynastic histories report that 300,000 soldiers, as well as 500,000 conscripted slaves, convicts, and local laborers, worked 10 years to complete the Qin wall. Later Chinese scholars cited the wall's expense, and the estimated thousands of deaths that occurred during its construction, as examples of Qin tyranny.

---

develop a solar calendar, which is crucial to determining appropriate planting and harvesting cycles.

The archeological remains of the northern Chinese city of Yin, located just outside modern-day Anyang in the upper Yellow River basin, represent the evolution of these earlier sites into impressive imperial cities. At its peak between 1400 and 1050 B.C.E., Yin served as the capital city of the Shang **dynasty** (1766–1122/1027 B.C.E.) and covered roughly 10 square miles (26 sq km). The complex consisted of a palace, royal ancestral shrines, and 80 accompanying residences. The site also contains several dozen royal tombs, including that of the wife of the emperor Wu Ding (r. 1200–1181 B.C.E.), discovered in 1976. In the tomb were the remains of 16 servants and six pet dogs (buried as sacrifices to serve her in the afterlife); 468 bronze ritual objects; many inscribed oracle bones and elaborate jade, stone, and bone carvings; bronze weapons, including a wooden-handled bronze-bladed dagger, the preferred battle weapon of the period; and 6,900 cowrie shells, which served as money.

These remains reveal much about **aristocratic** court life of the **era**, which formed the model for imperial courts of later Chinese dynasties. The elites of the Shang dynasty court were surrounded by luxury and aided by numerous servants, who were bound in their service to the elite, even in death. The era's religious practices included the reading of oracle bones to predict the future and the performance of elaborate rituals that required finely crafted ritual paraphernalia. People believed in an existence after death, in which the dead lived much as they had in their earthly existence, with aristocrats needing servants, pets, ritual items, and even money to maintain their lifestyles.

The imperial grandeur that is displayed in the remains of the Shang court reached new heights under the Qin dynasty (221–206 B.C.E.) and its elaborate capital at Xianyang near modern Xian. The most famous project of the first Qin emperor, Shihuangdi (r. 221–210 B.C.E.), was the Great Wall, erected across China's northern border to protect his realm from attacks by seminomadic warrior tribes from the surrounding grasslands of central Asia and Mongolia. Continuing the Shang and Qin initiatives, successor dynasties would also build, refurbish, or expand imperial capitals, restore and extend the Great Wall, and commission elaborate tombs to house deceased rulers and elite.

EARLY SITES IN KOREA AND JAPAN

Korea's earliest archeological sites, discovered at Yang'yang-gun and Osan-ni in the province of Kangwon, date from 8000 to 5000 B.C.E. They contain flat-bottomed pottery decorated with relief designs. Between 5000 and 1000 B.C.E., Jeulmun earthenware appears in western and southern coastal regions of Korea. These wide-mouthed storage and cooking vessels, named after the Korea site of their original discovery, are decorated with patterns of diagonal lines made with a comblike instrument. They are associated with the spread of evolving settled agriculture societies during this era.

Remains from Korea's Mumun pottery period (1500–300 B.C.E.) show that, by this time, Koreans had become millet farmers. The era is also well known for its large settlements and megalith, or large stone, burial sites found in the Liao River basin of North Korea. The elite were buried in tombs using upright stones supporting a horizontal slab. Another form of burial for elites and commoners used stone cists (underground burial chambers lined with stone) and earthenware jar coffins. Bronze ritual objects, pottery, and jade ornaments similar to those found in the early Chinese imperial tombs have been recovered from these first Korean tombs, reflecting that Koreans at this time shared similar beliefs about an afterlife with their Chinese neighbors.

Japan's earliest development mirrors that of Korea in the dates of its evolution from a hunting-and-gathering culture to a settled agricultural economy. Its first artifacts are associated with the Jomon culture (10,000–300 B.C.E.), named for its widespread and distinctive *jomon,* or "cord-marked," clay pots and figures, decorated using sticks wrapped in cord. Shell-covered trash mounds of Jomon sites include animal bones, tools, weapons, pottery, and jewelry, which are appropriate to that era's hunting, gathering, and fishing society. The first such site to be discovered by archeologists was excavated near Iwajiku in 1949.

The Yayoi civilization in southern Japan (ca. 300 B.C.E.–C.E. 300) introduced wet-rice cultivation, and, like those of their Korean neighbors, the archeological sites associated with this early settled wet-rice society contain bronze ritual artifacts and iron tools and weapons. Yayoi archeological sites are concentrated in the coastal regions of Japan's three southern islands that share the Inland Sea. Those in Yayoi society, inspired by their contemporary Korean neighbors, built large earthen mounds, some surrounded by water moats, over the tombs of their elite. These tombs include clay figurines depicting mounted male warriors that are the subject of much debate among archeologists. Some believe this statuary represents the era's ruling elite as Japanese mounted warriors, while others assert that it represents victorious invaders from Jin Korea, who introduced their culture to Japan.

See also: Agriculture; Angkor Wat; China; Culture and Traditions; India; Indian Ocean Trade; Japan; Java; Korea; Micronesia; Society.

FURTHER READING

Higham, Charles. *Archeology of Mainland Southeast Asia.* Cambridge: Cambridge University Press, 1989.

Imamura, Keiji. *Prehistoric Japan: New Perspective on Insular East Asia.* Honolulu: University of Hawaii Press, 1996.

Kim, H.J. *Pre-History of Korea.* Honolulu: University of Hawaii Press, 1978.

Yang, Xiaoneng. *New Perspectives on China's Past.* New Haven, CT: Yale University Press, 2004.

Art and Architecture

South Asia's Hindu and Buddhist traditions established artistic standards and principles that formed the foundation for much of ancient Asia's art and architecture. These principles were most fully expressed in Chinese imperial art and architecture, which were influenced by Indian Buddhist traditions and in turn inspired China's Korean, Japanese, and Vietnamese neighbors.

CHINESE ARTISTIC TRADITIONS

The ideas of the Chinese philosopher Confucius (Kungfutzu, 551–479 B.C.E.) shaped China's early architecture. Confucianism emphasized the importance of social order and hierarchy. As a result, China's imperial courts and their accompanying ritual and urban complexes celebrated the role of the Chinese emperor as the source of an orderly and productive Chinese society. China's architecture also celebrated orderly use of space, consistent with what became known as *feng shui,* the practice of placement and arrangement of space to achieve harmony with the natural surroundings.

Feng shui was reflected in the placement of public buildings. Rather than a random development, the city was laid out in a grid pattern on a north-south axis. North was positive, sacred, and traditionally associated with the realm of the supportive ancestors and celestial divine. South was negative, potentially dangerous, and associated with malevolent spirits and threatening outsiders. East and west were the middle ground where the sacred and the secular intersected. Burial grounds, as in the case of the royal tombs, were placed outside of this orderly urban ritual, administrative, and residential realm, because they contained the unpredictable spirits of the dead.

Urban Architecture

Cities of the Tang era (C.E. 618–907) built on the earlier Chinese court art traditions that date to the Shang dynasty (1766–1122/1027 B.C.E.). They made a conspicuous public statement about orderly Chinese society and became the architectural models for Chinese capital cities at Kaifeng (then called Pien-ching) in northern China (C.E. 960–1127), Hangzhou in southern China (C.E. 1127–1279), and Beijing (C.E. 1271–1644). They also inspired Kyongju, the capital city of Unified Silla Korea (C.E. 668–918) and the Nara and Kyoto capital cities of imperial Japan (C.E. 710–1185).

Tang cities, which were protected by defensive walls and gates, also were based on the cardinal points of the compass. The Tang imperial city of Changan (modern-day Xian) had major east-west and north-south thoroughfares that defined the subdivisions of the city. The imperial palace compound was in the north; beyond the palace and outside the northern city walls was an imperial park that included a large artificial lake, which served as a royal hunting preserve and private space for the emperor and his court.

At the extreme north of the city was the emperor's private residential compound, in a garden-like setting, complete with carefully placed groupings of plants and rocks and winding streams and pathways. These natural elements satisfied the emperor's need for a sense of a universal order beyond the secular orderliness of his surrounding imperial compound. Symbolically, the emperor alone, in his residential compound, was able to bridge the two realms.

IMPERIAL TOMBS

Chinese imperial tombs commemorated the secular accomplishments of an emperor and insured that the emperor became a benevolent ancestor. The early underground tombs, which date to the Shang era (1766–1122/1027 B.C.E.), were constructed in the form of a Chinese house. The "home" of the deceased replicated the imperial household, with inner and outer chambers flanked by side corridors and rooms containing grave offerings. Intricate bronze vessels, weapons, carved jades, and ceramic objects were placed near the coffin to provide comfort and protection in the next world. The walls of the burial chambers were often decorated with carved or painted scenes that depicted popular legends or daily life.

The underground tomb of the Qin dynasty monarch Shihuangdi (r. 221–210 B.C.E.) near modern Xian in northern China features a huge underground chamber containing an army of life-sized clay figures to "guard" and "serve" the emperor in the afterlife. The Han era (206 B.C.E.–C.E. 220) is especially known for its tomb paintings, which display the first elements of Chinese landscape painting, in contrast to the portrait art that dominated the Han palaces.

Tang-era (C.E. 618–907) royal tombs featured large commemorative archways leading into "urban" areas, complete with broad avenues ("spirit ways") containing larger-than-life human and animal statuary, ritual halls, and elaborate gardens. These avenues led to the burial mound, which was located above the tomb entrance. A vertical shaft connected the mound to an underground burial chamber. In front of each Tang tomb stands a focal memorial stone marker (stela) that proclaims the worldly accomplishments of the deceased. Tang tombs are also known for their *sancai,* three-colored glazed pottery figures of horses and human figures that were intended to accompany the deceased in their death.

Landscape Painting

Traditional Chinese landscape painting, which had its roots in the wall murals of the Han era, developed its "classical" style in the reign of the Tang dynasty. It was heavily influenced by Buddhist and Daoist traditions that minimized the importance of humanity and asserted the prevailing power of nature. For example, although a painting may depict the emperor's court activities, it is done in a setting in which all the participants, rulers as well as commoners, are considered. The surrounding landscape in such a work typically includes the rural communities surrounding the court, its urban centers, and the representative landscapes of a region. Traditional Chinese scroll paintings show little concern for perspective, the creation of a realistic scale, or conveying a sense of hierarchy. All elements, human and natural, are treated with the same care by the artist; none is emphasized as being more important than another.

ARTISTIC TRADITIONS OF INDIA

Architecture and art in India reflected the ideals of early Vedic religious traditions, which promoted the moral superiority and spiritual leadership of the priest over the secular authority of a monarch. This emphasis on the sacred was consistent with the central notions of India's indigenous Hindu and Buddhist religious traditions, which taught that humanity was impermanent. In southern Asia, temples took precedence over the construction of elaborate palace complexes and royal tombs.

Buddhist Art and Architecture

India's early architectural and artistic traditions developed following the founding of the Buddhist religion in the fifth century B.C.E. The best-known Mauryan-era (ca. 400–180 B.C.E.) Buddhist structures include inscribed stone pillars roughly 60 feet (18.3 m) tall, strategically erected throughout north India to establish the legitimacy of the Mauryan king Asoka (ca. 273–232 B.C.E.) and his patronage of the Buddhist religion. Typical of Indian artistic tradition, the inscriptions diminish Asoka's secular accomplishments in favor of highlighting his patronage of Buddhism. The inscriptions begin by acknowledging Asoka's glorious military victories and his inspired secular leadership, but then proclaim that Asoka ascribed no great significance to these accomplishments. Instead, the inscriptions praise Asoka for regarding an orderly secular world as his greatest achievement, as the necessary precondition for his subjects to achieve spiritual salvation. Thus Asoka, like other Mauryan kings, supported a mixture of secular art and sacred art and architecture.

TURNING POINT

Todaiji Temple

The Todaiji Buddhist temple in the central Japanese city of Nara was built in c.e 743, when Buddhism was the Japanese state religion and Nara was the residential capital of the Japanese emperor and his court. The temple building and its statue are modeled on the art and architecture of contemporary Tang China (c.e. 618–907). The temple was built to symbolically unify the Japanese elite and all the Buddhist temples that were spread throughout Japan under the centralized political and spiritual leadership of the Japanese emperor Shomu (r. c.e. 724–749). Japanese legend records that 2,600,000 people participated in its construction.

The Todaiji temple contains the massive Daibutsu ("Great Buddha") statue, which stands 49 feet (15 m) in height and is the world's largest cast bronze Buddha. The giant Buddha statue is housed in a wooden building, which at 157 feet (48 m) high is the world's tallest wooden building. The statue's ears are 8.25 feet (2.5 m) long; its hands can hold 20 people. It weighs 500 tons (455 m tons). Great thick wooden pillars hold up the structure. One of these in the rear of the temple has a hole through it, said to be the size of the Buddha's nostril. By tradition, if a person can pass through this hole, he or she is said to be a candidate for heaven.

Since the temple was built, the Daibatsu has been repaired several times after damage caused by earthquakes; its head has fallen off at least once. While the base of the statue dates to the eighth century, the upper portion, including the head, was recast in the late twelfth century. The Todaiji temple that remains today was rebuilt in 1709, after the existing wooden building burned in a late sixteenth-century fire. Following that fire the Buddha statue had remained uncovered for more than a century.

The Buddha is seated in a meditation posture appropriate to the Daibutsu Buddha, who in Buddhist tradition is the source of truth and knowledge. The "Cosmic" Buddha sits on his lotus throne (symbolic of purity and the foundation for the "flowering" of knowledge), presiding over the various levels of the universe. The Buddha's outstretched hands symbolize his willingness to offer truth and knowledge to his faithful devotees.

The notable architectural remains of the Mauryan era include large hemispherical earthen mounds, or *stupas*. Dating as early as about 461 b.c.e., these mounds are associated with events in the life of Buddhism's founder, Siddhartha Gautama (563–483 b.c.e.), known as the Buddha or "Enlightened One." One of the most significant mounds is located at the Mahabodhi temple complex at Bodhgaya (near modern-day Varanasi in northern-central India), the site where the Buddha is said to have achieved enlightenment. According to tradition, Asoka founded the Mahabodhi temple complex. A large stupa at nearby Sarnath, where the Buddha preached his first sermon, predates Asoka but benefited from his patronage. It is also the site of one of his pillars, which was once topped by a lion capital. The central image on the flag of India is taken from one of the Sarnath columns. It represents Asoka's 24-spoke *chakra,* a traditional **Sanskrit** symbol that denoted Asoka's "wheel of energy."

Additional Influences

India's further architectural evolution resulted from the introduction of religious **iconography** in the second century b.c.e. At this time, statues representing Buddhist spiritual concepts became common and inspired Hindu artists to create their own divine statuary and temples. The new popularity of statuary was influenced by the Macedonian king Alexander III, the Great, who invaded northwest India in 327–326 b.c.e. After Alexander's death four years later, some of his generals established their own domains in India's borderlands, and their Greek culture influenced regional art.

Indian statuary of this time represents an adaptation of the Greek tradition, which realistically portrayed gods and goddesses in contemporary human form and dress. This tradition is represented in the second- and third-century B.C.E. Gandharan and Kushana icon art produced on India's northwestern frontier. The most interesting remaining statuary from this period portrays the Buddha as ethnically Western and in traditional Greek dress.

India's new art and architecture also drew inspiration from new forms of religious devotion that developed in the second century B.C.E. The Bhakti devotional tradition in Hinduism and the Mahayana Buddhist tradition in Buddhism advocated the devotee's potential to embrace the divine through personal devotion and moral commitment, expressed by gifts, prayer, and ritual performance.

The earliest Indian temples were third century C.E. Buddhist and Hindu meditation sites excavated into the faces of mountains in northwest India, where the monastic compounds consisted of one or more chapels for worship. The oldest chapels contain representations of the Buddha in abstract, as a focal stupa crafted out of solid stone. Later depictions of the Buddha and the Hindu gods Visnu and Siva take the form of statuary, accompanied by images of Mahayana Buddhist and Hindu divinities. Buddhist and Hindu texts were also depicted in carved stone and in paintings on shrine walls. Five hundred years later, freestanding Buddhist shrines and Hindu temples across India adopted and adapted the art and architecture portrayed in these early mountain temples.

In northern India, a fluted melon-shaped cushion called an *amalaka* crowned most Hindu temples; in south India, rounded *stupi* topped the spires. These decorations reflected an adaptation of earlier temple art that culminated in a depiction of the *linga* (the male phallus), a symbol of the Hindu god Siva, the lord of fertility. Hindu temples usually included the image of such a divine being, with a spire above the image pointing to the god's celestial home, and a hall in front of the image for worshippers. Preliminary iconography, stone and cast-metal (normally bronze) icons, and wall murals inspired by the oral and textual traditions of the temple's focal divine prepared the worshipper to embrace the Lord in his inner sanctum.

EARLY INDIAN ARTISTIC LEGACY IN ASIA

India's art and architecture inspired artisans in Sri Lanka, where Buddhist art and architecture reached new heights. The great Buddhist stupa at Anuradhapura (built about 249 B.C.E.) is said to have been built initially after Buddhist monks sent by the Mauryan king Asoka converted Sri Lanka. In its final twelfth-century form, the stupa is taller than all of the ancient Egyptian pyramids except for the Great Pyramid at Giza.

From the third century C.E., artisans in the new monarchies of Southeast Asia also redefined and modified Indian temple art to fit their own cultural needs. Among the initial ritual complexes, the ninth-century C.E. Borobudur in central Java set the standard. The worshiper symbolically enters the Borobudur as a pilgrim, who physically and spiritually moves from the material secular world to the abstract realm of the divine. The pilgrim encounters elaborate stone relief depictions of the Indian Buddhist texts at the Borobudur's base, moves through intermediate terraces of Mahayana Buddhist statuary, and finally reaches a large culminating stupa at its top. Cambodia's twelfth-century C.E. Angkor Wat, dedicated to the Hindu god Visnu, and the Mahayana Buddhist Angkor Thom Bayon are the most impressive among the subsequent temple sites. These and other temples of that era in mainland Southeast Asia and Java still drew their inspiration from the Indian architectural tradition, but prominently incorporated local variations that were consistent with local cultural heritage.

Indian statuary and temple art also spread to China in the first century C.E., following the Silk Road from northwest India across central Asia. This pathway to China was marked by Buddhist pilgrimage and monastic sites, and accompanying statuary art and wall murals. Among these was Bamiyan, Afghanistan, which had two massive early sixth-century stone Buddhas, one standing 180 feet (55 m) and the second 121 feet (37 m). The fifth-century

Longmen Grotto complex in China's northwest Henan Province consists of more than 100,000 statuary images in a series of caves and temples. Here, the Indian Buddhist stupa had transitioned into *pagodas,* or multitiered towers, which would become the distinctive element in Buddhist temples throughout eastern Asia.

See also: Angkor Wat; Buddhism; China; Culture and Traditions; Hinduism; India; Japan; Java; Korea; Language and Writing; Society.

FURTHER READING
Craven, Roy C. *Indian Art.* London: Thames and Hudson, 1997.
Rawson, Philip S. *Art of Southeast Asia.* London: Thames and Hudson, 1990.
Stanley-Baker, Joan. *Japanese Art.* London: Thames and Hudson, 2000.
Watson, William. *The Arts of China to AD 900.* New Haven, CT: Yale University Press, 1995.
Watson, William. *The Arts of China 900–1620.* New Haven, CT: Yale University Press, 2000.

Australia

Island continent located in the southwestern Pacific Ocean, first settled by humans between 50,000 and 40,000 B.C.E. Two major geographical and climatic changes significantly shaped prehistoric Australia. The first was the continent's physical separation from Asia about 10,000 B.C.E. The second took place between 3000 and 1000 B.C.E., with the drying of swamplands, vast lakes, and forested zones that once covered substantial areas of Australia's interior. This left Australia covered largely by semiarid grasslands and a marginally productive, dry interior known as the Outback. Aboriginal adjustments to this changed habitat became the basis of early Australian culture.

EARLY POPULATIONS

The earliest aboriginal Australians likely migrated from Southeast Asia across a land bridge that once joined Australia and the Asian continent before the most recent **ice age**, which ended about 10,000 B.C.E. The earliest archeological remains of human settlement in Australia date from 50,000 B.C.E. in northwestern Australia (the Kimberley Range); from 40,000 B.C.E. in the Lake Mungo area of southwestern Australia; and from 30,000 to 20,000 B.C.E. in several regions of northern and southern Australia (Kenniff Cave, Koonalda Cave, Puritjaira, and Cave Bay), inhabited by an early aboriginal civilization collectively called "Gracile."

These earliest aborigines were joined after 10,000 B.C.E. by Torres Strait fishing populations, many of whom made the relatively short voyage to Australia across the Timor Sea from New Guinea. Anthropologists generally consider aboriginal Australians and the Torres Strait Islanders as two dis-

tinct groups, with different linguistic traditions. The Torres Strait Islanders are ethnically related to Papuan people of Melanesian heritage in New Guinea, whereas genetic evidence suggests ethnic ties between Aboriginal Australians and other aboriginal populations distributed across Asia. Despite these distinctions, long-term contact between the two Australian groups, as well as isolation from outside cultural influences, led them to develop broad cultural similarities.

Economic Practices

Prior to contact with Europeans in the eighteenth century C.E., most **indigenous** Australians were **seminomadic**, following seasonal sources of food over a fairly defined territory; none practiced settled agriculture. Indigenous Australians hunted animals of all sizes, from relatively large game, such as kangaroos and emus, to smaller prey, such as snakes, birds, turtles, and even insects. Despite

Some aboriginal rock paintings found in Australia, such as the one shown here in Kakadu National Park in the Northern Territory, date back as early as 50,000–40,000 B.C.E. The paintings often represent significant figures or events in the mythical aboriginal past, called the "Dreaming" or "Dreamtime." (Ira Block/National Geographic/Getty Images)

the popular image of the boomerang as the weapon of choice, indigenous Australians relied mainly on the spear for hunting. Indigenous hunters developed the *woomera,* or spear-thrower, to launch spears with greater force. Ancient Australians who lived in coastal areas and along rivers became expert fisherman; one community near the present-day city of Victoria even practiced eel farming.

A period of rapid social and cultural change appears to have occurred in Australia between 3000 and 1000 B.C.E., about the same time as severe environmental changes. This period was marked by greater human intervention in the environment, accelerated population growth, increased trade between indigenous groups, and the development of more sophisticated stone tools. During this

time, Australians also domesticated the dingo, a wild dog used to assist in tracking and hunting game.

Cultural, Religious, and Artistic Practices

Indigenous Australian societies featured complex kinship relations, and marriages were especially subject to strict rules. In central Australia, for example, men were required to marry women who were their distant cousins. Men and women who were eligible for marriage would gather annually at a festival (*corroborees*) at which goods were traded, news exchanged, and marriages arranged. These practices were designed to ensure that individuals married outside of their own family group,

LINK TO PLACE

Fossils: Australia and the Americas

Australia's oldest and most famous fossil remains, dating to 110 million years ago, are the jawbones of two mammals that were monotremes, or egg-laying mammals related to the platypus. Fossil evidence indicates that in North America at about the same time, 95 million years ago, marsupials, mammals with pouches that were early relatives of the American possum, were dominant. The first fossil evidence of marsupials in Australia dates only to 55 million years ago, leading scholars to conclude that the kangaroo was not native to Australia. Instead, it likely evolved from early marsupials that migrated to Australia at a time when it was joined to the continents of North and South America. Other fossil remains that have been found on all three continents, for example the remains of an early hoofed mammal known as the condylarth, support this conclusion.

Scholars assume that at some point in time Australia, South America, and Antarctica broke away from North America to form the ancient continent called Gondwanaland, a process that was completed between 550 and 500 million years ago. At that time, Australia and South America had similar animal populations. Roughly 40 million years ago, South America, Australia, and Antarctica separated into individual continents. In South and North America, placental, or live-bearing, mammals became dominant over the other mammalian species, while in Australia marsupials such as kangaroos, koalas, Tasmanian devils, and wombats won out, perhaps because of significant geological and environmental changes to which the marsupials were better able to adapt. These changes included a shifting climate and falling temperatures in Antarctica and the lower regions of South America, and a decrease in the number and types of predators in South America and Australia.

thus increasing the genetic health and diversity of the population.

Indigenous Australian society did not feature individual ownership of land, but did recognize group use rights, in which one group recognized the right of another to territory that was marked by natural geographic boundaries, such as rivers, lakes, and mountains. Elders passed this knowledge of the group's boundaries down to the next generation through song, dance, art, and storytelling.

Storytelling and art were also used to preserve indigenous traditions of the people regarding the origins, history, and relationship to the natural world. Indigenous Australians call the beginning, or creation, of their world the "Dreaming" or "Dreamtime." At this time, they believe, "ancestors" rose from below the earth to form various parts of nature, including animals, natural formations, and the sky. Humans and nature are thus one and the same; rock formations and rivers are ancestor spirits that remain spiritually alive. For example, the Nyungar people of western Australia believe that a high ridge known as the Darling Scarp represents the body of a snakelike creature, called a *wagyl*, that created the rivers and land formations in the region during the Dreamtime. It is said that the wagyl's tracks formed the sand dunes and its body the river beds, and where it stopped to rest it left bays and lakes. As it periodically moved from under to above the earth's surface it formed the rocks into hills, and its scales fell off to create forests and wooded areas.

Rock carvings and paintings discovered in the Bradshaw Cave in the Australian Northern Territory depict a wide variety of subjects. The earliest images, which date to as early as 50,000 to 40,000 B.C.E., include images of hunters or warriors; animals such as wallabies, turtles, and fish; and even the skeletons of animals and humans. Later images, made after European contact, show pigtailed European visitors, sailing ships, and individuals carrying firearms. These images at first carried religious significance, and also represented important

MIGRATORY ROUTES OF ABORIGINAL PEOPLES TO AUSTRALIA AND PACIFIC MIGRATIONS

The earliest aboriginal peoples likely migrated from the Eurasian continent across a land bridge into the Australian mainland and Tasmania between 50,000 and 40,000 B.C.E. The Europeans first discovered Australia in the 1600s but did not establish settlements there until the late 1700s, and the first British settlement was established in 1788.

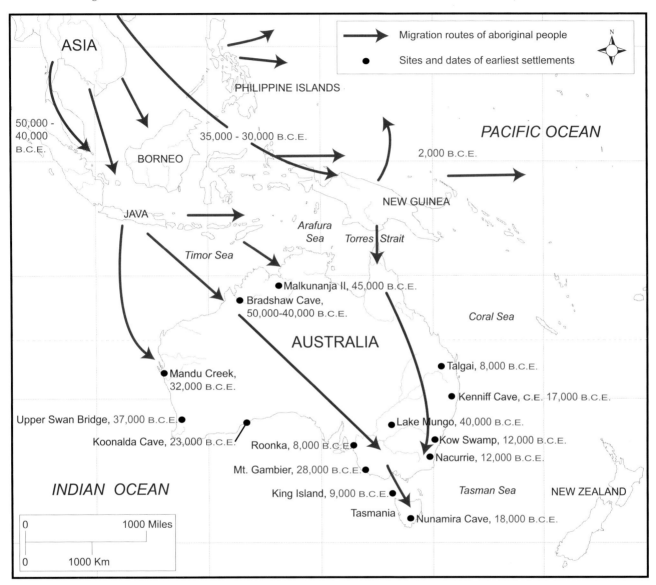

events in the lives and history of these people. They told stories about Dreamland, marked territorial land use rights, and served as reference points for those traveling across the Australian landscape.

EUROPEAN ARRIVAL AND IMPACT

Although Dutch navigators charted the coasts of Australia during the seventeenth century C.E., the first significant contact between Europeans and Australians occurred after Captain James Cook's claim of Australia for England in 1770, followed by the first British settlement of Australia, at Botany Bay, in 1788. Archeologists estimate that the indigenous Australian population in the late eighteenth century was between 300,000 and 1 million people. Over time, the Europeans absorbed the indigenous people into their newly created Western European–style communities, killed them, or drove the local populations from the more productive coastal areas. As Europeans began to explore and settle the inland grasslands, the indigenous peoples were

RISE OF AUSTRALIA

CA. 55,000 B.C.E. Earliest evidence of marsupials in Australia

CA. 50,000–40,000 B.C.E. First evidence of settlement by humans

CA. 40,000 B.C.E. Evidence of earliest settlement of southern Australia

CA. 30,000–20,000 B.C.E. First evidence of "Gracile" populations, ancestors of the Australian Aborigines

CA. 23,000 B.C.E. Earliest evidence of a human cremation in Lake Mungo region

CA. 10,000 B.C.E. Migration of Torres Strait fishing population to Australia

CA. 3000–1000 B.C.E. Prehistoric Lake Mungo dries up; the natural environment begins to stabilize; domestication of the dingo

C.E. 1606 First Dutch contact with Australia; continuing periodic coastal trade between Australian aborigines and the Dutch East India Company

C.E. 1770 Captain James Cook claims Australia for England

C.E. 1788 First English settlement at Botany Bay

---

pushed out of those productive lands as well. The remaining indigenous peoples were forced onto marginal lands considered by Europeans to be uninhabitable, such as the Great Sandy Desert, located in the northwestern Australian state of Western Australia.

See also: Aboriginal Peoples; Myths and Epics.

FURTHER READING

Mulvaney, John, and Johan Kamminga. *Prehistory of Australia.* Washington, DC: Smithsonian Institution Press, 1999.

Nile, Richard. *Australian Aborigines.* New York: Steck-Vaughn, 1993.

Smith, W. Ramsay. *Myths and Legends of the Australian Aborigines.* Mineola, NY: Dover, 2003.

Buddhism

Religion, widespread throughout Asia by the fourteenth century C.E., based on the teachings of a sixth-century B.C.E. Indian prince, Siddhartha Gautama, who renounced a life of comfort and power to seek truth. Ultimately, he claimed to achieve nirvana (**Sanskrit** for enlightenment), an understanding of the universal order and of humankind's relationship to it, and was thereafter called the Buddha, or the "Enlightened One."

Forsaking his own immediate salvation (a spiritual escape from the realm of human existence to a realm beyond), the Buddha taught 45 years until his death, or *parinirvana* (complete enlightenment). Following his death in ca. 483 B.C.E., his disciples formed a Buddhist monastic order, or *sangha,* which spread the faith throughout India.

INITIAL SPREAD

Buddhist monks spread the Buddha's "Middle Way," which preached the moral reform of existing

Buddhism originated in northern India during the fifth century B.C.E. and eventually spread throughout southern and southeastern Asia, China, Japan, and into what is now Indonesia. Chiang Rai, Thailand, is home to the contemporary statue of the Buddha shown here. (Dennie Cody/Taxi/Getty Images)

society and humanity's imperfect religious practices. Monks sent by the Mauryan ruler Asoka (r. ca. 273–232 B.C.E.) had converted Sri Lanka's elite by 249 B.C.E., the initial date of the Great Buddha temple at the Sri Lankan capital of Anuradhapura.

With the opening of the overland Silk Road trade route between India and China (138–126 B.C.E.), many sojourning traders and residents along the central Asian caravan route converted to Buddhism. The early caravan towns, such as Sogdiana (modern-day Bukhara in Uzbekistan) supported Buddhist temples and pilgrimage centers, where an international community of monks traveling the route periodically studied.

Buddhism gained a foothold in Han-era northern China (206 B.C.E.–C.E. 220), and, in a time of turmoil, gained numbers of converts after the Han **dynasty** fell in the early third century C.E. At that time the Chinese city of Luoyang, located at the end of the Silk Road, became a noted center of Buddhist learning. There, scriptures transported overland from India were translated into Chinese. At roughly this same time, local Kushana rulers at the western end of the Silk Road constructed a 180-foot-tall (55-meter-tall) Buddha statue at Bamiyan in what is now central Afghanistan.

Buddhist pilgrims traveling the **maritime** trade route between India and China in the third century introduced Buddhism to Southeast Asia, where several rulers converted to the faith. Leaders of early states in Sumatra and Java supported pilgrimage centers for Buddhist monks traveling between major Buddhist monastic centers in China and southern Asia. By the fifth century C.E., Nalanda, near modern-day Patna in northern India, had become the foremost international center of Buddhist scholarship. It would remain so until the twelfth century, at which time the decline of Buddhism in India forced a relocation of the center of the Theravada Buddhist church (a conservative, traditional style of Buddhism that teaches meditation for creating good karma) to Sri Lanka. Similarly, Mahayana Buddhist scholarship (a more liberal, innovative style of Buddhism that teaches that people are already enlightened beings but do not realize it) moved from India to China, which was the home of several pan-Asian Buddhist sects. Among these China-based Buddhist schools was the Chan Buddhist meditation sect, which was founded in China between C.E. 420 and 479, and then became the favored Buddhist sect, known as Zen Buddhism, among Japan's *samurai,* warrior, elite from the late twelfth century.

DOCTRINE

Buddhism offers spiritual refuge from the imperfection and subsequent chaos of everyday existence in the Three Jewels: the Buddha, his teachings, and the sangha. Buddhists consider these to be alternate paths to the elimination of human suffering. The Buddhist devotee might seek the mercy and intervention of the Buddha himself, immerse him- or herself in the study of and mediation on his teachings, or commit to the counsel of the learned Buddhist monkhood.

The Buddha's teachings and early Buddhist practices were compiled in a series of texts. The most important of these is called the Three Collections (*Pitakas*), which contain the Buddha's teaching (*sutra*), the laws of the sangha (*vinaya*), and Buddhist philosophies (*abhi-dharma*). The three collections, together with the later "three practical educations"—ethics (*sila*), meditation (*samadhi*), and scientific wisdom (*prajna*)—comprise the basic doctrines of Buddhism.

A Buddhist must accept the Four Noble Truths: (1) the world is filled with suffering; (2) suffering is caused by greed (craving or attachment); (3) to eliminate greed is to eliminate suffering; and (4) greed and consequent suffering is avoided by following a path of moral behavior and thought, known as the Eightfold Way. The Eightfold Way includes the elements of Right (meaning "spiritually pure") View, Right Intent, Right Speech, Right Action, Right Livelihood, Right Effort, Right Mindfulness, and Right Concentration.

Buddhism prescribes a lifestyle accompanied by meditation. Although Buddhist monasteries and monastic activities lie at the core of the religion, anyone can follow the Eightfold Way. Meditation under the guidance of a senior monk, however, helps to train the mind's powers of concentration. An individual with a properly trained mind can discover the true nature of his or her desire for earthly pleasures and eliminate them. This includes rejecting purely intellectual attachments such as philosophical or religious beliefs. By eliminating desire, it is believed that humans can achieve nirvana and release themselves from the cycle of death and reincarnation in which one repeatedly experiences mortal suffering.

INFLUENCE

The Buddha's teachings were revolutionary within India because they rejected the assumptions of the existing Hindu social hierarchy. Buddhism denied the sacred authority of the Hindu religious texts whose teachings dominated ancient Indian society. It also was antagonistic to the elaborate rituals that were the cornerstone of the Hindu partnership between priests and aristocrats. The Buddha did not so much challenge as ignore the special role of

GREAT LIVES

The Buddha

In 563 B.C.E., according to Buddhist tradition, the historical Siddhartha Gautama was born to the queen and king of a small clan state in northern India. At birth, it is said, Siddhartha Gautama appeared fully formed and immediately took seven steps, a sign that he would become either a great king or a great religious teacher.

At age 19, Siddhartha Gautama married the Princess Yasodhara; ten years later, she gave birth to a son. Having fulfilled his family obligation to provide a male heir, Siddhartha Gautama began to wander outside the palace compound, where he confronted images of sickness, poverty, and death. These images distressed Gautama, who began to see the world as a place filled with evil and misfortune. He also saw a wandering holy man with no material possessions who nevertheless seemed filled with inner peace.

Impressed by the holy man's demeanor, Gautama determined to follow in his footsteps. Completely abandoning material possessions, Gautama

spent the next six years attempting to conquer his worldly attachments, such as the desire for food, sex, and comfort. He sought out and studied under the greatest religious teachers of his age, and tried all the rituals and disciplined yogic exercises prescribed by the developing Hindu religion—to no avail.

Finally, in frustration, he sat under a Bodhi tree ("tree of wisdom") near the modern-day Indian city of Varanasi. For 49 days and nights he meditated in silence, enduring temptations from the evil spirit Mara. At sunrise on the fiftieth day he woke as the Buddha, the "enlightened one." He then rose and set out to teach humanity his enlightened "Middle Way," a moral life without extremes, based on the notion that a lifetime of sorrow could be negated by eliminating human greed. The Buddha spent the next 45 years spreading his message throughout northeastern India, accompanied by a band of monk disciples who continued to preach the Middle Way following his death in about 483 B.C.E.

priests in this system as the holders of the keys to salvation, as well as the privileged religious and social status of those claiming aristocratic descent. In contrast to Hindu society, Buddhism was inclusive of all social strata and promoted a communal lifestyle that violated the prevailing practice of occupational and gender separation.

Debate about whether or not it was necessary to follow a monastic life in order to achieve enlightenment was a major issue in early Buddhism. It was also the basis of an eventual split between Theravada Buddhists, who said that one had to be a monk to attain full enlightenment, and Mahayana Buddhists, who argued that the path to enlightenment was equally open to laypeople. Initially, the Theravada Buddhist sangha had assumed the major leadership role in the development of the Buddhist Church. By the second century B.C.E., however, some monks felt that the Buddhist sangha had

themselves become a new religious elite, little different from Hinduism's Brahmin priesthood. The reformist monks formed the rival Mahayana ("Universal or Greater Vehicle") Buddhist sangha, calling the coexisting older monastic Buddhism Hinayana ("Lesser or Individual Vehicle"). The Mahayana monks took their missionary activities beyond the walls of the monastic compound to work directly in lay communities.

Over time, followers of the Mahayana tradition began to worship the Buddha himself, who might be asked to grant divine favors. In these Mahayana teachings, the Buddha had five states of existence (the five Tathagata): the Historical Buddha Siddhartha Gautama, the Cosmic Buddha Dainichi, the Amitabha or Amida Celestial Buddha, the Bhaisajyagu Healing Buddha, and the Maitreya Future Buddha. These are all central figures of worship in Chinese, Japanese, and Tibetan Buddhism.

Mahayana followers believe that the Buddha was assisted by *bodhisattvas,* or male and female "saints." Like the Buddha, the bodhisattvas had achieved nirvana in this lifetime but had chosen to remain temporarily earthbound to assist humanity in their quest for salvation. At death, the bodhisattvas became divine assistants to the Buddha. Gods of other religious traditions, such as the Shinto spirits in Japan, were incorporated into Buddhism as lower-ranking bodhisattvas.

Vajrayana Buddhism offers an alternative path to enlightenment through the use of special techniques, chants, and rituals known collectively as tantra. Theravada and Mahayana Buddhists believe that it takes many lifetimes to reach nirvana, but Vajrayana followers claim that a person can achieve full enlightenment in a single lifetime through the use of tantra techniques. Despite these differences, Vajrayana Buddhists believe that Theravada and Mahayana doctrines form the basis of Vajrayana practice and that they are all legitimate paths to enlightenment.

See also: Angkor Wat; Art and Architecture; China; Culture and Traditions; Hinduism; India; Japan; Java; Religion; Silk Road; Society; Sri Lanka; Vietnam.

FURTHER READING

Gombrich, Richard F. *How Buddhism Began: The Conditioned Genesis of the Early Teachings.* London: Routledge, 2006.

Robinson, R.H., and W.L. Johnson. *The Buddhist Religion.* Belmont, CA: Wadsworth, 1988.

China

The dominant force in shaping eastern Asian civilization culturally, politically, and economically in the premodern era. From about 4000 B.C.E., prehistoric settled farming communities developed in northern and central China, in the Yellow and Chang River basins. At first these took the form of tribal and regional clan states; around 2200 B.C.E., they emerged as Asia's earliest imperial government.

Early Chinese learned to cultivate dry rice (millet), sorghum (grain-bearing grass), and wheat sometime after 4000 B.C.E., and these grains became their dietary staples. They also built a network of dikes to protect their crops from the devastating annual flooding of the Yellow River plain. Many historians believe that the magnitude of coordinating the construction and maintenance of these Yellow River dikes necessitated the emergence of China's earliest imperial government, the legendary Xia dynasty (ca. 2200–1766 B.C.E.). The events of this era are portrayed in numerous Chinese folktales that relate the mythical accomplishments of China's first emperors, the importance of ancestor worship and animistic forces in the everyday lives of the Chinese people, and the development of regionally powerful clans.

FROM TRIBE TO EMPIRE

Recorded Chinese history begins with the Shang dynasty (1766–1122/1027 B.C.E.), which reigned over the northern Yellow and Chang River basins, eventually settling in its sixth imperial capital at Yin, modern Anyang. Shang farmers cultivated dry rice and wheat and raised domesticated livestock, while the aggressive Shang warriors expanded the borders of their empire by attacking neighbors to acquire land, resources, and slaves. The Shang dynasty was especially noted for the development of bronze technology and the use of elaborate bronze vessels in religious and state rituals.

Clan States

The subsequent era of the Zhou dynasty (1122/1027–403 B.C.E.) began with the overthrow of the Shang rulers by one of several militant regional clans. From their imperial capital near modern Xian, Shang rulers reigned over a network of semi-autonomous regional clan states. Chinese historians

MILESTONES IN ANCIENT CHINESE HISTORY

CA. 4000 B.C.E. Settled farming communities develop in the Yellow and Chang River basins

CA. 2200–1766 B.C.E. Legendary Xia dynasty establishes China's first imperial government

1766–1122/1027 B.C.E. Shang dynasty marks beginning of recorded Chinese history

1122/1027–403 B.C.E. Zhou dynasty establishes imperial authority over a network of subordinate regional states

CA. 500s B.C.E. Origins of Confucian philosophical tradition and Daoist religion, doctrines central to subsequent Chinese secular and sacred tradition

403–222 B.C.E. Era of Warring States follows collapse of Zhou authority; six powerful warlord states vie for control over China

222 B.C.E. Qin state emerges victorious over its rivals and establishes ruling dynasty

206 B.C.E. Han Gazou leads overthrow of Qin state; establishes Han dynasty

206 B.C.E.–C.E. 220 Han dynasty; China annexes Mongolia and Korea and opens Silk Road trade route to the West

C.E. 220–581 China undergoes extended period of disorder following collapse of Han dynasty

C.E. 581–618 Sui dynasty restores imperial authority

C.E. 618–907 Tang dynasty; era of Chinese openness to new ideas and cultural innovations

C.E. 907–960 Regional states establish autonomy during Period of Five Dynasties and Ten Kingdoms that follows fall of Tang dynasty

C.E. 960–1279 Song dynasty, especially noted for artistic achievements in literature, painting, dance, and drama, as well as technological innovations such as gunpowder and moveable type printing

C.E. 1252–1279 Mongol lord Kublai Khan wages prolonged war against the Song, ultimately conquering China and founding the Yuan dynasty

C.E. 1279–1368 Mongol Yuan dynasty aggressively attempts to expand Chinese territory into what are now Myanmar and Vietnam and launches failed amphibious invasions of Java and Japan

C.E. 1368–1644 Ming dynasty marks return to ethnic Chinese rule; policy of commercial and cultural exchange leads to period of economic prosperity and social stability

---

characterize this as a network of city-states, emphasizing the emergence of important regional urban centers. Western historians often describe them as "feudal states," because the Zhou dynasty created a network of subordinate regional states under a landed aristocracy, comparable to the socioeconomic organization of Europe during the Middle Ages.

The Zhou era was also the classical age of Chinese intellectual inquiry. Both the Confucian philosophical tradition and Daoist religion originated in the sixth century B.C.E. Confucianism and Daoism proposed alternate paths to human fulfillment. While Confucianism advocated commitment to a hierarchical secular social order, Daoism emphasized that humans should withdraw from the affairs of everyday life to celebrate the ultimate reality and preeminence of nature.

TURNING POINT.

Chinese Civil Service

Chinese civil service examinations were recorded as early as 165 B.C.E. The resulting appointments filled vacant government positions on the six imperial bureaucratic government boards: personnel, rites, public works, war (provisioning the military rather than commanding it), revenue, and justice. Appointees served at one of three levels of government: local, provincial, and the imperial court. Applicants underwent written examinations; passing each of three exams qualified the candidate for successively higher government appointments.

In theory, the Chinese civil service was open to any adult male, regardless of wealth or social status. In practice, however, preparing for the exams was costly and time consuming. Because China lacked public schools, candidates had to study under the direction of a private tutor. As a result, most successful candidates came from a hereditary class of wealthy landholding gentry, who had the resources to afford private education. Aristocrats had an additional incentive to fill the posts: at least one family member from each generation was required to pass the exams in order for a family to maintain their aristocratic status. However, passing the exams was no guarantee of personal success. Because there were not enough positions to employ all qualified applicants,

only about 5 percent of those who took the exams passed them and received government posts.

The civil service and examination systems were also the critical means by which the Chinese government maintained the loyalty of the elite classes, or *shih*. Only those who had passed the exams, whether or not they received government positions, were allowed to communicate directly with the government. Thus, non-shih had to secure the services of non-officeholding shih in order to have dealings with the government. Shih businessmen frequently received profitable government contracts and commissions not available to non-shih.

The system, however, often produced too many expectant shih, who believed they were entitled to receive benefits as the government's local agents. In fact, many shih depended on commissions as a valuable supplement to the family's land-derived income. Dynastic decline normally coincided with the court having too few rewards to distribute in order to retain the loyalty of the shih. As the opportunities for appointments or rewards diminished, the elite began to think in terms of their self-interest rather than remaining loyal to the imperial court, hastening the dynasty's fall from power.

In the late fifth century B.C.E., the Zhou confederacy collapsed, leading to the Era of the Warring States (403–222 B.C.E.), when six regionally powerful warlord states competed in a series of battles and began to **annex** their smaller neighbors. In the late third century, the Qin state's forces emerged victorious under the leadership of the general Qin Shihuangdi (r. 221–210 B.C.E.), who became the first Qin emperor.

Qin China

Qin Shihuangdi organized the former clan states into new territorial provinces, in part to break up the longstanding regional associations of the

hereditary family clans. Three state officials supervised each province—one to administer the civil administration (for example, justice, police affairs, public works, record-keeping), a second to manage provincial finances (collecting and redistributing taxes), and a third who was in charge of provincial troops. Each official was encouraged to report the activities of the others to the emperor, which in effect created a system of checks and balances. This system of provincial appointments became the basis of China's imperial bureaucracy, which was initially filled with candidates favored by the emperor.

The Qin state minister Li Si (280–208 B.C.E.) played a significant role in imperial administration,

The ancient Chinese were great technological innovators, creating engineering marvels such as the Great Wall of China and the Grand Canal, pictured here. Begun in the fifth century B.C.E., the canal at one time reached a length of 1,500 miles (2,400 km) and connected six Chinese river systems. (Yann Layma/The Image Bank/Getty Images)

attempting to standardize not only Chinese weights and measures, but also life in general. His administrative innovations were based in the school scholars call Confucian Legalism, which advocated a strong interventionist state rather than a disengaged imperial authority that ruled by moral example. To ensure a singular and unchallenged Qin authority, Li Si banned and ordered the burning of books that expressed dissenting political views. When Shihuangdi died, Li Si tried to assume power, but because the Chinese had turned against the Qin policies that Li Si had worked so hard to support in the past, Li Si's efforts failed. The aristocracy were unwilling to entrust power to someone who held the now unpopular Qin views.

Han Gazou (r. 206–195 B.C.E.), a man of peasant birth, led the armies composed of disaffected Qin subjects that deposed the Qin and established a new dynasty. The new Han emperor and his succes-

sors (the Han dynasty ruled from 206 B.C.E. to C.E. 220) initially moderated the Qin centralization by temporarily allowing the old clan-based gentry to administer the new territorial divisions. Han rulers, however, gradually reintroduced the Qin administrative innovations, which they saw as the only logical means to administer their vast domain.

HAN, TANG, AND SONG CHINA

The high point of the Han dynasty is associated with the emperor Han Wudi (r. ca. 141–87 B.C.E.), who built on his predecessors' successful consolidations. He annexed Mongolia and Korea, and successfully stabilized China's western border. A series of military victories resulted in a peace settlement with the central Asian steppe tribesmen who threatened China's western borders. This settlement also allowed the opening of the Silk Road trade route, as the tribesmen agreed to protect travelers on the overland passageway that connected China to India, Persia, and the Roman West.

Han Wudi modified the Qin Confucian state, instituting a three-part national government consisting of the bureaucracy, the imperial court, and a professional military. The main qualifications for appointment included demonstrated ability and meritorious service; social class or status played no role in the selection process. Under Han Wudi, the state controlled and regulated commerce, notably to ensure that grains and other basic commodities such as salt were available at a reasonable price in the marketplace, that merchants conducted their business fairly, and that the government would have access to iron for its military needs. He also implemented Confucian **historical analysis**, which looked upon the past, especially historical figures, as the source of lessons for the present.

Han emperors faced periodic rebellions, including an uprising led by the peasant Wang Mang that temporarily overthrew Han rule (ca. C.E. 9–23). The victorious peasant armies, however, were unable to establish stable leadership, and Han forces restored the dynasty. However, the emperor's relatives, landed elites, Confucian bureaucrats, and the palace corps of eunuch imperial guards all periodically plotted to control the court's policies. This internal intrigue toppled the Han dynasty in C.E. 220; a series of smaller states run by warlords replaced the centralized empire.

Disorder, Displacement, and Change

With the fall of the Han dynasty, northern China faced 400 years of periodic raids by warriors (among these eastern Hun **seminomadic** tribesmen from the steppe grasslands of central Asia), and warfare among the powerful regional warlords. Buddhism spread from India to China, offering many Chinese a more satisfying religious solution to the generalized disorder than did local beliefs. For example, Buddhism offered the promise of an afterlife that Daoism did not. Traditional Chinese Confucianism strongly promoted involvement in **secular** affairs, but this focus was inconsistent with an age in which the secular realm was seen as particularly corrupt.

A large-scale exodus of the old Confucian aristocracy south of the Chang River helped to spread Buddhism beyond northern China at this time. It also resulted in the spread of Han culture into southeastern China, which previously had been under Han political authority but had retained most of its local culture. Denied access to the central Asian Silk Road, the Han elite were forced to find a new way to satisfy their desire for imported luxury goods. This led directly to the development of the Indian Ocean **maritime** trade.

Return to Imperial Order

Dynastic stability returned under the Sui (C.E. 581–618), whose military victories allowed them to consolidate their authority over northern and central China. The Sui, like the Qin, were aggressive in reestablishing dynastic order. The most noteworthy achievement of the Sui was the construction of the Grand Canal, which linked the productive eastern Chang basin to Beijing in the north. This allowed surplus wet-rice production from southern China to reach needy consumers in northern China. Increasing the volume of accessible rice in the north stabilized the price, ensuring that consumers throughout the realm could afford to buy rice.

The Sui ultimately overextended, committing vast human and financial resources in their resurrection of the Han realm and incurring heavy military expenses to secure China's western frontier. Popular revolts, assassinations, and internal disloyalty provided the opportunity for the Sui regional governor Li Yuan (C.E. 566–635) to seize authority and restore order under the new Tang dynasty (C.E. 618–907).

The Tang dynasty is frequently referred to as China's "Cosmopolitan Age" because of its openness to new ideas and cultural options. People of diverse ethnicity flowed into the capital city of Changan (modern Xian) by way of the reopened Silk Road. The Tang state institutionalized the Confucian examination system to secure qualified candidates for public office. In contrast to the Han-era exams, which tested the candidate's memorization, the new neo-Confucian examinations forced candidates to apply what they had learned by writing essays that addressed difficult situations they might face. This would demonstrate their ability to resolve real problems once they received political appointments.

CHINESE DYNASTIES, 1122 B.C.E.–C.E. 1365

Early Chinese history is marked by the transitions from one imperial dynasty to another, especially as seen in the changing borders of China's empires. The earliest dynasties were centered in the north. China reached its height during the Yuan dynasty.

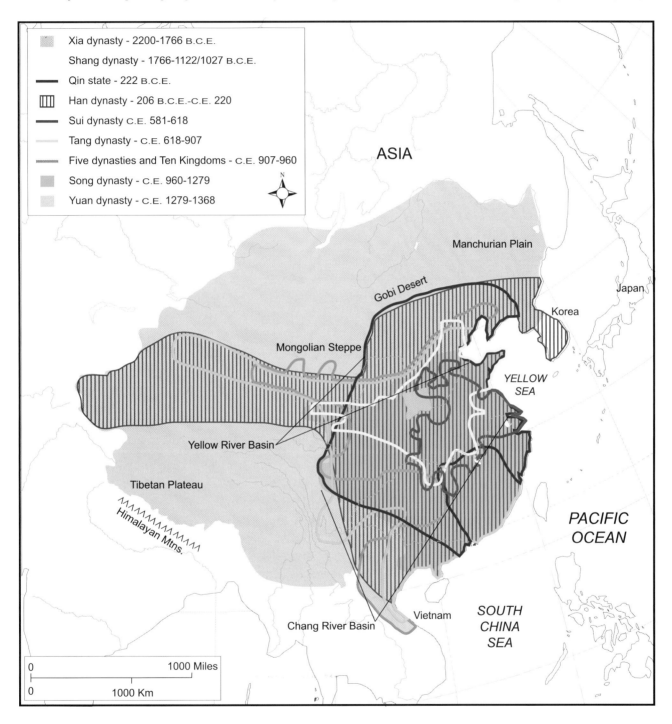

Legend:
- Xia dynasty - 2200-1766 B.C.E.
- Shang dynasty - 1766-1122/1027 B.C.E.
- Qin state - 222 B.C.E.
- Han dynasty - 206 B.C.E.–C.E. 220
- Sui dynasty C.E. 581-618
- Tang dynasty - C.E. 618-907
- Five dynasties and Ten Kingdoms - C.E. 907-960
- Song dynasty - C.E. 960-1279
- Yuan dynasty - C.E. 1279-1368

Like the Sui, the Tang ultimately collapsed due to the financial drain of funding troops needed to defend China's northwestern borders. After the dissident An Lushan led a temporarily successful military rebellion against the Tang in 755–757, later Tang emperors became overly dependent on the support of regional governors. Tang authority collapsed in 907, as the regional governors established their own autonomy in what is known as the Period of Five Dynasties and Ten Kingdoms. Ultimately one of these, the Song, renewed dynastic authority in 960.

The Song dynasty (960–1279) applied the broadly based neo-Confucian logic that human creativity stimulates human intelligence to constructive activity. During the Song era, such constructive activities included developing new technologies, among them printing with moveable type, gunpowder weapons, and improvements in navigation. The Song era is especially known for its artistic achievements, notably its literature, poetry, paintings, and contributions to the development of Chinese classical dance and drama. It was an age in which the traditional classes and genders more openly mixed, as merchants and gentry in particular shared in literary conversations at popular teahouse cafes. Urban residential districts became open to cross-class residence based on wealth rather than on birthright. Indeed, retrospective Chinese accounts of the Song criticized the dynastic leadership for being overly "relaxed," thus making China vulnerable to foreign invasion.

CONQUEST AND RESTORATION

The Mongol conquest of 1279 shocked the Chinese, who never before had been subject to rule by non-Chinese. The Mongols were warriors from the steppes of northern central Asia, whose forces conquered and temporarily controlled almost the entire Asian continent by the late thirteenth century. The Mongol lord Kublai Khan waged a prolonged war against the Song from 1252, finally completing his conquest in 1279 and founding the Yuan dynasty (C.E. 1279–1368).

The Yuan rulers, who were marginally literate warriors, recognized that they needed help from Chinese bureaucrats to rule successfully over China's vast non-Mongol population. They were suspicious of the Chinese Confucian gentry, however, so they frequently recruited foreigners from among their other realms to assume top-level administrative posts. Seeing how readily the Yuan adopted China's existing governmental system, em-

ployed its Confucian bureaucrats, and accepted its cultural practices, the Chinese concluded that their civilization must be the best in the world. Such cultural arrogance would prove a long-term liability as later Chinese dynasties turned inward, shutting off the country from outside influences and innovations.

The Yuan were aggressively expansionist. Following his conquest of China in 1279, Kublai Khan sent his troops south to fight in what are now Myanmar and Vietnam. The Mongol fleet also carried troops to attack Vietnam and Java. All of these attempts to extend Yuan power were costly failures, especially Kublai Khan's disastrous invasions of Japan in 1274 and 1281. Kublai Khan's successors found themselves weakened by his debts and increasingly isolated as the Mongol realm fragmented into regional kingdoms in the fourteenth century. These developments, paired with general Chinese dislike for their alien rulers, left the Yuan vulnerable to overthrow by resurgent Chinese forces led by Ming generals.

The Ming dynasty (C.E. 1368–1644) was intent on reestablishing the pre-Yuan Confucian bureaucratic system. The Ming emperors attempted to restore the Tang system instead of maintaining the more "relaxed" policies of the Song, whom they held accountable for the fall of China to the Mongols. The Ming also followed in the footsteps of the Yuan in their early foreign initiatives. In 1405–1433, Ming rulers sent General Zheng He (1371–1433) and his fleet of more than 300 warships into the Indian Ocean as a declaration of China's interests beyond its borders. After Zheng He's death these voyages ceased. In part this was because conservative Confucian political factions convinced the Ming emperors that such internationalism was too expensive and unnecessary. Some also argued that it was detrimental to China's military priority, which was defending its northern borders from barbarian invasions. Thereafter, Ming military investments focused on rebuilding the Great Wall and preparing for an invasion from the central Asian steppes.

In 1500, Ming China had the resources and productivity to provide for its society's basic needs. Rather than retreating into isolation, it maintained diplomatic and commercial contacts with its neighbors. It openly solicited imported luxuries, not just in satisfying the desires of Chinese consumers, but also because overseas trade was a major source of the Chinese government's tax revenue. Ming China was the source of products such as porcelain, silk, and tea that the remainder of the world desired. The international demand for these products benefited Chinese producers and merchants, as well as the Chinese government. This commercial prosperity, paired with China's broad range of previous societal innovations, reinforced China's cultural self-confidence, creativity, and desire to avoid the costly wars of its past.

See also: Agriculture; Archeological Discoveries;

Buddhism; Confucianism; Culture and Traditions; Huns; Indian Ocean Trade; *Pax Sinica;* Silk Road; Society; Technology and Inventions; Tools and Weapons.

FURTHER READING
De Bary, William Theodore, and Irene Bloom, compilers. *Sources of Chinese Tradition.* 2nd ed. New York: Columbia University Press, 1999.
Ebrey, Patricia Buckley. *China: A Cultural, Social, and Political History.* Boston: Houghton Mifflin, 2006.
Hucker, Charles O. *China's Imperial Past, An Introduction to China's History and Culture.* Stanford, CA: Stanford University Press, 1994.

Confucianism

A once-dominant ancient Chinese religion based on the teachings of the sage Confucius (Kungfutzu, 551–479 B.C.E.). Unlike other teachers of the time, Confucius believed that it was possible for all people, regardless of their station in life, to do right. He taught "right relations," which included benevolence, respect for superiors, and piety.

THE CONFUCIAN IDEAL
Confucianism is a set of ethical rules or a moral philosophy rather than a formal religion. It avoids discussion of a divine being and is vague in its views of the afterlife and otherworldly matters. The Confucian ideal is a ranked or **hierarchical** social and political order that is made up of status groups and graded roles, from the ruler at the top through officials and gentry (a landed and educated elite) to the family head. According to Confucian philosophy, the key to effective authority is setting a good example through "right relationships" in order to ensure "virtuous behavior."

In Confucian **doctrine**, the individual is like a stray nail sticking up that needs to be pounded down in order to protect the group's common interests. Confucianism encourages the subjection of the individual to the greater good of the family and society. Individualism and freedom are seen as the consequence of selfishness and a lack of rules. The result

of both is chaos and anarchy, or lawlessness, from which everyone suffers. Society then, through a set of laws, must evolve its own balance between individual actions and the need to protect the group.

Confucius believed that a formal legal code and the threat of punishment are no guarantee of individual virtue or social harmony. He also believed that, in a properly run society, rules and punishments are ineffective and unnecessary. In the ideal Confucian order, people *want* to do right, which is achieved only by making the Confucian ethical code of correct social relationships a part of one's own thinking. Violence is only a last resort, when the social system has broken down.

TWO SCHOOLS OF BELIEF
Early Confucianism, as popularized in the writings of the scholar Mencius (Meng Tzu, ca. 371–289 B.C.E.) presents a highly optimistic view of humanity and society. Later Confucian scholars, collectively

GREAT LIVES

Confucius

According to tradition, the Chinese sage Confucius was born about 551 B.C.E. in the feudal state of Lu in what is today Shandong province. His father, who was 70 when Confucius was born, died when the child was three, and Confucius's mother brought the boy up in poverty. Although details of his life are shrouded in uncertainty, he appears to have worked a variety of jobs as a young man, including a shepherd, a cowherd, and a bookkeeper. He eventually obtained a government position as an administrative manager in the state of Lu, and at age 53 he was appointed the state's Justice Minister. He left that position for reasons that are unclear, but that may have been related to the enthusiasm with which he promoted his beliefs to his superiors.

After leaving Lu, Confucius traveled to a number of states in northern and central China, hoping to interest rulers in implementing his ideas. Although he was unsuccessful in gaining official recognition, Confucius attracted a large number of adherents among China's intellectual classes, many of whom occupied influential government positions. His disciples promoted and spread his ideas and later compiled the *Analects,* a collection of sayings and short dialogues that form the primary source for information about Confucius and his philosophy. Confucius died in about 479 B.C.E., and it would take another 300 years for his ideas to be widely adopted in China. His teachings continue to influence Chinese society today and have also spread to Taiwan, Japan, Korea, and Vietnam.

known as "legalists," had a very different perspective. They argued that humans drift naturally toward chaos and thus require an intervening force, or the threat of force. Confucian legalists believed that people need a formalized code of law to achieve and maintain universal social harmony.

Both traditions, however, affirmed peoples' right to rebel against immoral or unjust rulers, leaders who had forfeited the "Mandate of Heaven" by their own lapse from virtue. While loyalty to superiors was the basic commandment of Confucianism, commitment to moral principle could prevail, especially in times of corrupt leadership. This situation, however, presented individuals with a severe dilemma—loyalty to leader versus commitment to moral principle. Consequently, civil disobedience was extremely rare, and, however unjust, authorities (from the emperor at the top to one's parents on the bottom) were rarely challenged.

POLITICAL, SOCIAL, AND RITUAL TRADITIONS

Confucian ethics were eventually incorporated in the Chinese imperial examination system during

the reign of the Han emperor Wudi (r. ca. 141–87 B.C.E.), with officials selected from among the educated classes. The result was a system that was, in theory, open to candidates of any social class or rank. Because China had no public schools, however, only the wealthy were able to afford the education needed to pass the exams. The gentry thus dominated the examination system and the Chinese bureaucracy. The entry of upwardly mobile lower-class individuals, although not impossible, was extremely rare.

Confucianism taught followers to honor hard work, achievement, material prosperity, and the enjoyments that "self-cultivation" produced. Confucians especially revered bearing children and attaining an old age of leisure surrounded by one's successful descendents. According to Confucianism, the natural world was the orderly model for the human world. Nature was thought to be a nurturing power, not a hostile one, to be admired and preserved, and to which people should adjust rather than attempt to conquer. Natural calamities, such as floods, droughts, or earthquakes, were commonly taken as the consequence of heaven's displeasure at the lack of virtue among China's rulers.

In the Confucian view, time was cyclical, and there was a repetitive rhythm to both natural and human existence. For example, Confucianism recognized the inevitability of the fall of a dynasty due to what the Chinese referred to as the "fat cat" syndrome. According to this syndrome, China's virtuous leadership should maintain order and anticipate natural disasters, for example, by initiating innovative public works projects and storing surplus production in prosperous times. Instead, rulers often chose to use public funds to pay for their luxurious lifestyle. Confucians argued that such nonvirtuous leaders were destined to fall.

Confucianism was also China's "state religion," in which the emperor presided over rituals at the imperial capital. These rituals were to intercede with heaven or to commemorate imperial ancestors to secure general public welfare: good harvests; rain; and the end to floods, epidemics, famine, and civil chaos. Sometimes the rituals were designed to acknowledge the inappropriate or unethical behavior among the ruling elite in the hopes of persuading heaven to restore society's prosperity.

The Confucian assertion that heaven is an impersonal force superior to humankind did not adequately explain spiritual existence, so many people turned to other religions, while continuing to maintain their Confucian beliefs and ritual practices. For example, many people embraced the Daoist naturalist philosophy and the Buddhist explanation of the afterlife. Daoism and Buddhism both depend on a formal priesthood and sets of universal rituals. Daoist and Buddhist temple worship encouraged Confucians to build their own temples, where illustrious figures of the local past were granted imperial recognition and were eventually worshipped as the community's imperially sanctioned guardian deities. Chinese folk religions, which invoked divine intervention through offerings to local spirits or deceased ancestors, also claimed many adherents.

Popular Confucianism extended respect for the contemporary elders to those who had gone before, as the ancestors became valued models, and ancestral rituals at small household and community shrines kept their memory alive. It was the duty of the eldest son to perform rituals on the death of his father, through successive generations, keeping the ancestral chain intact and thus ensuring family continuity. Maintaining the family line was so important that the greatest sin under Confucianism was to have no descendants (specifically male offspring because women left their parental family at marriage and became members of their husband's family). This attitude has perpetually favored sons and has encouraged couples to conceive as many children as necessary to produce a male child.

The ancient teachings of Confucius have defined traditional values and the ideas of proper behavior in modern China. Although once out of favor in the People's Republic of China, Confucian practices have become more visible in the past two decades, and live on in modern Taiwan, Korea, Japan, Vietnam, and the overseas Chinese communities resident in Southeast Asia.

See also: Art and Architecture; China; Culture and Traditions; Japan; Korea; Society; Vietnam.

FURTHER READING

Ebrey, Patricia. *Confucian and Family Ritual in Imperial China.* Princeton, NJ: Princeton University Press, 1992.

Elman, B. *A Cultural History of Civil Examinations in Late Imperial China.* Berkeley: University of California Press, 2000.

Mann, S., and Y. Chang. *Under Confucian Eyes: Writings on Gender in Chinese History.* Berkeley: University of California Press, 2001.

Miyazaki, Ichisada. *China's Examination Hell: Civil Service Exams of Imperial China.* Translated by Conrad Schirokauer. New Haven, CT: Yale University Press, 1981.

Culture and Traditions

Before C.E. 1500, local innovation and adaptations of the advanced cultural forms found in India and China characterized Asian society. The northern Indian Hindu-Buddhist culture of Gupta India spread to southern India in the sixth century B.C.E. and then to Southeast Asia. A century later, Korea and Japan adopted many aspects of the Chinese civilization of Tang China and adapted them to local life.

These diverse ancient societies were marked by increasing political, economic, and societal centralization, often the result of military conquest. Rulers of the Mauryan **dynasty** in India (founded about 400 B.C.E.) and the Qin dynasty in China (founded about 221 B.C.E.) were the first Asian leaders to take the title of emperor rather than king, considering themselves entitled to this lofty title as a consequence of their military victories and **annexations** of rival kingdoms.

In the aftermath of these dynasties, Chinese and Indian cultures took different courses. Indian culture was dominated by Hindu and Buddhist traditions and therefore became centered in temples rather than the royal court beginning in the Gupta **era** (ca. C.E. 320–550). Chinese culture, on the other hand, remained controlled by the **monarch** and his court, and therefore, from the Tang era (C.E. 618–907) on, was dominated by **secular** ideals rather than religious customs.

GENDER AND FAMILY LIFE

Official Indian and Chinese government texts drew a portrait of societies in which men were active in the realm outside the house and the women prisoners in it. Popular stories, legal documents, and other local accounts, however, demonstrate that there was not such a clear division of labor. Asian women were often economically active in the marketplace, profiting as matchmakers and serving as midwives delivering babies. Girls could learn to read and write from their educated fathers and brothers.

Chinese and Indian women often exercised substantial power within the family political arena, depending on their position in the extended family's **hierarchy**. Mothers were involved in the selection of marriage partners for their children and in the use of family income as this directly related to their children's marriage prospects.

Wealthy families could afford to keep their wives and daughters at home, while the less economically advantaged could not. In early China and India, it was not unusual for women to outlive their husbands, because women commonly married older men. Although both societies frowned on remarriage, widow remarriage was not unusual when the woman's surviving family was not able to support her and her children or did not have a male of sufficient age to insure the family's future.

Chinese women who had married a prosperous husband faced the likelihood that their husband would take at least one concubine. According to Chinese tradition, the wife should not be jealous because her family rank and that of her children were always above that of the concubine and her children. In practice, an attractive and younger concubine might have more influence on the husband than did the wife, despite the concubine's lower rank.

Having married children ensured a woman's future. Daughters-in-law were obliged to do most of the cooking and housekeeping, allowing the grandmothers to enjoy their grandchildren. Many elite women were literate and served as their grandchildren's first teachers, and also composed poetry and carried on correspondence with other women using a secret "woman's language," a kind of coded adaptation of standard Chinese understandable only to those familiar with the code.

During the Song dynasty (C.E. 960–1279), foot binding became popular, as Chinese men of the

Ceremonies that mark important life transitions, such as marriages and funerals, typically feature traditional social customs and rituals. This Hindu bride-to-be in Bombay, India, follows the ancient practice of decorating her hands with henna, a reddish-orange plant dye. (Roger Ressmeyer/Louie Psihoyos/Science Faction/Getty Images)

time considered small feet on women to be particularly attractive. Over time, however, the practice became a mark of social distinction, elegance, and beauty that eventually spread among all classes. Mothers bound their daughters' feet between the ages of five and eight, using long strips of cloth to keep their feet from growing, and to bend the four smaller toes under to make the feet narrow and arched. An aristocrat's feet were bound so tightly that she could barely walk and had to depend on servants. The feet of lower status women were bound less tightly, because they needed to work in the household and perform farming chores, despite their handicap. The practice of binding typically resulted in physical deformity and often led to degenerative diseases of the feet.

LEGAL CULTURE
Classical Chinese law was shaped largely by the Confucian legalistic tradition that advocated a rigid written legal code to maintain political power and social control. In contrast to the Chinese tradition of civil law, countries in southern Asia and most of neighboring Hindu-Buddhist Southeast Asia based their legal codes on the *Dharmasastra* Hindu texts that developed between 600 B.C.E. and C.E. 500. The *Dharmasastra* texts defined universal obligations and penalties, but these were always subject to local caste and religious codes that defined proper morality, duty, and obligations.

Chinese Legal Culture
The Chinese legal system tended more toward a

"rule by law" rather than a "rule of law." This required severe penalties that would discourage disobedience: public humiliation, hard labor, physical mutilation, banishment, slavery, or death.

The Confucian moral code advocated continuous self-cultivation and the performance of one's proper social role in a hierarchically structured society. Aggressive selfish behavior was unacceptable. Because criminal activity was considered the byproduct of improper family management of its individual members, the relatives of a convicted criminal could also be punished.

Most labor penalties lasted from one to six years; mutilation could include shaving the offenders' beard or head, branding, cutting off a nose or foot, or castration. The sentence of death could take several forms, including being torn apart by horse-drawn chariots, although decapitation and hanging were the usual norms. Penal labor was the usual penalty for theft or other civil crimes. Even those who were required to pay fines might have to work off the sentence over a stipulated term of servitude. Those with servants or wealth could receive credit for work performed by others in their place. Males might redeem their relatives by performing services on their behalf.

Laws were intended not only to regulate common people but also to constrain officials. There were rules for keeping accounts, supervising subordinates, managing penal labor, conducting investigations, and appropriately dealing with the public. Officeholders who violated this code of conduct were fined, lost their official positions, might be reassigned to a bureaucratic post on a distant frontier, or, in extreme cases, could be executed.

The Chinese legal system depended on magistrates who were state bureaucrats rather than appointees who had local roots. Private lawyers were prohibited, because they were considered to be social parasites whose involvement was more likely to result in further disputes than in a peaceful resolution. The government magistrate was both the judge and prosecutor (Chinese law thought the accused was guilty until proven innocent), but he was expected to thoroughly investigate a case and to impose a fair sentence. A case could be reopened if one party claimed to be the victim of injustice. To negate corruption and wrongful verdicts, the Chinese state held the magistrate absolutely responsible for mistakes of law or fact, regardless of good intentions or absence of malice. To protect themselves from reprisals, magistrates tried to avoid accepting formal complaints and instead devoted most of their efforts to the mediation of settlements rather than formal litigations inside their courtrooms.

The Chinese legal system made allowances for or penalized criminals according to the extenuating reasons for a crime. Among these was the failure to avoid inauspicious days in taking an action, improperly sacrificing to and burying the dead, and in marrying—all of which allowed the demons and maligned spirits to work their will. An individual's crime might also be blamed on another family member who was negligent in his or her ritual actions, thus making the guilty relative unknowingly vulnerable to a maligned spirit's reprisal.

By the Tang Dynasty era (C.E. 618–907), under the *Tang Code with Commentaries* (624), there were three mandatory automatic reviews of a sentence of death before an execution could take place. Family members could appeal any conviction all the way to the emperor, but they were subject to the risk of punishment if their appeal was ruled to lack merit.

Indian Legal Culture

In the *Dharmasastra* religious tradition, there was no hierarchy among the caste tribunals, and village and marketplace councils had overlapping legal jurisdictions. Every social group was allowed to formulate and apply its own customs and conventions. Law was not rigid but could be changed according to fluctuating local needs and to achieve the best interests of the local community. Ultimately, Indian courts made decisions consistent with the interests of the most powerful among the community's members, whose prominence rested on a combination of their political, economic, religious, and hereditary stature. Most local legal decisions resulted in expulsions and boycotts rather than the fines or the severe physical penalties that were typical of the Chinese court system. In theory, only a royal court could impose a death sentence.

A royal court of justice consisted of a king or emperor or his designated agent assisted by learned

Hindu and Buddhist clerics. Local justice could be appealed to royal courts, where kings made practical legal decisions based on their sense of common usage rather than a written code of law. For a case to go all the way to the royal court was highly unusual and put the community at risk because the king's justice would not necessarily conform with the community's interests. While the king was supposed to pass judgments consistent with the *Dharmasastra* and local traditions, ultimately kings made legal decisions based on their own best interests. Thus, it was likely that a community would choose to reach a local resolution rather than having the outcome dictated by the king.

MATERIAL CULTURE

By C.E. 1500, mainstream Asian cultures had adapted either the Indian or Chinese traditions, or mixtures thereof. As Asian societies became more centralized and commercialized, larger numbers of the local population were producing for the market, allowing Asians to enjoy a higher standard of living. Residents of the new urban centers as well as their networked rural hinterlands began to expect access to a wide variety of foods and material products. Among the consumables in high demand were Indian cotton and Chinese silk; Chinese, Thai, and Vietnamese porcelain ceramics; and Southeast Asian spices and exotic scented woods that had a variety of culinary, medicinal, and ritual uses.

Asians at this time expected to dress and eat better, and to enjoy some degree of luxury that had previously been available only to societal elite. A higher percentage of public literacy, combined with the development of the Asian printing industry, made affordable publications available to the general public, who were able to enjoy a wide range of popular literature and traditional classics. The newly affluent also patronized artists who, in the Chinese artistic tradition, created landscape paintings, scroll art, and portraits for eastern Asian consumers; and in the southern Asian artistic tradition, local artists produced religious and heroic art that was modeled on that of neighboring Persia.

Asian culture in C.E. 1500 was thus marked by wider consistency among increasingly integrated societies, as previously isolated regions and their populations linked into "national" cultures. There was also wider cross-cultural linkage between China and its neighbors in Korea, Japan, and Vietnam. Similarly, the populations in southern and Southeast Asia commonly shared in the Hindu and Buddhist traditions, and those in maritime Southeast Asia were beginning to accept Islamic cultural alternatives.

See also: China; Confucianism; Hinduism; India; Japan; Korea; Language and Writing; Slavery; Society.

FURTHER READING

Chamberlayne, Y., II. *China and Its Religious Tradition.* London: Allen and Unwin, 1993.

Cohn, Bernard S. *India: The Social Anthropology of a Civilization.* Englewood Cliffs, NJ: Prentice Hall, 1971.

Ebrey, Patricia B. *China: A Cultural, Social, and Political History.* Boston: Houghton Mifflin, 2006.

Hall, Kenneth R. *Maritime Trade and State Development in Early Southeast Asia.* Honolulu: University of Hawaii Press, 1985.

Varley, H. Paul. *Japanese Culture.* Honolulu: University of Hawaii Press, 2000.

Genghis Khan *See* China; Mongols.

Golden Horde

Western regions of the Mongol imperial confederacy that once connected the Middle East to China, established by the conquests of the Mongolian conqueror Genghis Khan (r. c.e. 1206–1227). The Golden Horde, which consisted of the Caspian steppes, the Crimea, the northern Caucasus, and the Ural basin in what became western Russia, was home to a collection of seminomadic tribesmen, farmers, and townspeople. This confederacy was financed by collecting taxes from farmers and townspeople along the Silk Road across central Asia, which since the first century b.c.e. had served as the overland trade connection between Europe and eastern Asia.

In contrast to the Mongols, who eventually assimilated into the urban Chinese and Persian civilizations they conquered, the Turkish tribesmen who founded the Horde retained their seminomadic culture. Mongol chieftains (*khans*) ruled the Horde indirectly, employing subservient native princes to carry out their orders. Mongol residents (*baskaks*) and, later, nonresident representatives (*posoly*) supervised the activities of the khans.

The Golden Horde reached the height of its power under Allah Khan Ozbeg (r. 1313–1341). During his reign, the Mongol khans, baskaks, and posoly converted to the Islamic religion, in part to strengthen their ties with their powerful Islamic Mamluk Egypt-based neighbors to the southwest. However, they remained tolerant of their Roman and Orthodox Christian residents rather than forcing them to convert as well.

Despite regular succession crises and the late fourteenth-century victories of Samarkand-based Tamerlane (d. 1405), a Turkik-Mongol who claimed authority as the rightful descendent of Genghis Khan, the Horde remained in power until the reign of Akhmar Khan (r. 1465–1481). In 1471–1472, Prince Ivan III of Muscovy defeated Akhmar's troops, and Akhmar himself failed to recapture Moscow in 1480. The last remnants of the Mongol realm collapsed in 1502, when Ivan allied with the Crimean khan Mengli Girei to crush the Horde's remaining centers of power.

The Golden Horde left a mixed legacy. It is often portrayed as the "barbarous horde" in the tradition of Tamerlane, who collected 70,000 enemy heads when he conquered the Persian city of Isfahan in 1387, and constructed towers made from the skulls of those he conquered on many other occasions.

Although not gifted statesmen, the Golden Horde khans provided leadership and united diverse tribes and multiethnic societies. Despite the end of Mongol rule in China in 1368, the Horde maintained the Silk Road connection between the West and China until 1453, when Constantinople, modern-day Istanbul in Turkey, fell to the Ottoman Turks. The Horde were religiously and culturally tolerant, in contrast to their Christian neighbors in the contemporary West, who regularly persecuted Jews, Muslims, and sects considered heretical by the Catholic Church.

See also: China; Islam, Spread of; Mongols; Silk Road.

FURTHER READING

Halpern, Charles. *Russia and the Golden Horde: The Mongol Impact on Medieval Russian History.* Bloomington: Indiana University Press, 1987.

Ostrowski, Donald. *Muscovy and the Mongols: Cross-Cultural Influences on the Steppe Frontier, 1304–1589.* Cambridge: Cambridge University Press, 1998.

Great Wall of China *See* Archeological Discoveries; Art and Architecture; China.

Hinduism

Religious and societal tradition that originated in southern Asia about 1600 B.C.E. but did not reach its inclusive form until the fourth century C.E., during the reign of the Gupta dynasty in northern India (ca. C.E. 320–550). This evolution of Hinduism paralleled the development of early Indian society from its **seminomadic** origins to its culmination in the Gupta age.

VEDIC ERA: RITUAL AND SOCIAL ORDER

Hinduism began with the entry of Indo-Aryan seminomads into northwestern India (modern-day Pakistan) from central Asia's steppe grasslands around 1600 B.C.E. The Indo-Aryans imposed their sacrificial religion on previous temple-based fertility cults. Aryans worshipped their family ancestors at household altars and held large-scale public celebrations of **celestial** divinities, especially the war god Indra. Aryan religion is described in the *Vedas,* four texts that contain sacred hymns, the details of ritual performances, and the essential Aryan beliefs that would become the foundation of Hindu orthodoxy.

The *Rig Veda* (ca. 1800–1300 B.C.E.) not only provides the earliest Aryan hymns but also describes the multiethnic agricultural society that formed after the Aryan invasions. According to its hymns, the original male (known as Parusa) was dismembered in a celestial sacrifice. His mouth became the *Brahmin* class (priests and religious teachers), his arms the *Ksatriya* class (warriors and rulers), his thighs the *Vaisya* (economic specialists such as traders, landholders, and those who owned livestock), and his feet the *Sudra* servants (those who labored on behalf of the top three social ranks).

The Aryan *varna,* or class, structure became the basis of the later Indian caste system, which categorized the occupational subgroups appropriate to the four varnas. This **hierarchical** social model was detailed in later teachings as compiled in the Hindu codebooks, the *Dharmasastras* and *Dharmasutras.* These legal texts defined the *dharma,* or duties and behavior, appropriate to each occupational rank.

In the initial Vedic **era** (ca. 1600–1200 B.C.E.) the king represented divinity and sponsored the great sacrifices that ensured his society's success. As Vedic-era society became more settled (ca. 1200–800 B.C.E.), the ritual functions performed by the king and the heads of prominent extended families became the duties of a professional Brahmin priesthood. The Brahmin's duties were detailed in

ORIGINS AND GROWTH OF HINDUISM

CA. 1800–1300 B.C.E. Composition of *Rig Veda,* early Aryan hymns describing basic religious concepts

1600 B.C.E. Aryans migrate to India from central Asia; Hinduism originates from mixture of existing Aryan and Indian beliefs

CA. 1600–1200 B.C.E. Early Vedic era; Aryan Hindu kings rule over what is now India

1200–CA. 800 B.C.E. Professional Brahmin priesthood assumes ritual functions once performed by India's Hindu kings and family heads

1000–600 B.C.E. Composition of the *Upanishads;* spread of ideas of reincarnation, *karma,* and yogic asceticism; acquisition of knowledge as an alternative focus to Brahmanical ritual; formalization of early caste system

500 B.C.E.–C.E. 200 Composition of the *Bhagavad Gita,* which becomes basis of Hindu *bhakti* devotional tradition

CA. C.E. 320–550 Gupta dynasty rules northern India; Hinduism achieves modern form

sacred texts, which described the ever more elaborate ceremonies necessary to ensure the success of Hindu society. The kings were now the potentially forceful upholders of dharma (dutiful behavior) and, in partnership with the priesthood, were the guardians of the social and sacred order.

Subsequent religious texts debated the appropriate behavior of a king. The *Dharmasastras* ("the laws of dutiful behavior") suggested that the best kings provided leadership by awe-inspiring moral example rather than by directly engaging in public activities. In contrast, the *Arthasastra* ("the laws of self-preservation") argued that successful kings needed to be more aggressive, leading their troops to conquer new territories, defending against invaders, and directly policing the social order.

THE UPANISHADS: KNOWLEDGE AND SALVATION

The literate, landed aristocracy that emerged between 1000 and 600 B.C.E. asserted its capacity for religious activity rather than depending on the ritual services of the Brahmin priest. The *Upanishad* sacred texts presented their case, proposing that knowledge was an alternative to ritual as one pursued ultimate liberation from the realm of humanity. In the *Upanishads,* the universe had its origin in a creative force, *Brahman,* which was thought of as a source of creative energy rather than as a divine being. Later Hindu art sometimes depicted *Brahman* as a cosmic egg, from which comes life.

From *Brahman* come the individual souls (*atman*) that take living form as humans or animals. According to the divine plan, each soul enters the realm of humanity with a duty (*dharma*) that is appropriate to its place in the hierarchy of existence. Thus, a laborer should not perform the duties of a priest; nor should a priest perform the daily tasks of the laborer. The point is that an individual should fulfill one's appropriate dharma; not to do so would jeopardize universal (divinely ordained) order. Actions are supposed to be those appropriate to one's dharma, but ignorance and illusion lead to improper behavior, or sin.

Because of this moral pollution, the initially pure soul is no longer able to return to the purity of *Brahman,* and thus the self (the soul) is plunged into a series of rebirths. Moral and immoral acts thus have consequences, resulting in a series of rebirths. The soul moves from one unfulfilled rebirth to another, in either human or animal form, as a result of merit or demerit accumulated in prior existences. Death is not tragically final but marks the passage of the soul from one temporary form of existence to another in its ongoing quest for purity and, therefore, salvation.

The *Upanishads* provide philosophical justification for caste and mandatory acceptance of one's place in the social hierarchy. They also provide a conceptual hierarchy that includes nonhumans. This explains why Hindus are frequently vegetarians; to kill and eat animals, which may possess the soul of an ancestor, is considered murder and cannibalism.

Later Hindu texts (*The Laws of Manu,* the *Yoga Sutras,* and the *Bhagavad Gita*) that elaborate on the *Upanishads* portray knowledge as an instrument for liberation from the cycles of rebirth. The consequence of liberation is the soul's return to *Brahman.* Knowledge is achieved by devoted physical and mental exercise (*yoga*) to eliminate the material and intellectual attachments that lead to illusion.

Only members of the three upper classes might achieve salvation at the conclusion of this lifetime by successfully passing through the four stages of life: student, householder, hermit, and ascetic. The ideal ascetic is the meditating intellectual who has withdrawn totally from society. By returning to the universal essence of *Brahman,* the permanent self ceases to exist and once again becomes part of the energy mass from which new souls will come.

THE BHAGAVAD GITA AND BHAKTI DEVOTIONALISM

In contrast to the ornate ritual traditions of the *Vedas* and *Brahmanas,* and the high-level intellectualism of the *Upanishads,* Hinduism developed a popular alternative. This alternative way is represented in the *Bhagavad Gita,* a subtext of the evolving *Mahabharata* epic tale that had its origin in the Vedic age. This epic poem, which tells the tale of the battle between two groups of Aryan warriors, was composed between 500 B.C.E. and C.E. 200. In it, the warrior hero Arjuna anguishes over his duty to kill. Lord Krisna intervenes, coming to earth as the divine persona of Visnu, one of the three supreme Hindu divinities, and assuming human form as Arjuna's charioteer and spiritual guide.

The *Gita* is a dialogue in which Krisna provides spiritual and philosophical guidance to the troubled Arjuna. The focal theme is unselfish action (or service), or disciplined action, in the performance of one's duty without expectation of reward. In the *Gita,* Krisna advises Arjuna to fight in the battle in performance of his duty as a warrior but to remain detached from the consequences. The practice of *karma yoga* in daily life makes the individual fit through action (in contrast to ascetic nonaction and meditation);

moral action is the ultimate pathway of devotion to Krisna alone as God.

The *Gita* episodes became the basis of the Hindu *bhakti* devotional tradition. Followers of this tradition had an obligation to fulfill their dharma, but they did so through a commitment to moral behavior rather than being consumed in the service of self or, even worse, taking excessive pleasure in one's actions. Rather than ritual or asceticism, the bhakti worshipper committed to moral behavior, devoted service to God, and a loving relationship in which pure love of God wipes out all bad *karma* (the force generated by a worshipper's actions).

Bhakti devotional movements focused on the divine Siva (the "destroyer" and lord of fertility) and Visnu, the "preserver," who, with Brahma, the god of "creation" (a personification of the Upanishadic Brahman cosmic force), form the Hindu divine trinity (*Trimurti*). Each has *avataras* (male, female, and animal personas) and their subordinate divine (for example, Ganesa, Siva's elephant-headed son). Bhakti tradition does not conceptualize salvation as the achievement of nonexistence, or a passage to a heaven, but as a release in which the devotee becomes absolutely One-with-the-Lord, through an intense love in which two become one.

See also: Culture and Traditions; India; Java; Religion; Society.

FURTHER READING

Klostermeier, Klaus, K. *A Survey of Hinduism.* 2nd ed. Albany: State University of New York Press, 1994.
Lipner, J.J. *Hindus.* New York: Routledge, 1993.
Michaels, Axel. *Hinduism.* Translated by Barbara Harshav. Princeton, NJ: Princeton University Press, 2003.

Huns

Nomadic pastoral populations that, in the fourth century C.E., moved from the central Asian steppe grasslands into northern Iran and modern-day Afghanistan. Called *Xiongnu* by the Chinese, *Chionites* by the Greeks, and *Hunas* by Indians, the Huns launched a series of attacks in the fifth and sixth centuries C.E. against the settled **agrarian** societies of the Roman West, Persia, and Gupta India.

This image depicts Attila the Hun (ca. c.e. 406–453), known as the "Scourge of God," whose nomadic mounted warriors devastated eastern Europe and reached the gates of Rome in the mid-fourth century c.e. According to tradition, Pope Leo I (d. c.e. 461) convinced Attila to spare Rome and abandon his invasion of Italy. (HIP/Art Resource, NY)

 **GREAT LIVES**

Attila the Hun—"Scourge of God"?

Western history and tradition refers to Attila (ca. c.e. 406–453), the fearsome leader of seminomadic steppe warriors known as Huns, as the "Scourge of God." His name is associated with cruelty and savage barbarism. Some of this negative portrayal, however, results from the biased writings of contemporary Romans who were subject to his conquests, and those who held him accountable for the destruction of Roman civilization. Later writers conflated Attila with other steppe warlords such as Genghis Khan (r. c.e. 1206–1227), who also had a reputation for savagery and bloodlust.

By contrast, the Roman historian Priscus, who visited Attila's camp in 448 on a diplomatic mission accompanying the Byzantine emperor Theodosius II, left a record that is filled with admiration for Attila. He praises Attila's personal stature and accomplishments as an able general who had united the various Germanic tribes and led them to impressive victories over the previously invincible Romans. Priscus also reports meeting with an eastern Roman captive resident in Attila's stockade residence, who had become content to live among the multiethnic residents of Attila's base and had no desire to return to the Roman realm.

The most famous of the Hun leaders was Attila (ca. C.E. 406–453), who led the western Hun hordes, then based in Eastern Europe, to victories against the Roman Empire. After his death, large segments of the Hun horde settled in Pannonia, east of the Danube River in modern eastern Austria and Hungary. Shortly after settling in this region, the Hun Empire fell apart as better-organized and militaristic steppe peoples, including early Bulgarians from the East, moved into the region.

In Asia, several waves of eastern Hun invasions were defeated by the Persian Sassanid Empire in the early fourth century. In 392, another Hun horde seized the regions of Bactria and Gandhara on the northwestern border of India. From there, they launched regular attacks against the Gupta rulers on India's northwestern frontier from the mid-fifth to the mid-sixth centuries. The Gupta kings successfully prevented Hun armies from entering the Ganges River plain, but the continuing effort drained the Gupta realm's resources and led to the end of the dynasty by about 550.

The original language of the Huns has been lost; following their invasions, Huns absorbed the languages of the regions they conquered or settled. The eastern Huns used the Bactrian script and language, which was a mixture of the Greek and Persian languages. They also imitated Persian coinage, and followed several of their predecessors' cultural practices, including cremation of the dead, use of the straight sword and compound bow, and the strange custom of artificially elongating their skulls upward, which is depicted in their coinage portraits.

Hun warriors were expert horsemen; each kept several small, tough horses. Warriors in battle would make quick cavalry charges, shooting arrows at their enemies, then retreating to mount a new horse. Using his string of horses, a Hun warrior could continue charging indefinitely. Opponents feared the Huns so much that many paid tribute to avoid being the target of Hun attacks. Until the time of the Mongols, most Eurasian populations saw the Huns as the ultimate symbol of ferocious barbarian cruelty and deceit.

Tributary payments by their neighbors, use and sales of war captive slaves, and the collection of ransom on war prisoners subsidized a comfortable lifestyle. Huns lived most of their lives in tents, some quite large, that were lavishly furnished. They traded horses and furs for grain, weapons, and luxuries such as Chinese silk.

See also: India.

FURTHER READING

Grousset, Rene. *The Empire of the Steppes: A History of Central Asia.* New Brunswick, NJ: Rutgers University Press, 1988.

Thompson, E.A. *The Huns.* Cambridge, MA: Blackwell, 1999.

India

A country that is a critical center in the development of Asian civilization, India has served as a cultural innovator, a recipient of external culture, and the source of cultural inspiration for other countries of the region and the world.

Before C.E. 1500, a series of invasions and migrations by seminomadic outsiders from central Asia and neighboring Persia into the Indian subcontinent played a significant role in laying the foundation of modern Indian society. By 1500, these indigenous and foreign groups had intermixed to produce an Indian society characterized by wide regional variation in ethnic, cultural, and linguistic traditions.

Geographical and climatic differences between northern India and the remainder of the subcontinent influenced India's early history. Northern India's broad river plains, drained by the Indus, Ganges, and Brahmaputra rivers, supported the concentrated settlement of farming populations, who provided a stable economic base to sustain India's early empires, the Mauryans (ca. 400–180

MILESTONES IN ANCIENT INDIAN HISTORY

CA. 2500–1800 B.C.E. Early urban centers arise in Indus Valley

CA. 1600 B.C.E. Seminomadic Aryans from southern Russia migrate to India and impose authority over existing populations

CA. 1600–600 B.C.E. Mixing of Aryan and Indian cultures produces foundations of Hindu religious beliefs and caste system of social stratification

CA. 600 B.C.E. Regional kingdoms begin to emerge in northern India's Ganges River plain

CA. 400–180 B.C.E. Mauryan regional clan conquers its competitors to establish rule over India

326 B.C.E. Macedonian king Alexander III, the Great, invades Pakistan and western India; his survivors establish Indo-Greek states in the northwest region

CA. 273–232 B.C.E. Mauryan Empire reaches it height under Asoka, who adopts Buddhism as the favored religious tradition of the state

CA. 180 B.C.E.–C.E. 320 Mauryan Empire collapses; India enters prolonged period of division and rule by competing regional kingdoms

CA. C.E. 320–550 Gupta kings establish control over north Indian Empire and adopt Hinduism as state religious tradition; Gupta rule considered the "classical age" of ancient Indian culture

C.E. 550–606 Repeated invasion attempts by seminomadic Huns leads to fall of Gupta empire and period of political disorder

C.E. 606–647 Military leader Harsa briefly reestablishes central authority in India

C.E. 647–1010 North India reverts to period of regional rule by states controlled by military leaders; now south Indian states emerge

C.E. 1010–1206 India comes under the rule of a series of early Muslim rulers

C.E. 1206 First dynasty of the powerful Delhi Sultanate established by Qutb-ud-din Aibak

C.E. 1206–1290 Slave dynasty, successors of Qutb-ud-din Aibak, rules India

C.E. 1290–1320 Reign of the Khilji Turks

C.E. 1320–1413 Reign of the Tughlaq Turks

C.E. 1336–1565 Powerful Vijayanagara Hindu military monarchy in south India

C.E. 1414–1451 Reign of the Sayyid Turks

C.E. 1451–1526 Reign of the Lodi Turks

C.E. 1526 Afghan leader Babur overthrows the Delhi Sultanate and establishes Mughal dynasty (1526–1857)

B.C.E.) and the Guptas (ca. C.E. 320–550). The rivers fostered economic and social exchanges, ensuring a more or less common culture among those who lived within the river system.

ARYANS, VEDICS, AND MAURYANS

Around 1600 B.C.E., migrating seminomadic Aryans from southern Russia's steppe grasslands entered India through the Hindu Kush mountain passes. They imposed their authority over India's settled agriculturalists, the remnants of a networked urbanized society in northwestern India's Indus Valley (2500–1800 B.C.E.). During the next 1,200 years, the nomads mixed with India's indigenous peoples, as settled agricultural society gradually spread from west to east in the Ganges River plain of northern India.

Linguistically, the Aryan's **Sanskrit** language displaced the previous use of Dravidian languages in northern India, but preexisting Dravidian cultures remained in widespread use in southern India. Religiously, Aryan worship of male **celestial** divinities mixed with local worship of female fertility deities; these female divinities became the wives and female companions of the Aryan gods. The cultural mix of Aryan culture with local culture, a process called Sanskritization, also resulted in the Aryan religion's inclusion of assorted local **animistic** spirits: ancestors, animals (cattle, birds, snakes), and various natural forces (wind, water, fire). The end product was the variety of divine beings that are still worshiped as the diverse personalities, incarnations, and subordinate deities of Visnu, Siva, and the Buddha.

Socially, the mixing of populations resulted in the Indian caste system, which developed from the **hierarchical** ordering of Aryan society. Priests and religious teachers were *Brahmins;* kings and their elite warriors were *Ksatriya;* commercial specialists, landholding elite, those who controlled livestock were *Vaisya;* and the supportive worker/laborers were *Sudra.*

By about 600 B.C.E., regional kingdoms began to emerge in northern India's Ganges River plain. These were dominated by landholding family clans that had appropriated the new mixed culture. By 400 B.C.E., the Mauryan clan had conquered its competitors, ruling from the urban center they called Pataliputra (present-day Patna). Their realm was located in the strategic central Ganges River plain, where its rulers could control communication networks throughout the subcontinent.

Mauryan India reached its peak under the emperor Asoka (r. ca. 273–232 B.C.E.), a great military conqueror and social innovator. Asoka initially fought against the regions bordering his realm, notably in 265–264 B.C.E. against the Kalinga realm on India's eastern coast, south of the Ganges River mouth. He **annexed** Kalinga after what his **inscriptions** estimate to be 100,000 Kalinga deaths, then resettled Kalinga's remaining populations in his territorial core. Asoka's inscriptions indicate that he converted to Buddhism shortly after his victory, and that he successfully promoted the faith's socially inclusive religious **doctrines**. Buddhism was more tolerant of social diversity than was the rigid caste-based order advocated in the *Dharmasastra* texts, and allowed Asoka to culturally unite the diverse populations that were now included in his vast domain.

During his reign, Asoka supported the development of Mauryan cities and promoted trade, implemented a universal law code and a realmwide judicial system, and initiated a partnership with the Buddhist church. Asoka sent Buddhist monks as his personal agents throughout north India, to minister to local populations while tending to the state's business. Monks also served as his international envoys to neighboring realms. Asoka was widely idealized throughout Asia following his death as the *cakravartin,* the universal **monarch** whose personal achievements and high ethical standards were the model for other kings.

NEW INVASIONS, THE GUPTAS, AND THE DELHI SULTANATE

After the Mauryan Empire split into regional kingdoms around 180 B.C.E., India was subject to new invasion attempts, migrations, and cultural infusions from the northwest until C.E. 320. This **era** resulted in the mixture of newly arrived and existing cultures on its modern-day Pakistan frontier. Among those who had an impact were the remnants of the armies of Alexander III, the Great, collectively called the Indo-Greeks (180 B.C.E.–C.E. 10). They had remained behind as rulers of Greek colonies on India's northwestern frontier after Alexander's 326 B.C.E. victory against Mauryan forces in what is now Pakistan. The Indo-Greeks initially competed for influence with the central Asia–based Scythians, then with the Iran-based Parthians to the first century C.E., and later with the Afghanistan-based Kushana, who held parts of the northern Ganges River plain from C.E. 105–250.

During this transitional era, Greek and Persian religious and artistic heritage influenced India's evolving Buddhist and Hindu traditions. This was especially the case as Greek tradition reinforced local adoption and adaptation of **icon** worship, evident in the earliest statuary representations of the Buddha in India's Gandharan art. It portrays the Buddha in Greek dress and with Greek physique, featuring long, dark hair and a mustache.

The origins of the Gupta Empire (ca. C.E. 320–550) are vague, although **historical research** suggests that the Gupta kings originated in the Bengal region. They established their empire by conquering the old Magadha political center of the Mauryan kings in the central Ganges River plain region. The Gupta kings, who claimed to be the heirs to the Mauryans, restored centralized authority, once again centered at the Mauryan capital city of Pataliputra.

Marking a break with the ultimately failed Mauryan past, Gupta kings patronized Hinduism. By the early fourth century C.E., Hinduism had developed as an inclusive mix of traditional Brahmanical ritual and scholarship and popular devotional worship of Hindu divinities. Gupta India is considered India's classical age, marked by its rulers' patronage of Hinduism and its religious and literary accomplishments. The Gupta age witnessed the composition of the highest quality Sanskrit language poetry, literature, drama, and religious texts.

Gupta rule ended around C.E. 550, as a result of the more than 100-year drain of public resources for the defense of India's northwestern frontier against the repeated invasion attempts by seminomadic eastern Huns. There was a brief renewal of centralized authority under the military leader Harsa in the early seventh century (r. C.E. 606–647). Harsa claimed that he had restored the Gupta realm, but his was a military rather than a civilian administration. After his death, north India once again lapsed into regional states dominated by similar martial kings or chiefs.

At the turn of the millennium, north India faced a new onslaught from the northwest by Muslim invaders. Most of these were Turks from central Asia who entered India via India's northwestern passageways. Between 1010 and 1525, a series of Muslim dynasties rose and fell. In 1206, the Ghurid warrior Qutb-ud-din Aibak (r. 1206–1210) took Delhi and founded the first of several dynasties known as the Dehli Sultanate. Qutb-ud-din Aibak's successors, collectively known as the Slave **dynasty**, reigned from 1206 to 1290. In turn, the Khilji Turks reigned from 1290 to 1320, followed by the Tughlaq (1320–1413), the Sayyid (1414–1451), and the Lodi Turkish rulers (1451–1526). Finally, in 1526, the Afghanistan-based Babur, an Afghan heir to the Mongols, defeated the Lodi armies and initiated the Mughal dynasty (1526–1857).

Some scholars characterize the Delhi Sultanate as a succession of Turkish dynasties that ruled over largely Hindu subject populations in northern India, exacting taxes in return for protection. Despite this seeming separation between ruler and ruled, Muslims and Hindus began a productive intercultural dialogue typical of the earlier eras of cultural integration. The key difference is that the Muslim rulers allowed Hindus greater opportunity to retain their cultural traditions, as long as they submitted to Islamic sovereignty.

See also: Archeological Discoveries; Buddhism; Hinduism; Huns; Islam to Asia, Spread of; Monsoons; Society.

FURTHER READING

Basham, A.L. *The Wonder That Was India*. New York: Grove Press, 1959.

Keay, John. *India: A History*. New York: Grove Press, 2000.

Wolpert, Stanley. *A New History of India*. New York: Oxford University Press, 2005.

Indian Ocean Trade

Commercial contact that linked the cultures along the coast of **maritime** Asia (India, Southeast Asia, China, Korea, and Japan) long before the arrival of Europeans in the middle of the second millennium C.E. By the first century B.C.E., the peoples and cultures of the Indian Ocean and the adjacent regions to its east were linked in a trade network that extended from the port cities of the eastern coast of the African continent all the way to Japan and Korea.

INTERNATIONAL TRADE ROUTES OF THE PEOPLES OF ASIA, CA. C.E. 1500

The multiethnic trade centers of Southeast Asia and the coastal regions of China, Korea, and Japan functioned as part of a great integrated trade network rooted in the Indian Ocean. The alternative east-west overland route was known as the Silk Road, which connected China to northern India, Persia, and the Arab capital at Baghdad.

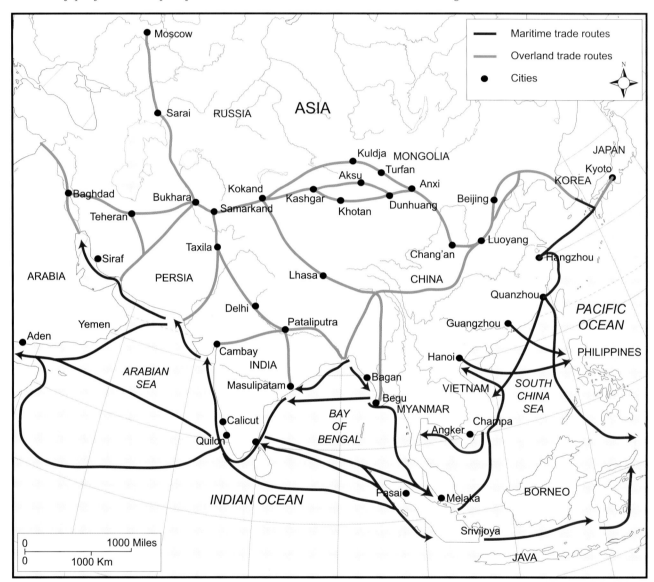

Initially, the greatest volume of maritime trade took place between the Middle East and India, as China's trade with the West depended more on the overland Silk Road until the early third century C.E. Maritime traders brought India's pepper, cotton **textiles**, and bronze statuary as far west as the Roman Empire. Indian statuary was even made to the specifications of Roman consumers. Exotic products from Southeast Asia and China, such as silk, incense, and spices, also made their way to Rome and other locations in the West.

China's earliest interactions with India intensified after the fall of the Han **dynasty** (206 B.C.E.– C.E. 220). At this time the China's elites, many of whom had relocated to southern China to avoid the chaos of the north, sought an alternative trade route to the West after the collapse of the Han dynasty rendered the central Asian Silk Road unsafe. They also sought to gain direct access to the homeland of Buddhism as the source of religious texts, religious **artifacts**, and ritual objects, and as a pilgrimage center where Chinese monks could study at the foremost centers of Buddhist scholarship. Later Tang (c.e. 618–907) and Song (c.e. 960–1279) governments took greater interest in commercial rather than religious exchanges with the regions to China's south. This interest stemmed from periodic insecurities along the old Silk Road across central Asia. Unsafe traveling conditions resulted in regular market shortages that left Chinese merchants unable to satisfy the **aristocracy**'s continuing demand for Western products.

The eleventh century witnessed a surge in the volume of Indian Ocean trade, thanks largely to the regional stability established over the Middle East by Muslim Abbasid caliphs (until 1258) and Seljuk Turks (1037–1219). Middle Eastern merchants flooded the Indian Ocean, seeking Asian goods in exchange for their own. This, combined with a stable China market, resulted in southern India and Sri Lanka becoming new international commercial hubs, filling roles as strategic intermediaries in the trade between the Middle East and Southeast Asia. In Southeast Asia, Java became prominent because of its central role in providing international access to the spices of the eastern Indonesia **archipelago**, then known as the Spice Islands.

By this time, regional centers began to function as part of one great, integrated Indian Ocean trade network. The increased volume of trade attracted a multiethnic community of trade specialists that included assorted Middle Easterners, Indians, Southeast Asians, and Chinese. All the sojourning traders made seasonal voyages using the Asian monsoon winds, which blew from southeast to northwest in June through August and then reversed, blowing from northwest to southeast in December through March.

Rather than navigate the entire length of the trade route, which might take two to three years, merchants specialized in shorter voyages in one segment, sailing to and from an adjacent region in

a single year. Traders would sell their goods to local intermediaries at their destination ports, who would then hold and resell them to merchants arriving later from other regional markets. For example, local intermediaries traded Middle Eastern glassware and Indian cotton textiles supplied by southern Asia–based seafarers for ceramics, silk, and spices brought by Chinese and Southeast Asian merchants.

In the early fifteenth century c.e., the new Ming emperors, who had come to power in China in 1368, sent the eunuch admiral Zheng He and his fleet of Chinese battleships to assert China's interests across the entire maritime network (1405–1433). Zheng He eliminated pirates and promised military assistance and continued Chinese support for local political regimes that guaranteed the regular flow of international products to China's ports. He also reinstated the Chinese tributary trade system, wherein Indian Ocean countries sent periodic embassies to China's courts to present diplomatic "gifts" of their prize marketplace commodities. In return, the Chinese emperor bestowed honorific material symbols and official proclamations that confirmed the local rulers' authority. Partly in response to these Ming initiatives, the fifteenth century in Asia witnessed substantial increases in trade volume, participants, and the diversity of traded commodities. This prosperity attracted the attention of Europeans, whose desire to acquire Asia's exotic commodities resulted in Europe's sixteenth century "Age of Discovery."

See also: Buddhism; China; Java; Melaka; Monsoons; Silk Road; Spice Trade; Zheng He.

FURTHER READING
Abu-Lughod, Janet. *Before European Hegemony: The World System 1250–1350.* New York: Oxford University Press, 1991.
Sen, Tansen. *Buddhism, Diplomacy, and Trade: The Realignment of Sino-Indian Relations, 600–1400.* Honolulu: University of Hawaii Press, 2003.

Islam, Spread of

The introduction of Islamic religion and culture from the Middle East, which profoundly affected the development of Asian civilizations from the eleventh to the sixteenth centuries C.E. While military conquest brought Islam to India, trade spread the faith throughout the rest of Asia.

Asian merchants and rulers initially adopted Islam because of the commercial advantage it brought in dealing with Muslim traders. Only later did Asian rulers oblige their subjects to convert to Islam. In some states, Islamic law and ritual also validated a society's break with a discredited Hindu or Buddhist past. Islam also served to legitimize and unify new states arising among tribal societies, such as the Mongols, which had no prior tradition of central authority.

CONVERSIONS

The initial Asian conversions to Islam took place following the Umayyad Arab conquest of Persia in C.E. 651, after which most Persians converted from Zoroastrianism to Islam. Persian merchants and missionaries traveling the central Asian Silk Road trade route through Afghanistan found resident Turkish tribesmen receptive to the new faith, in part because of the political and economic advantages that conversion provided relative to their Islamic neighbors: politically, those who shared the Islamic faith were likely to negotiate and form alliances rather than wage war on each other, and to offer a mutual defense against non-Muslims, and Islamic law forbade those who shared in the faith from taking advantage of a fellow Muslim in economic transactions, which was reassuring to long-distance sojourners trading with strangers. By 661, the central Asian caravan hub of Samarkand was already a noted center of Islamic scholarship, and soon other Islamic retreats appeared at major stopovers on the overland trade route between the Islamic Middle East and China.

Multiethnic Muslim traders first reached China during the Tang **dynasty** (C.E. 618–907), arriving either by the overland Silk Road or the Indian Ocean **maritime** route. They established small residential communities in major Chinese cities throughout the Tang and Song (C.E. 960–1279) dynasties. They became especially prominent under the Mongol Yuan dynasty (C.E. 1279–1368), although Yuan Muslims remained a small percentage of China's overall population. While the Yuan officially supported the Buddhist religion, their ruling elite included many Muslims with central Asian and Middle Eastern roots.

In the early fourteenth century, factions of the Mongol alliance based in central Asia established an **autonomous** Islamic confederacy known as the Golden Horde. The Golden Horde's conversion to Islam reinforced its independence from other Mongol tribes and established the foundation for an alliance with the Mamluk Turks, who bordered the Horde to the southwest.

As in China and India, small numbers of urban-based Southeast Asian rulers, elite, and commercial specialists converted to Islam. Local populations were slower to accept Islam because of their strong traditional loyalties to Hinduism, Buddhism, and local **animistic** faiths. Although Muslim traders from the Middle East, southern Asia, and China traded actively in Southeast Asia by the eighth century C.E., the first Southeast Asian coastal state to convert to Islam was Samudra-Pasai in northeastern Sumatra, in 1267. Brunei in northeastern Borneo followed suit in 1365, as did Melaka on the southwestern Malay Peninsula (1415) and Demak in northwestern Java (1475). In each of these port-states, Muslim rulers reigned over non-Muslim societies, and likely converted to Islam to encourage sojourning Muslim traders to transact their business in their port of trade rather than in that of a non-Muslim competitor. However, conversion may have also been due to genuine commitment.

In the early eleventh century, meanwhile, Muslim tribesmen from the central Asian steppes invaded India and established Islamic rule there; in 1206, Qutb-ud-din Aibak founded the first dynasty of the Delhi Sultanate, which lasted, under successive Islamic dynasties, until 1526. This succession of Turkish dynasties ruled over largely Hindu subject populations in northern India from massive walled fortresses. Both Muslim and Hindu communities in India adapted the Islamic artistic traditions of Persia, most notably in the development of "Persian miniature" religious and **secular** art.

CULTURAL CHANGE

There is no single Asian Islamic tradition. Throughout the continent, Islamic thought, practice, and ritual adapted to local circumstances and cultures. Asian Islamic societies did not develop in isolation, however, as Asia-based clerics regularly participated in the theological debates among leading Islamic scholars in Mecca and other major religious centers of the Middle East. Initially, conversion to Islam may have been a token gesture undertaken for economic, political, or social benefit. In addition to the noted ruling elite, the other major initial conversions took place among people of previously low social stature, who viewed their conversion to be a means to enhance their opportunities for personal gain.

The earliest Islamic scholars who traveled to central Asia, India, and Southeast Asia found the mystical traditions of Islam especially compatible with existing religious values, and thus promoted a modified version of Islam known as Sufism. The Sufi tradition blended Islamic and local values to win converts, rather than promote the more legalistic versions of Islam (Sunni and Shi'a). In Java, for example, the form of Islam that took root placed less emphasis on Islamic **doctrine**, but instead stressed the role of divinely empowered saints who allied with Java's new Islamic sovereigns to unite the natural and supernatural worlds. Java's Islam focused on rulers and clerics performing magical court-based Islamic ritual. Local converts retained their most valued societal practices and continued their worship of traditional spirits, which they believed were subordinate to the supreme Islamic divine being, Allah.

The Islamic dietary restrictions against eating pork were especially troubling in China and Southeast Asia, where pork was a dietary **staple**. In southern Asia and China, Muslim cultural practices regarding women reinforced preexisting limitations on women's activities outside the home—and went even further by suggesting that women should be veiled as well as secluded. Islamic doctrine was used to legitimize the subordination of women, to assert that a woman's primary duty was to marry and raise children (especially boys), and to assert that a woman's principal spiritual duty was subservience to her husband. At the same time, however, Islam brought a new emphasis on the equality of all before God, which had previously been advocated by Buddhists and in Hinduism's bhakti tradition. Islam's orthodox restrictions were not usually applied in Southeast Asia, where women regularly participated in the marketplace.

Moreover, the influence of Islam in Asia to the sixteenth century remained uneven. Northern India's majority Hindu population was subject to the authority of the Delhi Sultanate ruling elite. Central Asia's steppe populations had widely converted to forms of Islam that allowed them to retain most of their previous cultural practices. China had small Muslim communities that were largely composed of Islamic merchants and **artisans** who lived in most of its major urban centers. Southeast Asia had several conversions among elite members of its most prominent maritime trade centers, but as yet Islam had few nonelite followers there. Nevertheless, Islam was having a cultural impact on Asia, including the rise of new Islamic states, the importance of Islamic law as it reinforced Asian trade, and local interest in Islam as a new **monotheistic** alternative to the existing Asian religious faiths.

See also: Golden Horde; India; Java; Religion; Silk Road; Spice Trade.

FURTHER READING
Eaton, Richard M., ed. *India's Islamic Tradition, 711–1750*. New Delhi: Oxford University Press, 2003.
Hildinger, Erik. *Warriors of the Steppe: A Military History of Central Asia 500 B.C. to A.D. 1700*. New York: DaCapo Press, 2001.
Ricklefs, M.C. *Mystic Synthesis in Java: A History of Islamization from the Fourteenth to the Early Nineteenth Centuries*. Norwalk, CT: EastBridge Press, 2006.

Japan

East Asian island nation that evolved from a primitive hunting-and-gathering culture into a regional political and economic power between 1000 B.C.E. and C.E 1500. Japan's earliest history was influenced by extensive trade and cultural interactions with Korea, which was Japan's point of contact with the more advanced civilization in China.

YAYOI CIVILIZATION

Diverse and widely dispersed Japanese hunting, gathering, and fishing societies are collectively referred to as Jomon culture. Named for their distinctive cord-marked pottery, these societies date from roughly 10,000 B.C.E. to 300 B.C.E. The Yayoi period (300 B.C.E.–ca. C.E. 300), named for the town near modern-day Tokyo where archeologists first discovered distinctive pottery of that era, witnessed the introduction of Korean *sawah* (wet rice), bronze, and iron cultures into Japan. During the Kofun period (ca. C.E. 300–538), elite tribal clans, known as *uji,* achieved dominance over rural rice-cultivating peasants. The period is named for distinctive keyhole-shaped raised Kofun tombs, some as large as 440 yards (400 m) in length, located on the eastern Kinai plain on the Japanese island of Honshu, between the modern-day cities of Osaka and Nagoya.

The uji clans legitimized their supremacy by claiming that they were the sole intermediaries between humans and powerful spirits known as *kami.* The Shinto religion, which evolved during this time, ascribed great power to the kami, which included the spirits of departed relatives and divine spirits that animated natural forces. The uji claimed that only they could influence these spiritual forces to protect their communities. By about C.E. 400, the Yamato clan, centered in the region surrounding the modern city of Nara, forged a network among local uji clans through a combination of conquest, absorp-

tion, and incorporation of clan heads as government ministers. The ruling Yamato clan subordinated the other uji and claimed ultimate authority based on its direct descent from the sun goddess Amaterasu. Early Japanese emperors served as supreme priests, who recognized and ranked the local shrines that were subordinate to the imperial shrine.

Following a war over imperial succession in 587, the Soga uji clan took over the day-to-day affairs of the early state. The Yamato emperors became figureheads who spent most of their time performing state Shinto rituals, while the uji clans were assigned specific tasks in the new imperial administration, for example, revenue management, rituals, and warfare.

YAMATO JAPAN

Prince Shotoku (r. C.E. 593–621) promoted the spread of Buddhism in Japan as a superior new magic that was successful in contemporary China. During the period and following, the Chinese Sui (C.E. 581–618) and Tang (C.E. 618–907) courts were blending Buddhism with the Confucian tradition. They successfully reconstructed their Chinese state, which had not had an emperor since the fall of the Han dynasty in C.E. 220.

Shotoku felt that Buddhism played a key role in the renewed Chinese Confucian social order that promoted the centralization of political power. With Shotoku's encouragement, clan leaders in Japan competed with one another to erect lavish local

MILESTONES IN ANCIENT JAPANESE HISTORY

CA. 10,000–300 B.C.E. Early hunting-and-gathering culture known as Jomon inhabits Japan

CA. 300 B.C.E.–C.E. 300 Yayoi culture marks transition to settled agriculture in Japan

CA. C.E. 300–538 Kofun period; elite tribal clans achieve dominance over rural rice-cultivating peasants; Shinto religion originates during this time; named after the mound-shaped tombs that were built for the elite class at this time

CA. C.E. 400 Yamato clan establishes authority over rival clans and forms first Japanese empire

C.E. 593–621 Reign of Prince Shotoku, who promotes spread of Buddhism in Japan

C.E. 645 Regional clans revolt, establish new imperial authority under the Fujiwara family

C.E. 710 Nara is declared permanent imperial capital, breaking the tradition of moving the capital upon the death of the emperor

C.E. 710–784 Nara-era court patronizes Buddhism, whose growing influence over the state becomes a concern for many Japanese

C.E. 784 Capital moved to Kyoto to distance government from influence of Nara-based Buddhist sects

C.E. 794–1185 Kyoto imperial era; imperial government becomes increasingly isolated from affairs in the countryside, leading to rise of local military leaders known as *shoguns*

C.E. 1185–1333 Kamakura Shogunate wields ultimate power; exercises authority through regional *samurai,* or warrior lords

C.E. 1274 AND 1281 Mongol invasions twice thwarted due to unexpected typhoons, which were dubbed *kamikaze,* or "divine wind," by the Japanese

C.E. 1338–1467 Ashikaga Shogunate fuses Japanese imperial court traditions with samurai culture, fostering notable achievements in art, architecture, drama, and literature

C.E. 1467–1568 Era of civil wars between competing samurai armies

C.E. 1603–1868 Tokugawa Shogunate restores central authority; retrains samurai warriors as scholar-bureaucrats; Japan becomes international political power and develops new urbanized culture under Tokugawa rule

shrines dedicated to the main Buddhist sects, whose central temple complexes in Japan were located in the imperial capital at Nara. Nara temples served as centers from which the competing sects spread their influence among the clans.

The uji families retained a large measure of power under Yamato rule by negotiating a partnership with the emperor and the Buddhist clergy to oversee various aspects of the state's ritual, military, and administrative affairs. The foundation for this new order was the "Seventeen Article Constitution" issued by Prince Shotoku in C.E. 604. This document, which promoted a mixture of Buddhism, Confucianism, and the Chinese model, replaced traditional **hereditary** ranks with new Chinese-style designations of senior, junior, upper, and lower grades. Buddhist priests and uji elite accepted their proper place in the new Yamato political and religious order.

In C.E. 645, the succession of a new emperor coincided with a revolt staged by several powerful uji clans. The uprising was led by the Nakatomi clan head Kamatari, who subsequently established a partnership with the new emperor, Tenchi. As the head of the retitled Fujiwara family, Kamatari implemented the new Taika ("great change"), reforms that were intended to eliminate what remained of Japan's old decentralized government. He also established a new capital at Naniwa (now within the modern city of Osaka), which was modeled on the contemporary Tang capital at Changan, now called Xian. The Taiho Code (710), issued by Kamatari's Fujiwara successors, further codified the new Japanese political order, formalizing the Yamato state structure that had emerged gradually over the previous century.

IMPERIAL RULE IN NARA AND KYOTO

Nara became the new imperial capital in c.e. 710 following the death of the emperor Tenchi. Prior to this time, the Yamato court moved whenever an emperor died to avoid ritual pollution associated with the deceased ruler. This once-common practice was abolished under the new Taiho Code, which proclaimed that Nara was to become the permanent capital.

Nara was the site of the realm's greatest Buddhist temples, such as the stunning Todaiji Eastern Great Temple and its Great Statue of the Buddha. The monks of six Nara-based sects competed for the patronage of the emperor and his elite but too often took this competition into the streets of Nara, where they regularly fought with one another. The revelation of a romantic affair between a Buddhist priest and an empress in the c.e. 750s reinforced public fears that Buddhism had become a threat to the civil order. When the priest and the empress attempted to overthrow the Fujiwara family, the imperial military intervened to occupy the Nara temples and to place the Nara priests under "house arrest." With the death of the empress, the new emperor Kammu (r. c.e. 781–806) and his Fujiwara advisers decided in c.e. 784 to move the Japanese capital out of Nara, leaving behind the tarnished reputation of the Nara-era court and the once-powerful Nara-based Buddhist sects. Nagaokakyo served as the capital for 10 years before the court relocated to Heian (modern Kyoto) in 794.

During the Kyoto imperial era (c.e. 794–1185), only two Kyoto-based Buddhist sects were officially recognized, and women were no longer allowed to hold the imperial throne. Kyoto imperial authority reached its height in the tenth century c.e., when the Fujiwara clan exclusively managed the affairs of the court on the emperor's behalf. Under the Fujiwara, which continued to dominate imperial government until c.e. 1160, the court became more and more insulated from the affairs of the countryside, which finally slipped from the direct authority of the court.

The decentralization of Japanese political authority was based in the *shoen,* or regional estates of the court elite. Lay officials managed the estates, which were intended to finance the needs of the court **aristocracy** as well as maintain order in the countryside. Military authority also decentralized to professional warriors called *samurai,* who formed military regiments led by a *shogun* ("military guardian against barbarian peoples"). The samurai protected Japan's core agricultural region from the periodic attacks of bandits who lived on the frontier. When the court finally collapsed in 1185, local civic officials, religious orders, large landowners, and Buddhist temples became the new centers of Japanese authority. They partnered with a new warrior elite, confirming the reordering of Japanese society that had emerged over the past century.

THE KAMAKURA AND ASHIKAGA SHOGUNATES

After c.e. 1185, a series of shoguns wielded ultimate political authority in Japan. The shogun received his authority from the emperor after winning battles against armed opponents. In theory, the emperor delegated to the shogun responsibility for running the Japanese imperial state. In practice, the local "stewards" (*jito*) and "constables" (*shugo*) who had managed the **aristocratic** estates during the imperial period assumed the day-to-day affairs of what remained of the Japanese state. The now-hereditary samurai military elite, ultimately bound by service contracts to the shogun, imposed local order.

The shogunate system depended on the shogun's willingness to acknowledge the local territorial rights of the samurai lords. For example, under

TURNING POINT.

The Divine Wind

The *kamikaze,* or "divine wind," is in recent times associated with Japanese pilots who flew suicide missions against American ships during World War II. The name, which refers to two of the most significant events in ancient Japanese history, represented to the Japanese the possibility of victory even in the darkest hour of impending defeat. The roots of the expression lie in the attempted Mongol invasions of Japan during the thirteenth century.

In C.E. 1266, Kublai Khan (ca. C.E. 1215–1294), ruler of the Mongol Empire, demanded Japan's submission to his newly established Yuan court. When Japan's Kamakura Shogunate (C.E. 1185–1333) refused, Kublai Khan launched an invasion force of 30,000 Mongol and Korean warriors. In 1274, the Yuan army landed on the west coast of the island of Kyushu at Hakata (modern-day Fukuoka). The Yuan military not only outnumbered the Japanese samurai, but also possessed superior tactics and weapons. However, severe weather wrecked many of the invading Chinese ships and threatened to isolate the Yuan troops from their supply lines. The Mongols ultimately were forced to retreat to southern Korea.

Seven years later, Kublai invaded Japan again, this time with a force of 140,000 Mongols, Chinese, and Koreans, carried in the largest fleet of ships ever assembled. Since the last attack, however, the Japanese had built a stone wall along the shoreline at the Mongol landing site at Hakata. They had also retrained their forces to fight in the group style of the Mongols rather than in the individual combat favored by the samurai. The Japanese defenders kept the Mongols contained on a narrow beachhead, while Japanese boats successfully raided the Chinese supply ships. Two months after the landing a typhoon struck, destroying most of the Chinese fleet and forcing the remainder of the Mongol forces to withdraw in defeat.

To the Japanese, this "divine wind" was no accident. It confirmed the Japanese belief that they were favored by the gods, who would always protect Japan against any outside threat. Interior threats, however, were another matter. Despite the Japanese victory, the Mongol war had bankrupted the Kamakura Shogunate, which subsequently fell to the Ashikaga shoguns (C.E. 1338–1467).

the Kamakura Shogunate (C.E. 1185–1333), regional samurai lords were submissive to the Kamakura shoguns, but were also allowed to maintain their own armies. The Kamakura Shogunate, based in Kamakura, southeast of modern Tokyo, was notable for its successful institution of the decentralized shogunate system. Under this system, educated samurai became hereditary administrators who managed the affairs of the Kamakura court. They served as a key source of contact between the shogun and his regional subordinates.

The Kamakura shoguns repelled Mongol invasions of Japan in 1274 and 1281, with considerable help from the *kamikaze* ("divine winds"), or severe typhoons that destroyed the invading Mongol fleets. However, the expense of maintaining a strong de-

fense against potential Mongol invasions undermined the Kamakura Shogunate. After defeating the Kamakura clan in C.E. 1338, the Kyoto-based Ashikaga Shogunate (C.E. 1338–1467) took power.

The Ashikaga era was marked by further decentralization of authority, but is especially noteworthy for its fusion of imperial court traditions with samurai culture. Japanese artists made notable achievements in landscaping and gardening, the evolution of the tea ceremony (and teahouses), Noh drama (marked by the performers' attempts to strictly control their expressions), and new forms of samurai-inspired literature. The Ashikaga era ended with a century of civil wars (C.E. 1467–1568) among rival samurai armies loyal to regional *daimyo* warlords intent on consolidating power.

Japanese religious practice often blends elements of Buddhism, Shinto, and traditional animistic beliefs. Each of the five levels in the Tosho-gu Shrine on Japan's Honshu Island (shown here) represents a different element of the natural world. (Demetrio Carrasco/Dorling Kindersley/Getty Images)

The new Tokugawa Shogunate (C.E. 1603–1868) that emerged from the wars restored the strong central authority that had eroded since the fall of the imperial court in C.E. 1185. It accomplished this reunification by retraining the hereditary samurai warriors to become educated scholar-bureaucrats, based in a network of new urban administrative and commercial centers. This successful transformation from a decentralized military order to a recentralized political, economic, and social system was the foundation for the rapid transformation of Japan into an international power in the late nineteenth century.

See also: Archeological Discoveries; Buddhism; Confucianism; Culture and Traditions; Language and Writing; Myths and Epics; Shinto; Society.

FURTHER READING

Brown, Delmer, John W. Hall, and Kozo Yamamura, eds. *The Cambridge History of Japan*. Vols. 1–3. Cambridge: Cambridge University Press, 1992–1999.

Duus, Peter. *Feudalism in Japan*. New York: McGraw Hill, 1993.

Schirokauer, Conrad, David Lurie, and Suzanne Gay. *A Brief History of Japanese Civilization*. Boston: Wadsworth, 2005.

Java

Island in what is now Indonesia that served as the center of maritime Southeast Asian cultural development starting in the fifth century C.E. Among Java's cultural artifacts are some of Asia's most impressive Hindu and Buddhist temples, which date from C.E. 600 to 1500.

EARLY BUDDHIST AND HINDU CIVILIZATION

Sanjaya (r. ca. C.E. 732–760), a patron of the Hindu god Siva, was the first significant Javanese monarch. He built his court and the first of Java's sprawling temple complexes on the sacred Dieng Plateau in northern central Java. Sanjaya was succeeded by a series of Sailendra monarchs (ca. C.E. 760–860), who followed his lead and built several major Mahayana Buddhist temples in central Java near modern-day Yogyakarta. These efforts culminated in the early ninth century with the Borobudur temple complex on the western edge of the Kedu Plain.

In the late ninth century, central Java–based Hindu kings defeated the Buddhist Sailendras and proclaimed their sovereignty over what they called the Mataram state (ca. C.E. 860–1000). These kings constructed their own impressive central temple complex dedicated to Lord Siva at Prambanan, north of Yogyakarta, near the volcanic Mount Merapi.

A devastating eruption of Mount Merapi in the tenth century temporarily made the central Java plains uninhabitable. This shifted the center of Javanese civilization east to the basins of the Brantas and Solo rivers. For a time, temples assumed less importance as statements of royal authority. Instead, kings through the reign of Airlangga (r. ca. C.E. 1016–1045) encouraged the spread of wet-rice agriculture in eastern Java, initiating the construction of new water management projects and mountainside wet-rice terraces to support the development of new village societies. The move to the east also allowed Javanese monarchs to exploit a strategic position adjacent to the international maritime trade route to eastern Indonesia's Spice Islands.

The Javanese monarchy split into competing factions following Airlangga's death, with kings identified by their association with two rival courts. One regional dynasty ruled from Kediri on the southwestern edge of the eastern Java river plain, and the other at Singosari to the southeast on the Malang Plateau.

MAJAPAHIT JAVA AND THE TRANSITION TO ISLAM

The Majapahit state (C.E. 1293–1528), based on the edge of the Brantas River delta west of present-day Surabaya, was the high point in the development of the Hindu-Buddhist civilization in the islands of Southeast Asia. Its kings came to possess a degree of direct administrative control over their subordinate regions in eastern Java that went beyond that of previous courts. They also established authority over the remainder of Java and claimed an overseas empire that included all of the islands that are now part of modern Indonesia, which they called Nusantara.

Local societies appropriated Majapahit's refined culture. The most notable of these was neighboring Bali, which still practices the Hindu religious traditions it inherited from Majapahit. Although the other eastern Indonesian archipelago islands did eventually convert to Islam, their ritual practices were still heavily mixed with a continuing worship of local spiritual forces, and their material culture (their dress, food, and court traditions) derived from those of Majapahit-**era** Java.

During the fifteenth century, Majapahit faced aggressive competition from the newly Islamic ports on Java's northern coast. In 1528, the court finally fell to a military coalition among these Islamic ports led by the Demak port-states. Thereafter, the Javanese gradually converted to Islam and shifted their political loyalties to the new Mataram Islamic court (ca. C.E. 1570–1755) that was based in the old central Javanese heartland. While outwardly Islamic, this new Mataram court retained most of the cultural characteristics of Java's previous Hindu-Buddhist age.

See also: Agriculture; Buddhism; Hinduism; Islam, Spread of; Language and Writing; Melaka; Spice Trade.

FURTHER READING

Kinney, Ann R. *Worshipping Siva and Buddha: The Temple Art of East Java.* Honolulu: University of Hawaii Press, 2003.

Tarling, Nicholas, ed. *The Cambridge History of Southeast Asia.* Vol. 1. Cambridge, MA: Cambridge University Press, 2000.

Junk *See* Technology and Inventions.

Khmer Empire

Ancient Southeast Asian kingdom (C.E. 802–1432), based in what is now Cambodia, that once included the adjacent regions of Thailand and Laos. Historians use the name Angkor ("city") to refer to both the ancient capital city and the ancient kingdom. The boundaries of the realm were never clearly defined, and Angkor is best understood as a confederation of populations willing to submit to a central authority.

Angkor was the successor to previous Khmer regional states centered in the upper Mekong River basin, which began to leave **inscriptions** in the sixth century C.E. In contrast, Angkor was centered on the northern edge of Cambodia's Great Lake, Tonle Sap. Its productive wet-rice agriculture depended on the annual monsoon season that flooded Khmer fields. Several rulers constructed enormous reservoirs and a network of canals around the capital city to provide a more secure source of irrigation for the rice paddies, and to reinforce the ritual symbolism of their capital.

The Angkor state was founded by King Jayavarman II (r. C.E. 802–835), who established the state *Devaraja* ("god-king") cult, which celebrated the unity of the Khmer people under the favor of the Hindu god Siva. Jayavarman's capital was at Hariharalaya, southeast of Angkor. Angkor became the realm's continuing capital under Yasovarman I (r. C.E. 889–900), and was named Yasodharapura in his honor. Suryavarman I (r. C.E. 1002–1049) extended Angkor's territory in all directions and consolidated its political authority. Suryavarman II (r. C.E. 1113–ca. 1150) defended Angkor against its Cham neighbors in central Vietnam, and also sponsored the construction of the Angkor Wat temple complex, dedicated to the Hindu god Visnu.

In 1177, forces from neighboring Champa raided Angkor, desecrated its temples, and carried off the state's wealth and significant numbers of its population. Jayavarman VII (r. C.E. 1181–ca. 1218) restored order through a series of military victories against regional opponents, then successfully defended his realm against the Chams. He also built a new capital city adjacent to Angkor Wat at Angkor

RISE AND DECLINE OF THE KHMER EMPIRE

c.e. 550–800 Pre-Angkor regional states arise in upper Mekong River basin

c.e. 802–835 Rule of Jayavarman II; founds the Khmer Empire and initiates the royal *Devaraja* Siva cult at Hariharalaya

c.e. 889–900 Rule of Yasovarman I; founds Khmer capital of Angkor

c.e. 1002–1049 Rule of Suryavarman I; extends the Khmer realm, especially to the north and west

c.e. 1113–ca. 1150 Rule of Suryavarman II; builds temple complex at Angkor Wat (which

means "city monastery") dedicated to the Hindu deity Visnu

c.e. 1177 Cham invasion devastates the Khmer realm

c.e. 1181–ca. 1218 Rule of Jayavarman VII; restores order and Khmer power; builds Angkor Thom (which means "Angkor the Great") and its Bayon Mahayana Buddhist temple complex

c.e. 1431 sacking of Angkor by Ayudhya forces from Thailand

c.e. 1432 Khmer political center shifts to Phnom Penh, after which Angkor is deserted

Thom, which he centered on the Bayon Mahayana Buddhist shrine.

Following the death of Jayavarman VII, the Angkor state gradually declined, evidenced by the decreased number of inscriptions recording state activities. When the Chinese envoy Zhou Dagua visited Angkor in 1295–1296, he described it as a royal city in decay, which he attributed to a series of exhausting wars against Thai armies.

The armies of the region of Ayudhya (in Thailand), based in the former north and west Angkor territories, sacked the Angkor capital in 1431 and brought an end to the Angkor-based Khmer realm. They carried Angkor's royal regalia back to the Thai capital, where it remains to this day as the symbolic source of Thai political authority. In 1432, Cambodian rulers, who also claimed to be Angkor's legitimate successors, established a new Khmer capital at Phnom Penh on the Mekong River.

See also: Agriculture; Angkor Wat; Sukhotai and Ayudhya; Vietnam.

FURTHER READING
Higham, Charles. *Civilization of Angkor.* Berkeley: University of California Press, 2002.
Snellgrove, David. *Angkor: Before and After: Cultural History of the Khmers.* Boston: Weatherhill, 2004.

Korea

Peninsula in northeastern Asia, first settled by migrating populations from Mongolia and Siberia from 7000–5000 b.c.e., and frequently thereafter ruled or influenced by neighboring dynasties in China. The first centralized states appeared in Korea by about 400 b.c.e. These states fought among themselves for control of the peninsula before uniting under the control of the Chinese Han **dynasty** in 108 b.c.e. During the next 2,000 years, a series of Buddhist and Confucian dynasties would rule the region.

ORIGINS

The legendary first Korean state was Old Choson, from an old name for Korea. ("Old Choson" distinguishes this legendary Korean civilization, associated with the fourth century B.C.E., from the later Choson state that began in 194 B.C.E.) This realm, in the northern Liao and Taedong River basins, struggled to remain independent from its powerful Chinese neighbor under the Han dynasty (206 B.C.E.–C.E. 220).

Around 194 B.C.E., an unsuccessful rebel against the Han dynasty fled to Korea and established an independent state named Choson based at Pyongyang, the modern capital of North Korea. The Han emperor Wudi (r. ca. 141–87 B.C.E.) conquered Choson in 109–108 B.C.E., and thereafter established several semi-independent military garrisons in northern Korea. The most powerful of these was the military commandery of Lelang (108 B.C.E.–C.E. 313) based at Pyongyang. Three Korean tribal warlord confederations (Mahan, Pyonhan, and Chinhan) occupied southern Korea, while rival alliances claimed other portions of Korea. During the Three Kingdoms Period (ca. C.E. 300–700), the southern confederations evolved into the central Paekche Kingdom, the northern Koguryo Federation, and the southeastern Silla Kingdom.

Koguryo, which consolidated its hold over the north following the fall of the Han dynasty in 220, was the most powerful of these kingdoms. After reaching its height in the fifth century C.E., Koguryo declined in the mid-sixth century, caught between the attacks of competing Chinese forces to its north and the rise of Paekche to its south. Paekche seized the Han River basin, but its success was short lived. An alliance between the new Chinese Tang dynasty (C.E. 618–907) and the southern Silla kingdom conquered Paekche in 668.

SILLA, KORYO, AND YI DYNASTIES

By 668, Silla had consolidated its authority over most of the Korean Peninsula. During the so-called Unified Silla **era** (C.E. 668–918), Silla rulers partnered with Korean Buddhists to administer their realm. They also established the Confucian Academy to train scholar-bureaucrats for a new civil administration, and experimented with a formal examination system to fill the civil service with qualified candidates. The resulting political system depended on *hwarang* (flower knights), a paramilitary youth organization that trained and educated the sons of the Silla elite. The hwarang instilled in their pupils the "bone-rank" system, a societal **hierarchy** of warrior-**aristocrats** based on birth.

By the 870s, powerful landholding regional clans began to challenge the Silla dynasty's central authority. Regional autonomy and limited court authority characterized the last 40 years of the dynasty, known as the Later Three Kingdoms era (878–918).

In 936, a former merchant named Wang Kon (877–943) rose to power, supported by regional Silla landlord clans. Wang founded the new Kaesong-based Koryo dynasty (from which the name Korea is derived). Koryo rulers abolished the Silla ranking system and replaced it with their own set of status distinctions. A literate class of bureaucrats who had passed the state's Confucian civil service examinations led Koryo society, in partnership with Buddhist clergy who had qualified by a separate examination. A privileged **hereditary** ruling class that included royalty, civil bureaucrats, military bureaucrats, and the Buddhist priesthood controlled the Koryo state's administration.

The Koryo civilian bureaucracy held authority until 1170, when the state's generals, supported by a network of military-bureaucrats, began a 20-year civil war in response to the increased concentration of power in the court. Other state bureaucrats who opposed court **absolutism** joined their ranks, and from 1196–1258 the Choe family clan of military dictators held power. The Mongols ended this period of military-bureaucratic partnership by invading Korea in 1258 against limited opposition. They restored the Koryo royal family, placing it under the watchful eye of a Mongol overlord. The Mongols extracted heavy taxes, labor, and military services from Koreans, especially during the era of the Mongolian military campaigns against Japan (1274–1281).

General Yi Song-gye defeated the remnants of Mongol authority in 1364, following the fall of the Mongol dynasty in China during the 1350s. After 28 years of civil war, he deposed the Koryo rulers in

1392, founding the Yi dynasty (c.e. 1392–1910), based at present-day Seoul, modern South Korea's capital. Yi Song-gye appeased the new Ming dynasty rulers of China (c.e. 1368–1644) by paying tribute and accepting subordinate status to China. Subsequent Yi and Chinese rulers described the relationship as that between "younger brother and elder brother."

Yi and his successors implemented a new Confucian monarchy and reduced Buddhism to a secondary religion. He seized church lands, closed temples, and placed the supervision of restricted Buddhist activities under the watchful eye of a newly empowered landowning aristocracy known as *yangban.* He and subsequent Yi rulers stressed Confucian ancestor worship and its rituals over Buddhist traditions. They also implemented a Confucian social code that discouraged social practices that had reinforced the autonomy of the traditional family clans, such as taking multiple wives, widow remarriage, and marrying within the family clan network. In return, the gentry were granted the hereditary right to both civil and military appointments. Confucian examinations and official appointments were only open to yangban candidates—in contrast to the Chinese Confucian examinations and bureaucracy that were in theory open to anyone.

Confucian art and literature replaced Buddhist art and culture in the early Yi era. However, the Yi monarch Sejong (r. c.e. 1418–1450) sponsored the development of a more independent Korean culture, based in the creation of a new Korean alphabet, known as *hangul,* which replaced prior dependence on Chinese writing.

In 1471, Yi monarchs adopted a national code that defined their Korean adaptation of Confucian government. The new code ignored traditional clan-based territorial divisions and reorganized Korea into eight provinces and subordinate counties administered by state bureaucrats rather than clan landlords. In theory the Yi monarch was supreme, but in practice he and his officials were examined by bureaucratic review boards (or censors) who had the authority to charge any state official, even the emperor, with misconduct or mismanagement. A guilty official was removed from office, his economic resources were confiscated, and he might even be imprisoned or put to death.

The first centuries of Yi rule were highly innovative and productive. Over time, however, the Yi system lapsed into aristocratic factionalism and administrative ineffectiveness, and it never fully recovered from an attempted Japanese invasion in 1592–1598. Despite this setback, the continuing prosperity of the Korean economy also contributed to the problems for the Yi rulers, as newly wealthy Korean farmers and a new Korean merchant class began to buy *yangban* status.

See also: Archeological Discoveries; China; Japan; Language and Writing.

FURTHER READING

Eckert, Carter J., et al. *Korea Old and New.* Cambridge, MA: Harvard University Press, 1990.

Holcombe, C. *The Genesis of East Asia, 221 b.c. to a.d. 907.* Honolulu: University of Hawaii Press, 2001.

Lee, Ki-Baik, et al. *A New History of Korea.* Cambridge, MA: Harvard University Press, 2005.

Pai, H. *Constructing Korean Origins.* Cambridge, MA: Harvard University Press, 2000.

Language and Writing

The frequent migrations of people and ideas throughout ancient Asia and the Pacific led to cultural mixing that produced a diversity of linguistic and literary traditions. The linguistic heritage in ancient China developed as a mixture of pictorial and symbolic representations of concepts rather than sounds, a heritage that was adapted by China's Korean and Japanese neighbors. In India, early written forms gave way to an alphabet in which each character represented a spoken sound. Indian and Southeast Asian writing traditions derived from early India's Hindu and Buddhist heritage. This was in sharp contrast to China and its neighbors, where literature addressed the **secular** order of humanity rather than focusing on religious concerns, reflecting China's Confucian tradition.

EMERGENCE OF WRITTEN LANGUAGE

The earliest Asian literature was composed in Chinese and in **Sanskrit** and Pali (a Prakrit, or local Indo-Aryan, language related to Sanskrit), the original languages of Hinduism and Buddhism. People in Korea, Japan, and Southeast Asia later modified the variety of Indian and Chinese scripts and texts to meet their own cultural needs.

South and Southeast Asian Scripts

Written script in India was late to develop relative to the rest of Asia. In the third century B.C.E., King Asoka erected pillars containing **inscriptions** in Prakrit, written in Brahmi script, which later developed into the Devanagari script that is used today by Sanskrit and Sanskrit-derived north Indian languages. South Indian languages, by contrast, derived from the Tamil language, which developed a different script tradition from the same Brahmi linguistic base. Southeast Asians also developed their own initial language scripts during the first millennium C.E. by adapting Brahmi script to their own local needs.

Chinese Written Language

Between 1500 and 1000 B.C.E., Chinese priests developed the earliest Chinese **pictographic** script. Modern Chinese script began to take shape as a more linear representation of the pictographs in *xiaozhuan* script around 700 B.C.E. The *lishu* script, which was better suited for rapid sketches because it used fewer strokes, became common after 500 B.C.E. The new script was more efficient for government bureaucrats in an **era** marked by significant increases in governmental authority.

LANGUAGE AND WRITING

CA. 1500–1000 B.C.E. Chinese priests develop the earliest Chinese pictographic script

CA. 800–600 B.C.E. *Brahmana* religious textual manuals composed in India

CA. 700 B.C.E. Linear *xiaozhuan* script develops in China

CA. 600–200 B.C.E. *Upanishads,* philosophical religious epics, composed in India

CA. 500 B.C.E. Simplified *lishu* script evolves in China

CA. 500 B.C.E.–200 C.E. Indian epic the *Mahabharata* committed to writing

CA. 400 B.C.E. The *Arthasastra,* early book of advice for rulers consolidating power, written in India

CA. 300 B.C.E. (*Li Sao*) *The Lament,* China's first extended epic poem, composed by Qu Yuan

CA. 250 B.C.E. Indian king Asoka (r. ca. 273–ca. 232 B.C.E.) erects pillars containing inscriptions in Prakrit script

CA. C.E. 100 Earliest Korean script, *hanja,* evolves from Chinese characters

CA. C.E. 1000 World's first novel, *The Tale of Genji,* written by Japanese courtesan Murasaki Shikibu

CA. C.E. 1200 Korean *kugyol* script develops from earlier *hanja* script

CA. C.E. 1420 Korean king Sejong (r. C.E. 1418–1450) commissions the development of a new Korean script, *hangul*

The continuing evolution of Chinese script was tied to the development of Chinese calligraphy, which placed focus on disciplined and continuous brush strokes. *Kaishu* ("standard script") appeared near the end of the Han dynasty (ca. 206 B.C.E.– C.E. 220). *Xingshu* ("running script"), a cursive version of kaishu appeared shortly thereafter. *Caoshu* ("grass script") developed among calligraphers in the fourth century C.E. as a continuous flowing brush script.

Korean and Japanese Scripts

Both the Korean and Japanese scripts developed from Chinese script. The earliest Korean script (*hanja*), which came into existence in the first century C.E., adapted Chinese characters that combined both sounds and meanings. In the thirteenth century, the *kugyol* script was introduced, in which characters distinguished between sound and meaning. At the time, classical Chinese was the preferred language in Korean literary culture. King Sejong (r. C.E. 1418–1450) of the Yi dynasty (C.E. 1392–1910), in his attempt to reassert an independent Korean

culture, commissioned the development of a new Korean script, *hangul.* Despite his attempts, Korean literature was still almost exclusively composed in Chinese until Korea achieved independence in 1945 and made hangul the official language. Prior to that time, where hangul appeared, it was paired side by side with Chinese.

Japanese writing and literature also derived from Chinese roots. In the fifth century C.E., the Japanese used Chinese characters (*kanji*) in a system called *kanbun*, "Chinese writing." Kanbun used Chinese characters to represent both ideas and syllables. Although kanbun used Chinese characters, it employed Japanese rather than Chinese grammar. Finally, a new writing system, *kana*, developed that used kanji to represent things or ideas, and simplified versions of the characters to represent sounds.

Hiragana writing, in which characters represent Japanese words, developed in the eighth century C.E. Many literate Japanese continued to use the older kanji system, while hiragana became associated with women's compositions. The *Tale of Genji,* sometimes

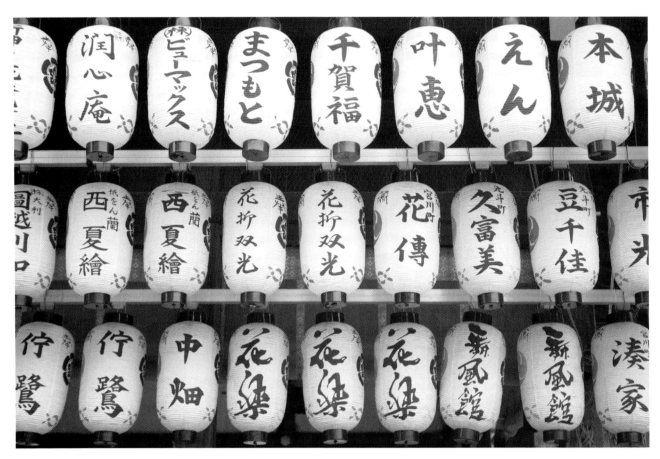

Several major Asian languages, including Chinese and Japanese, employ pictograms–characters that represent words or concepts–rather than letters. The characters on the Japanese lanterns shown here indicate the names of sponsors of the temple that contains the lanterns. (Karen Beard/Taxi Japan/Getty Images)

called the world's first novel, was written in hiragana by Murasaki Shikibu (ca. 1000), a resident of the Kyoto court (C.E. 784–1185). *Katakana* ("part kanji"), yet another option, used a Japanese script in which characters represented individual syllables. It was originally developed in the ninth century to aid in the pronunciation of Chinese Buddhist scriptures, but by the fourteenth century was in wider use.

LITERATURE

Philosophical, moral, and religious texts assumed great importance in the Asian cultural tradition. Literacy and learning were widely respected; even Japan's *samurai* warriors were literate and composed poetry. Despite the fact that women did not attend regular schools, they sometimes acquired literacy from family members. This was especially the case in imperial Japan. In India, where religion was such a focal part of life, most of the early literature was associated with India's Hindu and Buddhist traditions. In China, Confucian tradition favored philosophical texts that focused on human existence in this world rather than speculating on an afterlife.

Indian Literature

India's literary tradition began with oral compositions that by the fourth century B.C.E. were recorded as sacred Hindu texts composed in Sanskrit, Prakrit, and Pali. The earliest of these were the four *Vedas,* which recorded the mythology, rituals, ritual chants, and magical spells of Indian society from about 1600 to 1000 B.C.E. The *Brahmana* (800–600 B.C.E.), textual manuals for Brahmin priests, provided further detail for elaborate religious rituals. In contrast, the *Upanishads,* composed between 600–200 B.C.E., were philosophical, discussing the nature of the universe and the place of humans in it.

The *Upanishads* were foundational to the development of Hindu law, as they addressed good and evil, human morality, and duty. These themes were developed in contemporary and subsequent literature. The Buddha's teachings and the early interpretations of these by Buddhist monks (the *Sangha*) provided a Middle Way between Vedic ritual and the philosophical meditations of the *Upanishads,* as collected in the Buddhist *Pitaka* texts (ca. 500 B.C.E.). Early discourse on Hindu law developed in the *Dharmasastras* from roughly the same era.

The issues that were being addressed in these various religious texts were popularized in the *Mahabharata* epic tale about a legendary battle between two early Vedic-era tribes. The epic evolved as an oral text from roughly 1600 B.C.E., and, with later additions, did not reach its final form until roughly C.E. 200. The *Ramayana* epic poem, which dates from roughly 300 B.C.E., is a symbolic story about rightful human conduct that offers a glimpse into divine involvement in human affairs. Much like the contemporary *Bhagavad Gita* subsection of the *Mahabharata* epic poem, it supports Hinduism's developing Bhakti devotional tradition because it speculates on the human-divine relationship.

The *Arthasastra,* which is attributed to the fourth century B.C.E. Mauryan statesman Kautilya, critiqued the age of heroic chivalry that was portrayed in the *Vedas* and the *Mahabharata*. It also provided an alternative to the proposal in the *Dharmasastras* that kings should lead by moral example. Instead, it is a textbook for rulers consolidating power into a new imperial regime, in the tradition of the third-century B.C.E. Chinese text titled *The Book of Lord Shang,* by Li Si, the prime minister of China's Qin Dynasty (221–206 B.C.E.). The *Arthasastra* encourages rulers to seize, hold, and manipulate power, but it also advises that prolonged tyranny ultimately leads to popular rebellion. The wise ruler thus cultivates his subjects' respect by remaining directly involved in the affairs of state, administering justice, and even showing compassion when it is to his advantage.

India's early literary tradition culminated in the classical Sanskrit compositions of the Gupta era (ca. C.E. 320–550), notably the *kavya* poetry and drama of Gupta-era authors. These writings on love, nature, and morality were intended for recitation and performance, to bring an emotional response from their audience. Human emotions were personified in seasonal and day and night settings, as well as in birds, beasts, and flowers.

Chinese Literature

China's early literature focused on secular themes, particularly the conditions required for successful governance. Earlier oral mythological and historical tradition was codified in the era of the Zhou dynasty (1122/1027–403 B.C.E.) in the works that are collectively referred to as the Confucian Classics, attributed to the statesman and philosopher Confucius (Kungfutzu, 551–479 B.C.E.). These include the *Book of Songs* (a collection of mythical folk ballads), *The Book of Changes* (about magical spells), and the *Book of Rituals*. They also feature collections of historical documents; the histories of the Xia, Shang, and early Zhou dynasties; and a collection of Confucius's writings, *The Analects,* which were collated by his students after his death. All of these writings influenced the commentaries and philosophical writings of subsequent Confucian scholars in China, Korea, Japan, and Vietnam.

Confucian tradition dictated that early Chinese poetry conform to rigid standards and contain some moral lesson. *Li Sao (The Lament)* by Qu Yuan (ca. 340–278 B.C.E.) was China's first extended lyric poem. It addresses the sorrows of an exiled prince, who rides on dragons and serpents in his travels from heaven to Earth. The poem incorporates early Chinese legends and myths but above all explores the conflict between the individual and the group and ultimately asserts the hero's love for Chinese people.

The era of the Han dynasty (206 B.C.E.–C.E. 220) was notable for the development of Chinese governmental record keeping. These records initiated the tradition of compiling official dynastic histories, which typically were written by the succeeding dynasty. The first of these, *The Record of the Historian,* a Han-era history of the Qin dynasty, is attributed to the court historian of emperor Han Wudi (r. ca. 141–87 B.C.E.), Sima Qian. In the Han age, *yuefu,* popular narrative and lyric ("folksong") poetry, developed, as best represented in the *Flight of the Phoenix to the*

MAJOR LINGUISTIC GROUPS OF ANCIENT ASIA AND THE PACIFIC

Asian language families are many and diverse—from the languages spoken in the Philippines, Malaysia, and Indonesia, to the Sanskrit, Hindi, and Pali of South Asia, to the Sino-Tibetan and Austro-Asiatic languages of Southeast Asia, and the Indo-European and Ural-Altaic languages of central Asia.

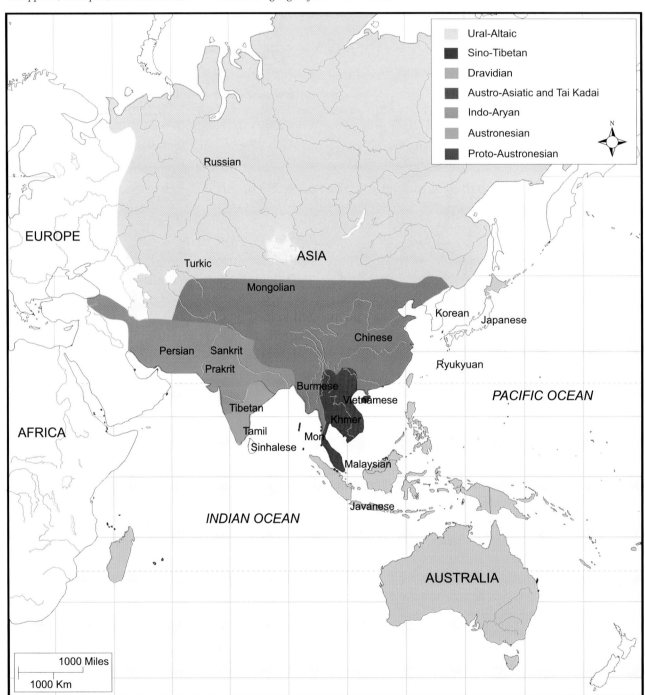

Southeast, a tragic tale of lovers under pressure from their parents and families.

Under the Tang (C.E. 618–907) and Song (C.E. 960–1279) dynasties, Chinese literary expression flowered in a wide range of neo-Confucian writings that attempted to blend Confucian and Buddhist traditions. Buddhism advocated literary creativity as an appropriate activity through which to explore the limits of the human mind. Such an activity also reinforced the traditional Confucian notion that humans should exercise the kind of self-discipline required of a serious writer. The perfected individual might then be a more productive member of society. Scholars, popular writers, and poets debated whether there should be a limit on government leadership and stressed the need to believe once again in the moral capacities of humanity. They argued for a less regimented society as the means to inspire human creativity.

Tang and Song texts were printed using carved woodblocks, which made written works widely available among an increasingly literate Chinese urban public. Among these were popular accounts of Buddhist pilgrims, printed encyclopedias, interpretive histories, and neo-Confucian philosophical essays. Tang-era writings still conformed largely to Confucian models, but Song era authors fully embraced creativity for its own sake. They even openly indulged in the subtle pleasures of life, which Confucian scholars regarded as dangerous to the welfare of humanity.

Chinese authors finally produced novels during the Yuan dynasty (C.E. 1279–1368), when two of China's "Four Classic Novels," *Water Margin* and *Romance of the Three Kingdoms,* were published. *Monkey, Journey to the West* (ca. 1590) and *Dream of the Red Chamber* (1792) are the other two, to which

many add a fifth major composition, *Golden Lotus* (1610). In each of these stories, the lead heroic characters all end as immortals or supernatural beings with magical powers. The novels blend traditional Chinese culture with Buddhism in their acceptance of the notion of reincarnation and *karma* (force generated by one's actions) that leads to the fate of the individual. They offer a commentary on Yuan social and religious conventions, often portraying the negative societal consequences of choosing individualism over the commitment to uphold the Confucian traditions of the past.

See also: China; India; Japan; Java; Korea; Myths and Epics.

FURTHER READING

De Bary, William Theodore, et al., eds. *Sources of Japanese Tradition.* Vol. 1. New York: Columbia University Press, 2001.

Embree, Ainslee, ed. *Sources of Indian Tradition.* 2nd ed. New York: Columbia University Press, 1988.

Lee, Peter H., Yongho Ch'oe, and Hugh H. W. Kang. *Sources of Korean Tradition.* New York: Columbia University Press, 1996.

Mair, V., ed. *Columbia History of Chinese Literature.* New York: Columbia University Press, 2002.

Mandate of Heaven

Political and social philosophy, or *tian ming* ("mandate" or "decree" of heaven), that served as the ancient Chinese explanation for the success or failure of Chinese civilization. The Chinese believed that a **dynasty** fell, or leaders failed, because they lost the moral right to authority that was given by heaven alone. In this view, heaven was not a personal god but an all-pervading cosmic power. Scholars of the Zhou dynasty (ca. 1122/1027–403 B.C.E.) developed this **doctrine** to explain the Zhou conquest of the previous Shang dynasty (1766–1122/1027 B.C.E.) and to legitimate their new dynasty.

Initially, this political theory argued that heaven was committed to the welfare of humanity. For this reason, heaven established rulers who assumed responsibility for the welfare of their human subjects. Heaven mandates that select people be in charge and supports rulers and their dynasties as

long as they rule justly, fairly, and wisely. If a dynasty or ruler ceases to rule justly or wisely, and begins to serve his or her own interests, heaven revokes the mandate, and the ruler or dynasty falls. Heavenly authority then passes to another family-based network, which is obligated to revolt against and overthrow the failed dynasty. The mandate is not equivalent to blind fate or destiny. Instead, it imposes a code of appropriate human behavior. Humans are free to rule justly or unjustly; they are even free to harm the people they rule. If they do so, however, their rule will come to a swift end as heaven passes on its mandate to another family.

In contrast, the concept of *ming,* or destiny, implies that certain events are beyond human control. Things that happen in the physical world—earthquakes, sickness, wealth, floods, famine, and other hardships—are the direct result of heaven's actions, and thus humans cannot affect them. Human misconduct, however, such as human abuse of the physical environment, can create imbalances in the physical world.

During the sixth century B.C.E., Confucius applied the concept of tian ming to human relations, insisting that each person was obligated to contribute to the welfare of others. According to Confucius, the Mandate of Heaven applied to all human obligations and actions. It postulated a moral order to the universe that paralleled the physical order and promised that humankind ultimately would achieve social harmony. Attaining proper human relationships (*li*) was thus the goal of tian ming.

Thus, human success was ultimately the consequence of successful human actions that were respectful of and in balance with the heavenly and natural orders. Human failure was equally the result of inappropriate human actions that were ultimately self-serving rather than sensitive to and focused on wider societal need.

See also: China; Confucianism.

FURTHER READING

Hucker, Charles O. *China's Imperial Past, An Introduction to China's History and Culture.* Palo Alto, CA: Stanford University Press, 1994.

Schwartz, Benjamin I. *World of Thought in Ancient China.* Cambridge, MA: Harvard University Press, 1985.

Melaka

Narrow, 500-mile-long (800-km-long) maritime passage separating the Malay Peninsula from the island of Sumatra. The strait takes its name from the port-based Malay state of Melaka (or Malacca). This state was founded in ca. 1390 by the Sumatra-based Malay prince Parameswara (d. 1414) who shifted his court to Melaka from what is now Singapore.

The Melaka Strait became the major shipping route between India and China in the fifth century C.E. At this time, Indian Ocean shipping shifted south from prior routes that involved stopovers and portages across the Malay Peninsula's Kra Isthmus. A maritime state, known to the Chinese as Srivijaya, dominated the strait from the fifth to fourteenth centuries C.E., until the establishment of Parameswara's realm. Less than 50 years later, Melaka had become the wealthiest commercial port in Asia. It served as both the connecting hub in the trade from India to China and the international source of Indonesian spices.

Melaka's initial success was a result of special diplomatic ties with China's Ming court. Merchants wishing to trade in China's ports were given special treatment if they first made stopovers in Melaka. In return, Melaka was obligated to keep the strait free of piracy, thereby assuring the regular flow of Western luxuries into China. Zheng He (C.E. 1371–1433), a famous Ming maritime admiral, visited Melaka several times between 1409 and the early 1430s with his fleet of ships. His voyages were intended to reinforce Melaka's position as China's favored Southeast Asian port of trade, as well as to ensure the security of the strait.

The Ming court ended its aggressive diplomatic voyages into the region in the 1430s and subsequently began to restrict China's overseas contacts. This led Melaka's ruler, Sri Maharaja (r. 1424–

1444), to convert to Islam (taking the name Muhammad Shah) in order to encourage the Muslim merchants who dominated the Indian Ocean trade to use his port. His patronage of Islam also served to legitimize and extend the Sultan's control over other ports in the region of the strait.

The Portuguese seized Melaka in 1511, wrongly believing that by holding Melaka they could monopolize Indian Ocean trade. As the Portuguese discovered, Melaka's power was based not on its military strength, but on its favor among the Asian commercial community. It prospered because it provided a secure and neutral marketplace for its diverse international community of merchants to exchange the profitable luxury goods demanded by consumers in both the East and the West. Although the Portuguese failed to develop a monopoly over Indian Ocean trade, they did build a profit-able commercial enterprise based in Melaka that allowed them to dominate the flow of Southeast Asia's spices to European marketplaces through the sixteenth century.

See also: Indian Ocean Trade; Islam, Spread of; Spice Trade; Zheng He.

FURTHER READING
Andaya, Barbara Watson, and Leonard Y. Andaya. *A History of Malaysia.* Honolulu: University of Hawaii Press, 2001.
Hooker, Virginia Matheson. *A Short History of Malaysia.* Sydney, Australia: Allen and Unwin, 2003.
Wheatley, Paul, et al. *Melaka: The Transformation of a Malay Capital, c. 1400–1980.* Kuala Lumpur, Malaysia: Oxford University Press, 1983.

Micronesia

Located in the western Pacific Ocean, an island chain settled by waves of Malayo-Polynesian and Melanesian seafarers beginning in roughly 4000 B.C.E. Modern-day Micronesia consists of the Marshall Islands, Guam, the North Mariana Islands, and the Caroline Islands, including Palau and the Micronesian Federated States of Yap, Chuuk, Pohnpei, and Kosrae. The inhabitants of these islands share similar ethnicity, but are culturally diverse because of their varying geographical and historical circumstances.

Austronesian-speaking voyagers from the Philippines settled Palau and the Marianas between 4000 and 1500 B.C.E. Later waves of Oceanic-speaking Melanesians from the South Pacific arrived in Yap between 1300 and 200 B.C.E., followed between 500 B.C.E. and C.E. 1 by a third wave of Melanesian voyagers who settled the Marshalls, Kosrae, and Pohnpei. Ancestors of the voyagers who settled these latter islands later migrated to other parts of the Carolines.

SOCIAL AND ECONOMIC ORGANIZATION

The people in Micronesian societies commonly lived in villages on the lower slope of mountains on the edge of coastal plains, where they could plant taro, a tuber, or rooted vegetable, that was their principle subsistence crop. Men and women had separate but equally important economic chores that ensured local prosperity. Before the arrival of Europeans, around C.E. 1500, men spent most of their productive time collecting fish, sea turtles, and octopus; they also harvested coconut and breadfruit trees, and hunted native animals, notably land snails and tropical birds. Women cultivated the land (for taro), gathered wild foods from the jungle, fished inland ponds, and wove cloth and mats from tree and plant fibers. Village houses were clustered in clan groups; the houses of clan chiefs and other community elders were built on wooden platforms, which also acted as community meetinghouses. Cross-family and clan social activities were based in male and female clubs that were graded by age.

POLITICAL SYSTEMS

The traditional political systems of Micronesia varied greatly. The society on Yap, for example, never had a strong, centralized authority. Order was concentrated around a local chief who shared power with a council composed of the heads of the family clans. Village societies were arranged in an island-wide ranking based on the debts owed by one village to others.

In contrast, the islands of Kosrae and Pohnpei were once ruled by supreme chiefs. Kosrae traditionally had a head chief who ruled the entire island, assisted by sectional chiefs. The head chief was entitled to receive a share of all local production (food or handicrafts) in payment for successfully leading the community. Pohnpei initially had several roughly equal confederated chiefs who had control over villagers in their region. They were assisted by "talking chiefs," chosen from the second-ranking family clan in each region, who acted as designated mediators if disputes arose between two regions. As in Kosrae, the two elite clan lines received payment in the form of a share of local production from the local non-**aristocratic** clans.

The Kosrae and Pohnpei supreme chief system reached its height, perhaps as early as the eighth century c.e., under a mysterious line of kings known as the Saudeleurs. These kings built a spectacular capital city at Nan Madol, on the southeastern shore of Temwen Island, off the coast of Pohnpei. The remains of this city consist of a coral reef of 92 human-made islets intersected by a network of artificially constructed canals and waterways, protected by seawalls of loglike basalt stone that are up to 50 feet (15 m) high and 20 feet (6 m) wide. The focal centers of this ancient city were the islet sites of elaborate funeral rituals, the residences of priests, and royal tombs, which were surrounded by the islet residences of state elite and marketplaces.

Much of Micronesian society and culture significantly changed after the 1525 arrival of the first Portuguese explorers in Yap. Early Portuguese and Spanish contact provided Micronesian societies with their first access to iron and also introduced domestic animals, such as goats, cows, and chickens, into the local economy.

See also: Polynesia.

FURTHER READING

Bellwood, Peter. *Conquest of the Pacific: The Prehistory of Southeast Asia and Oceana*. Oxford: Oxford University Press, 1979.

Quanchi, Max, and Ron Adams. *Cultural Contact in the Pacific*. Cambridge: Cambridge University Press, 1993.

Mongols

From the grassland regions (steppes) north of China, **seminomadic** population who, between c.e. 1206 and 1481, conquered and ruled the largest land empire in history. The Mongol Empire at its height stretched across Eurasia from China and Korea in the east to the Middle East and eastern Europe in the west. These **nomadic** clans, previously known as Tartars (after the central Asian tribe that had once controlled them), fostered cross-cultural exchanges between East and West, by being culturally tolerant, providing the opportunity for secure transit across Mongol-controlled territories, and recruiting non-Mongols into their administration.

CULTURE

The Mongols' success was based on their skills as warriors, and their great military advantages were mobility and superior cavalry tactics. They could cover 100 miles (160 km) in a day, carrying whatever small food rations and supplies they needed in their saddlebags and, therefore, never having to pause to wait for their supplies. They were the first to use signal flags to coordinate their battlefield actions. Their short, compound reflex bows allowed them to

⚔ ANCIENT WEAPONS

The Mongolian Bow

Until the development of breach-loading (cartridge) firearms in the 1800s, the ancient Mongolian composite bow was the most effective long-range tool in war and hunting. It was vastly superior to any military technology in the medieval West, including the famed English longbow.

The Mongolian bow was made of three layers: an animal horn or pounded bone outer layer covered a wooden birch core, and a back made of layers of sinew (animal gut) taken from deer, moose, or mountain sheep. The bow was then wrapped with boiled birch bark or fish skins to protect it from moisture. These layers were secured using glue made from boiled fish bladders, which was resilient and highly moisture resistant. Alternatively, the binding glue might be made from boiled animal hides, but this method was less durable and absorbed moisture.

After construction, the bow was wrapped in ropes and placed in a form to dry and harden at room temperature for a year or more. This made it extremely strong and allowed it to keep its shape and snap during years of shooting. The finished bow was normally about 5 feet (1.5 m) in length, and, when strung, it had a double curve, with the top and bottom of the bow bent away from the archer; this double curve gave the bow its power.

Compared to an English longbow that had a draw of about 70 to 80 pounds (32 to 36 kg), the Mongol bow had a pull of 100 to 170 pounds (45 to 77 kg), depending on the strength of the archer. The English longbow could shoot up to 250 yards (230 m), but the Mongol bow could hit a target at 350 yards (320 m) and well beyond. A thirteenth-century record of Mongol ruler Genghis Khan (r. c.e. 1206–1227) reports a shot made by one of his master archers that reached 428 yards (390 m).

Warriors, both male and female, always carried at least two bows, one for long-range shooting and another for close-range combat. The Mongol bow was shot from horseback by pulling the bow away from the string, rather than pulling the bowstring back. Skilled archers timed shots to release when their horses' hooves were in midair, to avoid distortion in aim when horse and rider hit the ground.

load and fire at full gallop. As a result, the Mongols lost few battles.

Local populations often chose to submit and pay **tribute** to the Mongols rather than fight them because of the Mongols' reputation for cruelty to defeated foes. This aura of terror was promoted by Mongol spies and agents, who spread horrific tales about their exploits. Nevertheless, the Mongols actively recruited local allies. The thirteenth-century Mongol victory over China depended largely on the Chinese technicians, siege engineers, gun founders, artillery experts, and naval specialists who helped them overcome China's heavily fortified cities, defended by gunpowder weapons and explosives. The Mongol conquest of China marked the first widespread use of cannon in warfare.

HISTORY

The Mongol realm came into existence under Temuchin (c.e. 1155–1227), who was proclaimed Genghis Khan, "universal sovereign" (r. c.e. 1206–1227), by an assembly of all Mongol chieftains. This assembly acknowledged Genghis's conquests of central Asia, the Near East, and eastern Europe, and his initial victories in northern China. His success was a result of his ability to unite the traditionally divided tribes living in modern-day Mongolia under his personal leadership and to reorganize them into 1,000-man fighting and administrative forces (*minggan*). To maintain order among his ranks, he introduced a code of law that provided examples of appropriate military and social behavior. The code emphasized loyalty to the Mongol military over family clans, promised reward for meritorious service

MONGOL EMPIRE AT ITS GREATEST EXTENT, CA. C.E. 1300

From the steppe populations on the northern border of China, the Mongols, a semi-nomadic people, eventually conquered and ruled the largest land empire in history. Mongolian territory stretched across Eurasia from China and Korea in the east to the Middle East and eastern Europe in the west. Wherever they ruled, the Mongols adapted to the culture and society they conquered.

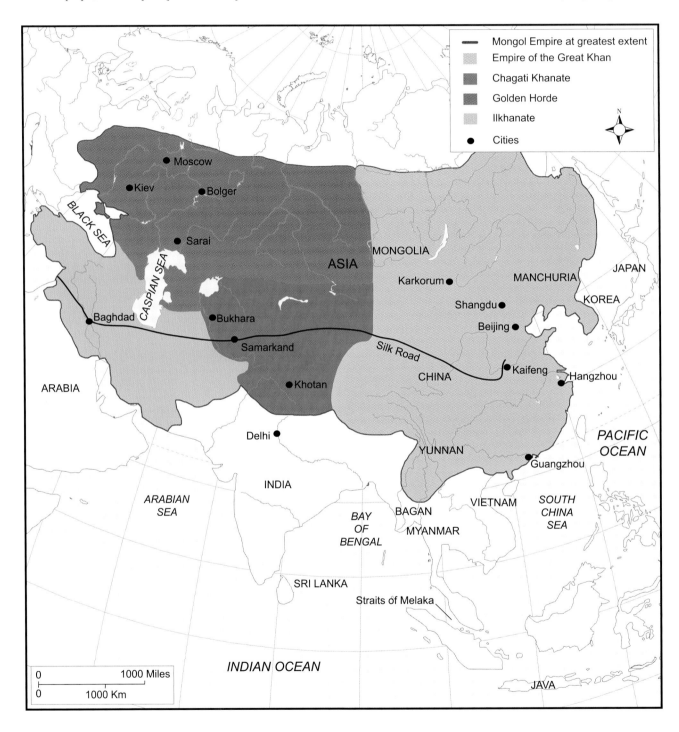

rather than **hereditary** social standing, and promoted ethnic and gender equality. Genghis's realm had four regional divisions (*khanates*): the Golden Horde in western Eurasia and Russia, the Ilkhans in modern-day Iran and the Middle East, the Chagatai in central Asia and Siberia, and what would eventually become the Yuan in China and eastern Eurasia.

The unity of Genghis's reign did not last long, however, as the traditional Mongol tribal assembly system never had a clear succession policy. After Genghis's death, the Mongol chieftains divided the realm among his four sons, each of whom were based in one of the four regions. They proclaimed Genghis's third son Ogedei (c.e. 1186–1241) as his successor, now titled Mongol "emperor."

Ogedei, who reigned from his base in central Asia, continued to coordinate the successful military conquests begun by his father. By the end of Ogedei's lifetime, the Mongol realm had nearly reached its peak, annexing most of modern eastern Europe and the Turkish peninsula in the west. His successors, however, were too involved in family feuds to continue the conquest of the West. When Ogedei died, Mongol troops that were advancing on Vienna in modern-day Austria withdrew from eastern Europe.

In China, Genghis Khan's grandson Kublai Khan (r. c.e. 1260–1294) succeeded Ogedei as emperor, but the other three regional khans largely ignored his authority. In c.e. 1279, Kublai completed the Mongol conquest of China and Korea and founded China's Yuan dynasty (c.e. 1279–1350). Kublai failed in repeated attempts to take Japan (c.e. 1274, 1281), Vietnam (c.e. 1281, 1283–1285), and Myanmar (c.e. 1277, 1283, 1287). He also sent an ill-fated fleet against Java in c.e. 1292. These unsuccessful military expeditions drove the Yuan government into debt that Kublai's successors were not able to overcome. A Chinese military alliance deposed the Yuan realm in 1350, ending Mongol rule in China.

Mongol rule of Persia (modern Iran) effectively ended in c.e. 1335, with the death of the Ilkhan monarch Abu Said (r. 1316–1335). Regional leaders established independent authority until Timur (Tamerlane), a Turko-Mongol leader based in northern Persian and Afghanistan, intervened from 1370 to 1405. Tamerlane also ended Mongol control over Central Asia and united the Turkestan regions under his control in the 1380s. The Golden Horde finally fell to aggressive Moscow-based Russian forces in 1481.

LEGACY

Wherever they ruled, the Mongols adapted to the more culturally sophisticated societies they conquered. Their administration depended on local officials, a few Mongols who became literate and adopted local cultural practices, and foreigners. Although they had previously worshiped a universal sky god as well as various ancestral and natural spirits, Mongol rulers later converted to Buddhism, Islam, and Christianity in the lands they conquered. They also entered profitable business partnerships, encouraged maritime trade initiatives, and patronized artisans and artists, whose efforts provided an important source of tax revenue to finance the Mongol administration.

Above all, the Mongols insured the security of the vital east-west Silk Road trade route across central Asia, which became an important means for cultural exchange. Regular Mongol-sponsored intellectual meetings between Persian and Chinese scholars, scientists, physicians, and agricultural specialists promoted the spread of knowledge throughout the Mongol realm.

See also: China; Golden Horde; Silk Road.

FURTHER READINGS

Hildinger, Erik. *Warriors of the Steppe: A Military History of Central Asia, 500 b.c. to a.d. 1700.* New York: DaCapo Press, 2001.

Ratchnevsky, Paul. *Genghis Khan: His Life and Legacy.* Translated and edited by Thomas Nivison Haining. Oxford: Basil Blackwell, 1992.

Rossabi, Morris. *Khubilai Khan: His Life and Times.* Berkeley: University of California Press, 1988.

Soucek, Svatopluk. *A History of Inner Asia.* New York: Cambridge University Press, 2001.

Monsoons

Seasonal winds that bring heavy rain from the Indian Ocean to Southeast Asia and the Indian subcontinent. The monsoons have dictated the yearly cycle of human existence in southern Asia for millennia. They have encouraged or discouraged human habitation and contributed to social organization and cultural innovation.

The term comes from the Arabic word *mawsim,* meaning "season," or "seasonal wind." The region has two monsoonal seasons. The summer, or southwestern, monsoon season lasts from late spring through August. The winter, or northeastern, monsoon occurs between October and December.

In summer, the dry landmass of Eurasia heats up and generates a mass of hot air. As this warm air rises, it creates an area of low pressure that draws in cooler air from the Indian Ocean. Cool ocean breezes blow over the continent from southwest to northeast, mixing with the continental warm air mass to produce heavy rain.

During late fall and winter, the central Asian landmass cools rapidly, producing cold, heavy air. The air pressure over the ocean decreases relative to that over the land, drawing cool continental air from the northeast back to the southwest. These winter winds are dry as they blow across the continent, but pick up moisture as they pass over the ocean. Upon encountering land, the moisture falls as rain in coastal regions such as southeastern India's Coromandel Coast.

Parts of east Asia's coastal regions, such as southern China, are subject to both monsoon seasons, making them agriculturally productive year-round. Others, notably India's southeastern coast and the Southeast Asian islands that lie south of the equator such as Indonesia, receive significant rainfall only during the winter monsoon. Farmers in southeastern India store rainwater from the winter monsoon in large tanks to make agriculture possible year-round. In other cases, depending on the proximity of the region to the equator, cultivation is possible during the dry winter season due to the continuing flow of water from the summer melting of snow in the Himalayas into the major river systems of China (the Yellow, Chang, and the multiple rivers of southern China) and southern Asia (the Indus, Ganges, and Brahmaputra).

Monsoons are necessary to support large populations in southern Asia, but they also can be extraordinarily destructive. Monsoons often bring floods that destroy crops and property and cause death from drowning, disease, or famine. The timing of the monsoons is uncertain, as is their duration and the amount of rainfall they bring. One year may bring floods while the next is marked by drought.

The development of wet-rice agriculture, which led to Asia's population boom, and the construction of elaborate dike networks to hold back seasonal monsoon floods are but two societal responses to the monsoons.

See also: Agriculture; Culture and Traditions.

FURTHER READING
McCurry, Steve. *Monsoon.* London: Thames and Hudson, 1997.
Parks, Peggy J. *Monsoons.* Farmington Hills, MI: KidHaven Press, 2006.
Wang, Bin. *The Asian Monsoon.* New York: Springer-Praxis, 2006.

Myths and Epics

Oral mythology told of the evolution of the earliest civilizations of Asia into settled agricultural communities. Over time, some of these folk traditions became the basis of more formalized spirit worship, as in, for example, Japan's Shinto tradition. Others were incorporated into more sophisticated narratives, as in India's epic poems *Mahabharata* and *Ramayana*.

Myths and epics popularized the cultural values of a society in a form that was accessible to even the uneducated commoner. They served to spread common cultural values among both the **aristocratic** and nonelite classes, as well as among both urban and rural populations. Indian and Southeast Asian kings and Chinese and Japanese emperors all claimed their authority as the legitimate heirs to the mythic figures of the legendary past. The epics might, as in the case of some sections of the Indian *Mahabharata,* consist of sophisticated philosophical discourse, but this was the exception rather than the norm.

FOLK DEITIES AND SPIRIT WORSHIP

Early Asian myths were oral tales that typically celebrated a culture's ancestral heroes or spirits of nature. Most ancient Asian peoples saw these forces as having powerful influence over their lives, and they created tales to explain and emphasize the role of those forces in everyday life. Myths were originally recited at public gatherings, perhaps around a communal campfire as was the case with the tales of ancestral heroes and gods featured in the Indian *Rig Veda*. The *Rig Veda* myths, which were first composed around 1800 B.C.E., focus on the spirits of the natural realm who are more or less subordinate to Indra, the supreme **deified** ancestor who is the lord of war. These myths were also recited in private and public rituals that were the foundations of Hindu religious tradition.

Many societies incorporated traditional, local myths and spirit worship into Buddhist, Daoist, and Confucian traditions, often adapting the ancient myths to reflect the beliefs and **pantheon** of the later religion. In such cases, the local spirits became subordinates of a universal **celestial** divine. In contrast, Japanese Shinto linked the early regional spirit cults to an **animistic** faith.

Shinto

Japan's folk deities were associated with the forces of nature, which had the capacity to help or harm early Japanese rural society. Japanese mythology begins with the creation myths about a divine brother and sister, Izanagi and Izanami, who created the Japanese islands and gave birth to the sun goddess Amaterasu, the guardian deity of the Japanese people, who lived in the "Land of the Rising Sun."

The Japanese spirit realm is populated by *Inari,* a complex of divine spirits associated with the power of abundance and food, especially rice. Inari are also often associated with the symbolic masters of transformation, *kitsune* (foxes), *tanuki,* and *tengu* (mountain and forest goblins). These figures have a longstanding connection to traditional **shaman** magic and the realm of ghosts, spirits, and demons. Male divinities are normally demons with flaming heads, fiery eyes, and swords. Female divinities often played more benevolent roles in human affairs. These include Kannon, the goddess of compassion and mercy who might intervene on humanity's behalf, and Shoki, the demon slayer. Some female divinities were said to bring misfortune, such as Adachigahara, who was fond of killing unattended children.

Chinese Folk Tradition

China's Confucian myths portray the early societal evolution of northern China in a series of tales about deified ancestors. These tales provided the foundation for the concept known as "Mandate of Heaven," wherein successful Chinese emperors are believed to be backed by celestial forces. The myths

Indian and Greek Epics

Greek and Indian epics both derive from an Indo-Aryan heritage that had its roots in the steppe regions of southern Russia. The Indian *Mahabharata* and *Ramayana* epics, which originated around 1600–1200 B.C.E., and the Greek epics that came to be known as Homer's *Iliad* and *Odyssey* (1100–800 B.C.E.), were originally oral compositions in verse form. In contrast to Homer's texts, which were in written form by 800 B.C.E., and despite the early development of Indian Sanskrit writing, the *Mahabharata* and *Ramayana* epics remained oral "works in progress" into the Gupta **era** (ca. C.E. 320–550). They still exist today in several versions that developed in both India and Southeast Asia. Thus, it is not technically correct to speak of "the" Indian epics.

In India and Southeast Asia, Indic epics are still vital, and their characters—Rama, Hanuman, Krisna, and Bima—are still worshipped as being divine. This is in contrast to the gods and heroes in the Greek epics, who are no longer a living part of the Greek culture. Rather, Zeus, Hera, Achilles, and others are said to be representative of the **classical** transition from belief in divine intervention to acceptance of humankind's accountability for its own successes and failures.

Both Vedic and Greek gods portrayed in the epics are beneficent beings who bestow prosperity and good fortune on their human followers. When evil occurs, it is not the work of the gods but the work of demons. The gods inevitably defeat the demons, whether in competitions that take place on earth or in the realms of the gods, and restore order to the realm of humanity. The divine beings are also moral and punish the sinful and wicked while rewarding the pious and righteous. But more important than being moral, they are mighty. They may do whatever they wish, and have imperfections, but have power over all creatures.

also served as examples and lessons on correct and incorrect human behavior.

Chinese mythology begins with the Three August Ones and the Five Emperors, who made society and culture possible. The August Ones, also known as the Three Sovereigns, are the god-kings who founded Chinese civilization. The Five Emperors are wise and morally perfect sages. They include the Heavenly Emperor Fuxi and his wife Nuwa, the first ancestors of humanity; the Earthly King Zhu Rong, who invented fire, which made the earth habitable; and the Human King Shennong, who invented farming. The most prominent among the Five Emperors was the Yellow Emperor, Huang Di, who invented weapons that allowed him to defeat the war god Chi You. This tale represents the victory of settled agricultural populations over neighboring **seminomads** who regularly raided China's earliest farming communities.

Another Chinese myth incorporated into Confucian, Daoist, and Buddhist traditions involves the Jade Emperor, the supreme divinity in Chinese folk religion. The Jade Emperor rules heaven and Earth assisted by a pantheon of divine civil servants. The members of the pantheon were humans who were made divine as a result of exemplary accomplishments during their lifetimes. This myth reflected and reinforced the Chinese practice of basing civil authority on merit, rather than **hereditary** entitlement.

The Eight Immortals also achieved exalted status by overcoming moral deficiencies such as drunkenness, dishonesty, and personal vanity during their lifetimes. Although they could not become gods, they resided at the Jade Emperor's court and could intervene on humanity's behalf to resolve seemingly lost causes.

The most prominent female divine in the Chinese tradition is Guanyin, the goddess of compassion and caring and a role model and **patron** deity for Chinese women. Guanyin especially supports the distressed and hungry, and gives comfort and aid to

The *Tale of Genji*, a mythical story from eleventh-century C.E. Japan, is often called the world's first novel. The scene depicted above shows Prince Genji, the story's hero, leaving the palace of his lover, Lady Fugitsubo. (Art Resource, NY)

the downtrodden. She has the ability to transform into any living creature to complete her task. She can help make women fertile, and is also concerned with the care of infants, especially newborns, who are particularly vulnerable.

EPICS

Throughout Asia, early oral myths evolved into oral epics that were eventually committed to writing. The most important of these stories describe the founding of the societies that produced them. As such, early epics conformed to the values and interests of the societal elite.

Japan, China, and Korea

Two early Japanese epic tales offer views into ancient Japanese elite society. Japan's *Tale of Genji*, often considered the world's first novel, captures the complexities of secluded court life in eleventh-century Japan. The *Tales of Heike*, written in the thirteenth century C.E., provides a view of court society in decay with its history of the Taira (Heike) family's fortunes in the Taira-Minamoto War of C.E. 1156–1185. This conflict marked the critical transfer of political authority from Japan's imperial court to the Kamakura Shogunate, a military dictatorship.

Korea's *Samguksagi* ("Chronicles of the Three States") and *The Legend of Tangun* (the history of the founding of the ancient Choson state in the twelfth century B.C.E.) are compilations of earlier tales. Like Japan's eighth-century *Kojiki* (*Record of Ancient Matters*) and *Nihongi* ("History of Japan"), they were intended to provide the ruling families of Korea and Japan with distinguished ancestral histories. The thirteenth-century Koreans went further in their epic study of *King Tongmyong* (C.E. 1168–1241), which reviews the founding of Koryo sovereignty.

China's earliest known epic was the fourteenth-century C.E. *Romance of the Three Kingdoms,* which recounts the fall of China's Han dynasty and the period that followed (C.E. 150–280). The text is a window into the Chinese past, a commentary on Chinese political philosophy, and ultimately a reflection on politics in the Yuan era (C.E. 1279–1368) during which it was written. All Chinese knew the main characters of the tale. Cao Cao, the founder of the post-Han Wei regional state (C.E. 220–265) is the classic arch villain. The three early heroic champions of the rival Shu state (C.E. 221–265) are Liu Bei, who fights to uphold the traditions of the past, and his able and loyal generals Zhuge Liang, who defeats the evil Cao Cao, and

Asian Creation Myths

Asian myths typically explain that humans came into existence by the actions of a god or gods that established a continuing bond between the world of humanity and the world of the divine. They also indicate that the creator established a hierarchy in which humans exist below the gods and other supernatural beings but above animals and plants. The societies that created these myths applied this idea of order and hierarchy to human relations; most ancient Asian cultures were marked by strict social stratification.

One of China's several creations myths is representative of those of other Asian civilizations in its explanation of an original source of human existence. In this tale, which was incorporated into Chinese writings by the sixth century B.C.E., Pan Gu was the first living thing. He evolved from a giant nurturing cosmic egg, which contained the opposing forces of *yin* and *yang*. Yin and yang fell from the egg, and yin formed the earth and yang the sky. When the egg hatched, Pan Gu became the source of the third element of the trinity of earth, sky, and humankind.

Japan's origin myth, which appears in an eighth-century C.E. Japanese chronicle collection, differs from the Chinese myth in that the earth and sky are deities of different sexes—male sky and female earth—which produce human offspring. Instead of yin and yang, the sea is said to be the creative source of energy that made human existence possible. In the Japanese creation myth, the god Izanagi and goddess Izanami stir the waters of the earth to produce the island of Okonoro, from which they later create the Japanese islands. The divine couple then populates the islands with their many children, including the sun goddess Amaterasu, from whom descended the emperors of Japan.

Guan Yu, who was deified as Guan Di, the Chinese god of war.

India

India's greatest epic is the *Mahabharata,* which tells of a civil war that took place in the Vedic age (ca. 1600–800 B.C.E.). The Pandava brothers, who emerge victorious over their rivals, the Kaurava, represent the various personalities of humankind and stand as models for appropriate human behavior. One brother, Yadhisisthira, is pious, righteous, and gentle, but a little negative in character. Bhima is physically imposing, rough, and gluttonous, but very intelligent. Arjuna is the great warrior—principled, generous, and brave. Notable narrative episodes tell legends of the Indian gods, as well as stories that serve as commentaries on proper and improper behavior.

The *Ramayana,* a symbolic story about rightful human conduct dating to about the third century B.C.E., is just as significant to Indian epic literature as the *Mahabarata.* The *Ramayana* focuses on Rama, a prince who slew many demons that had been attacking local villagers. To avenge his fellow demons' deaths, Ravana, the demon king of Lanka (Sri Lanka), kidnaps Rama's wife, Sita. Rama and his brother, Laksmana, ally with Sugriva, the king of the monkeys, and his general, Hanuman, to find Sita. After tracking Sita to Ravana's palace, Rama, Laksmana, Hanuman, and their army of monkeys kill Ravana and his followers and rescue Sita.

Although Ravana had not mistreated or even touched Sita, Hindu sacred law forced Rama to refuse Sita as his wife, because she had lived with another man. In anguish, Sita threw herself on a funeral pyre (a fire built to burn the bodies of the dead, following Hindu custom). This act was expected of loyal wives, who sacrificed themselves to join their deceased husbands in the afterlife. In Sita's case, however, it was as an act of penance to cleanse herself of her perceived wrongdoing. The fire-god Agni, however, refused to accept her self-sacrifice and Sita lived. Interpreting this as a sign of

Sita's innocence, Rama and Sita renewed their marriage vows and returned to Ayodhya to righteously rule as king and queen. The tale was written as a critique of the unintended consequences of strict Brahmanical law.

The *Mahabharata* and *Ramayana* epics were models for other south Asian regional epic literature, as well as for the localization of these epics into the language and cultural traditions of Southeast Asia. The most notable of these local efforts are the Javanese *kakawin* epic poems from the eleventh through the fifteenth centuries C.E., which retell the Indian classics in the Javanese language and a Javanese setting.

See also: China; Confucianism; Hinduism; India; Japan; Java; Korea; Language and Literature; Mandate of Heaven; Shinto.

FURTHER READING

Creese, Helen. *Women of the Kakawin World: Marriage and Sexuality in the Indic Courts of Java and Bali.* Armonk, NY: Sharpe, 2004.

Davis, Edward L. *Society and the Supernatural in Song China.* Honolulu: University of Hawaii Press, 2001.

Tambiah, Stanley J. *Magic, Science, Religion, and the Scope of Rationality.* Cambridge: Cambridge University Press, 1990.

New Zealand

Southern Pacific islands located southwest of Australia that were settled between the twelfth and fourteenth centuries C.E. by migrating populations from Polynesia known as Maori. New Zealand is known by its native population as Aotearoa, literally "land of the long white cloud."

EARLY SETTLEMENT

New Zealand's earliest known settlements date to the Archaic Maori era, which began around C.E. 750. At this time, Polynesian settlers of unknown origin lived on New Zealand's South Island. Archeological evidence and local legend suggest that these earliest settlers depended on hunting the moa, a now-extinct flightless bird that was as large as four feet (1.2 m) tall and grazed on the open grasslands of South Island. The largest populations of this moa-hunting people lived in camps along the eastern coast of the South Island. According to Maori legend, the earliest inhabitants of South Island eventually killed off the moa bird population, forcing the settlers to maintain their settlements close to the coast, depending primarily on the sea for their survival. Later, as confirmed by archeological evidence, other Archaic Maori became fishermen on the North Island's western coast around Mount Taranaki.

According to Maori mythology, the adventurer Kupe led a tenth-century expedition to New Zealand in double outrigger canoes from the Maori homeland, which most scholars identify as the Society Islands of the southern-central Pacific. Legend holds that Kupe found the island uninhabited. The beginning of the larger and more well-attested Maori migration occurred during the twelfth century, led by the legendary chief Whatonga and his grandfather Tai.

Archeological discoveries confirm kernels of truth in these legends, such as evidence of short-term tenth-century Maori settlements in the Bay of Islands on New Zealand's northern tip, and evidence of gardening at Urimatao on Moturua Island. However, other than these sites, there is little evidence of settlement on the North Island until the twelfth century C.E. The best archeological evidence suggests that the first group of voyaging Maori populations arrived in the twelfth century and settled the Dargaville area on the North Island's western coast. From there they moved farther south, building fortified villages at Rawhiti and Manawaora.

In this period, known as the Classic Maori age, Maori left the coasts to settle the interior. New food crops were introduced, notably taro, yams, and gourd, but especially *kumara,* a variety of sweet potato and the only tropical plant to flourish in New Zealand's cool climate. According to local legend, the Polynesians brought the kumara to New Zealand from their original island homeland.

Maori Culture: Ancient and Modern

The centerpiece of a Maori community is the *marae,* or meeting ground, where a range of activities takes place according to traditional practices. These celebrations include funerals, weddings, tribal reunions, and an annual cycle of other rituals. The marae, which symbolizes group unity, normally consists of an open grassy area in front of a large, carved wooden meetinghouse.

Community elders manage the marae, where they pass along group traditions and cultural practices to the young by teaching oral folktales, songs, and the traditional arts of weaving and woodcarving. Among the most important lessons taught at the marae is distinction between *tapu,* that which is sacred, and *noa,* that which is held in common. A person, object, or place that is tapu may not be touched or even approached except according to specific rules and prohibitions. By tradition, community members of lower rank may not touch the tapu objects of those of higher rank, as those of higher birth may not touch the tapu belongings of those in the lower ranks. If a person of low status touches the glass of a higher-ranking person, for example, the drinking vessel must be destroyed.

Some objects, for example, a ritual basket, a water vessel, or a sacred axe, are so tapu that they are considered dangerous to all except qualified priests. In previous times, failure to honor such an important tapu would pollute the sacred object, place, or person and was punishable by death. To not honor such tapu offended the gods and was sure to bring negative societal consequence. Noa, however, are free of such prohibitions, and are available to all regardless of rank, as common community property.

As the new crops took hold, societies gave up their nomadic camp culture and unfortified villages, and began to build fortified settlements. They also developed an efficient underground storage system that allowed them to harvest the fragile kumara tubers before the first frost and allow them to ripen during the cold winter months. Stored crops fed the local population in the winter, and the surplus was replanted in the spring. Some successful groups began to live in unprotected villages, whereas others continued to occupy strongly fortified villages.

The final settlers from Polynesia landed in the Bay of Islands area in the late fourteenth century, where they intermarried with the established Maori settlers. By the time the first Europeans arrived in the late sixteenth century C.E., most Maori lived on the tropical North Island's northern coastline. Today, most Maori live on the North Island, representing 14 percent of New Zealand's total population.

CULTURE

The great diversity among Maori ancestral arts, crafts, languages, and ways of life reflects cultural differences related to geographical isolation and the varied dates at which the settlers arrived. These differences find expression principally through the distinction between northern and southern Maori culture. For example, while there is a single Maori language, there are separate northern and southern Maori dialects, and nine known regional variations of the northern dialect.

Maori community life centered on a yearly cycle of group performances and rituals held at local meeting grounds, which symbolically bonded individuals to the local community. Community assemblies convened inside a large wooden hall adjacent to the meeting grounds, where speeches, songs, recitations of Maori myth, and ritual processions took place. These proceedings frequently ended in gift exchanges between the meeting hosts and their guests, acknowledged by a ceremonial touching of noses, and a concluding ceremonial sharing of food.

Maori religion is based on Polynesian myth, which explains that humans and every other aspect of nature are descended from Sky Father and Earth Mother. There was a subsequent competition between two of

their children, the fierce Tumatauenga (god of war), and his wise brother Tane Mahuta (god of the forest), who ultimately prevailed. Tane Mahuta's son Maui eventually "fished Aotearoa up" from the sea (a symbolic explanation for New Zealand's volcanic origin).

Archeological evidence demonstrates that there are elements of truth in the symbolic Maori creation myth. The Archaic Maori lived in fortified villages, as protection against their neighbors. Later arrivals, by contrast, lived in unfortified villages. Maori understand this archeological evidence as demonstration that the earliest inhabitants were in agency with Tumatauenga, the destructive god of war. In contrast, the new arrivals were committed to the wise Tane Mahuta; they eventually prevailed and thereafter both groups of Maori learned to live in peace.

See also: Polynesia.

FURTHER READING

Belich, James. *Making Peoples: A History of New Zealanders from Polynesian Settlement to the End of the*

Nineteenth Century. Honolulu: University of Hawaii Press, 1996.

Patterson, John. *Exploring Maori Values.* Auckland, Australia: Dunmore Press, 1992.

Pax Sinica

Political time, influential in pre-1500 Asia, when it was thought that the success and prosperity of the Asian continent depended on the existence of a strong and stable Chinese ruling dynasty. The rise of dynastic authority in China during the Han dynasty (206 B.C.E.–C.E. 220) coincided with increased prosperity throughout Asia. When Chinese dynasties fell, or during extended periods without strong dynastic authority, Asia tended to experience local economic difficulties and political strife.

Nineteenth-century Western scholars coined the term *Pax Sinica* to compare the periods of stable Chinese rule with the *Pax Romana* ("Roman Peace") established in the early years (29 B.C.E.–C.E. 180) of the Roman Empire. During the *Pax Romana,* Roman law and civic culture spread throughout the empire, helping to unify and pacify a diverse population of conquered peoples. Similarly, scholars believed, the Han dynasty united the diverse regions of China under its imperial rule, and used China's powerful political and economic base to impose its will on its neighbors. Like the Romans, the Chinese were able to maintain control with the threat of military force; subject populations were unwilling to challenge a well-armed, well-trained army. This threat formed the basis of the Chinese Tributary System.

Under this system, populations not directly subject to Chinese authority (such as those in Korea or Vietnam) were expected to send regular embassies to present tributary gifts—samples of local products that might be of interest to the Chinese—to the Chinese emperor. The emperor, in turn, presented the ambassador with a gift that symbolized Chinese approval of the local ruler's sovereignty. The ruler displayed the gift to his subjects as a public demonstration of the emperor's support.

Certain expectations accompanied imperial approval, notably that the ruler who gave tribute would ensure peace and stability in his realm in order to encourage peace among his neighbors. China also expected regular trade with tributary states. Exotic foreign products such as spices, aromatic woods, cotton textiles, jungle birds, and medicinal items were important markers of status in China and thus the foreign trade supported the luxurious lifestyle of China's elite. Just as importantly, mandatory foreign trade occurring at Chinese ports provided a vital source of government revenue.

The fall of the Han dynasty brought a drop in international trade, significant economic disruption, and political destabilization to Asia. The return of long-term Chinese dynastic authority under the Tang (C.E. 618–907) and Song (C.E. 960–1279) led to a prolonged period of economic and political growth throughout the region. The resumption and expansion of trade paved the way for development of an international communication network that brought the Buddhist faith to China. The newly converted Chinese authorities made their realm a center of Buddhist worship and scholarship.

The era of the *Pax Sinica* also witnessed the spread of Chinese Confucian culture to neighboring Japan (C.E. 710), Korea (C.E. 935), and Vietnam (C.E. 960), where the Chinese political system became the basis for successful local monarchies. Even the "barbarian" Mongol emperors during the Yuan dynasty (C.E. 1279–1368) adopted established Chinese political and cultural systems and successfully managed an empire that extended from China to the Mediterranean Sea.

The rulers of the Ming dynasty (c.e. 1368–1644) offered an even greater possibility of peace and prosperity in the early fifteenth century. At this time, well-armed Ming fleets sailed to the Middle East and Africa to eliminate piracy and other local threats to the vital Indian Ocean maritime trade route. The Ming withdrew from these overseas voyages in the 1430s to refocus their military spending on securing their northern borders against the raids of threatening central Asian steppe populations. Thus, when cannon-bearing Portuguese and Spanish ships entered Asian waters in the early sixteenth century they had no initial opposition, and their aggressive use of gunpowder to assert their economic interests marked the final end of the *Pax Sinica*.

See also: Indian Ocean Trade; Japan; Korea; Melaka; Mongols; Silk Road; Spice Trade; Vietnam; Zheng He.

FURTHER READING

Chang, Chun-shu. *The Rise of the Chinese Empire: Frontier, Immigration, and Empire in Han China, 129 B.C.–A.D. 107.* Ann Arbor: University of Michigan Press, 2006.

Hardy, Grant, and Anne Behnke Kinney. *The Establishment of the Han Empire and Imperial China.* Westport, CT: Greenwood, 2005.

Polynesia

Stretching from New Guinea east across the Pacific, a widely scattered group of islands that were populated by seagoing people with roots in Southeast Asia. After migrating from mainland Asia sometime before 10,000 B.C.E., some Polynesians left New Guinea around 1500 B.C.E. They traveled first to the Solomon Island chain, then to the Banks and Vanuatu archipelagos, and eventually as far east as Samoa and Hawaii. The name Polynesia refers to the shared cultural heritage of the islands, rather than any geographic or political unity among them.

Archeologists estimate that it took hundreds of years for the Polynesian migrants to reach the easternmost islands, some 2,000 miles (3,200 km) from their starting point off New Guinea. Hawaii was settled about c.e. 400 to 500, Easter Island about c.e. 400, and New Zealand about c.e. 1100–1200. Samoa, Fiji, and Tonga seem to have had special roles as the strategic points for the later voyages of migration, as they are mentioned in local traditions as points of origin.

Except for the sweet potato, all of the crops and domesticated animals of Polynesia (taro, bananas, yams, breadfruit, sugar cane, pigs, dogs, and chickens) came from Asia. Even the sweet potato likely was brought from its native South America by sojourning Polynesians. Scholars agree that the voyagers brought these foods with them, indicating that the goal of their trip was settlement, not simply random exploration.

The Polynesians navigated the Pacific in ingeniously designed and built double-outrigger canoes. These vessels consisted of two hulls connected with lashed crossbeams and covered with a central platform. Although referred to as canoes, these vessels were wind-driven, using sails made of natural fiber matting. The two hulls gave the craft greater stability and resiliency in the open ocean, as well as the capacity to transport people and supplies over long distances. A medium-size boat, 50 to 60 feet (15 to 18 m) long, could accommodate two dozen people and their belongings, including plants and animals to introduce on the new islands they settled.

Polynesian culture is based on family bloodlines and ranking of the different branches of ancestors. Rank often is related to previous islands of residence, and favors the earliest settlers over those who arrived later. Polynesians have a unique animistic religious outlook, in which sea creatures, birds, and the heavens are vital spiritual forces. The Polynesians view these oceanic creatures as having protected and guided the migrating voyagers in their travels. Polynesian religious tradition also celebrates a divine brother and sister, Ru and Hina, who navigate the earth to locate new islands for settlement. The sister, Hina, is said to remain as the moon, guiding voyagers across the ocean.

Today's Polynesian society and culture resulted from the mixing of populations and cultures over the centuries. These cultures and languages, which developed locally rather than being transplanted from Asia, commonly emphasize movement, heroic voyages of discovery, and observation of natural signs such as the stars and ocean currents.

See also: Micronesia; New Zealand.

FURTHER READING
Bellwood, Peter. *Polynesians: Prehistory of an Island People*. London: Thames and Hudson, 1987.
Campbell, Ian C. *History of the Pacific Islands*. Berkeley: University of California Press, 1990.
Irwin, Geoffrey. *The Prehistoric Exploration and Colonization of the Pacific*. Cambridge: Cambridge University Press, 1994.

Religion

Although drawn from a wide variety of local sources and traditions, ancient Asian and Pacific religions have long coexisted and influenced one another's beliefs and practices. Ancient practitioners of Hinduism, Buddhism, Confucianism, Daoism, and Shinto existed alongside one another as have followers of animist religions and ancestor worship cults. As a result, traditional beliefs about humankind's relationship with the spirits of the natural world occupy a central role in several major Asian religions.

Although similarities exist, this intermingling of indigenous religious beliefs throughout ancient Asia led most of the major religions of the region to develop several different forms, or schools of thought, with varying beliefs and practices. Faiths such as Hinduism and Shinto, which had no single founder, grew from an accumulation of beliefs and show significant regional variation. Even Buddhism, although based on the teachings of Siddhartha Gautama (ca. 563–483 B.C.E.)—the Buddha, or "enlightened one"—split into three major schools. In most places, local cultural notions shaped the form of the religion.

ANIMISM

Traditional Asian animism was based on local belief in spirits that populate the realms of nature and humanity. These spirits are revealed in dreams, trances, and a variety of supernatural experiences, including human encounters with ghosts or other spiritual presences. For example, ancient agricultural cults among the village sites of northern China's Yangshao culture (ca. 5000–2000 B.C.E.) assigned a special role to the spirits of the soil, plants, and weather, as well as to local guardian spirits associated with sacred rocks, trees, or sources of water. Local agricultural productivity was believed to result from a partnership between humanity and the spiritual forces of the natural realm. Similar beliefs were popular among the Jomon culture (ca. 10,000–300 B.C.E.) of Japan during the same time period.

Adherents of animistic faiths believed that spirits could flow from one realm of existence to another in ways that humans could not. Humanity occupied a middle realm between supernatural forces that inhabited both the darker regions below the earth and the celestial realms above it. Spirits that dwelled below the earth, such as fertility spirits, could be benevolent; others were potentially dangerous evil forces. Those who lived above the earth were generally beneficial to humans. In animist belief, humans cannot eliminate evil spirits but they can perform rituals to appease them.

Animistic "cults of the soil" were well established in India and China at the time settled agricultural communities appeared in both areas about

87

2500–1800 B.C.E. In these cults, a chief or priest served as the intermediary between the earth deity and ancestor spirits on the one hand and the human community on the other. This intermediary performed rituals and sacrificial offerings of food, animals, and even humans (slaves or war captives) to assure the fertility of livestock and crops and the general good fortune of the community. Prosperity was not seen as the product of human labor, but as the work of the gods. Economic productivity was thus the consequence of healthy relationships between humans and supernatural forces.

CHINESE ADAPTATIONS

In China, Daoism drew heavily on animistic ideas to promote harmonious coexistence between humans and nature. Lao Tzu, a semimythical scholar from the sixth century B.C.E., traditionally is credited with writing the founding text of Daoism, the *Tao te Ching*, although various authors likely produced the work over a period of many years. Daoism is based on the Dao, or "way of nature," a supreme natural force that produces and nurtures everything in the universe. Daoist teaching looks to nature for examples to illustrate its concepts and stresses that all living things, including humans, should strive to live in harmony with the Dao.

Confucianism, meanwhile, embraced traditional Chinese worship of ancestral spirits but redirected the focus to the world of the living. In Confucianism, observing correct familial relationships is seen to be key to an orderly and healthy society. This includes not only honoring deceased ancestors but also paying proper respect to parents and other living family elders. In broader society, this translates into respect for one's social superiors, particularly government officials. However, Confucius (Kungfutzu, 551–479 B.C.E.) believed that societal leaders should be selected on the basis of merit, rather than on the basis of wealth or noble birth. He advocated opening the Chinese civil service to all qualified applicants.

The Confucian state eventually appropriated many aspects of Chinese animistic faiths into a state cult, with the emperor serving a priestly role as supreme intermediary between ancestral spirits and humanity. Local government officials erected over 2,000 temples to Confucius after Confucianism became the state religion in 206 B.C.E. Imperial officials assumed roles as religious leaders in an attempt to focus religious practice on the state and its representatives.

INDIAN RELIGIOUS TRADITIONS

In India, Hinduism emerged as a result of the mixing of Vedic influences from central Asia with existing Indian animistic beliefs. The Aryan nomads who entered India about 1600 B.C.E. practiced a faith centered on the worship of male ancestors, and these ideas merged with Indian worship of female fertility spirits. For example, the stone *linga,* or male phallus, was portrayed united with the female vulva as the focal object of ritual fertility celebrations in animistic pre-Hindu India. Under Hinduism, these local divinities were transformed into universally powerful gods and goddesses. The linga, for example, came to symbolize the Vedic god Siva, who oversaw the realms of agricultural fertility and human health.

Hinduism did not develop a single tradition, however, and various strains of belief developed as a result of debate about the earliest Hindu texts, the *Rig Veda*. Although most Hindus acknowledge the ultimate authority of the *Rig Veda*, few Hindu sects base their ideas solely on its teachings. Most Hindus, for example, worship a pantheon of gods, while others practice monotheism, and some are even atheists. Local customs and culture shape individual beliefs about which god or gods to worship, which ritual practices are the most important, and how much social freedom is accorded to females.

Unlike Hinduism, Buddhism does not draw its inspiration from existing animist beliefs; however, it does not prohibit its followers from practicing animism. In fact, Buddhism is unique in that it allows its followers to worship any god or set of gods they choose. The goal of the Buddhist believer is to seek ultimate truth; how one achieves that goal is considered relatively unimportant. As a result, an individual who sacrifices to Hindu gods can be a practicing Buddhist as can one who worships at a Shinto shrine or one who ritually honors deceased ancestors. This tolerance and inclusiveness helped Buddhism spread widely throughout Asia after its founding in the fifth century B.C.E.

TURNING POINT.

Reincarnation

In Hinduism, reincarnation is believed to be the process of rebirth after death in another form. According to ancient religious tradition, reincarnation is a result of improper action during life, action that makes one's self or "soul" too impure to unite with the ultimate divine creative force, or *brahman*. Improper action is defined as concern for self over the common welfare of humanity, exemplified by actions such as incorrect thought, touch, sight, passion, material gluttony, or abuse of others.

Because of these sins, the polluted soul assumes various forms of life, human as well as animal, in a series of rebirths determined by one's accumulated negative actions over previous lifetimes. Release from the cycle of rebirth can be achieved only by giving up sinful behavior and committing the remainder of one's life to nonmaterial pursuits, such as disciplined meditation, which might lead to even higher levels of purity. India's Jain religion, founded in the sixth century B.C.E., goes beyond the Hindu tradition, proclaiming that rebirth is not limited to humans and animals, but might also take place among inanimate objects. Thus, a stone may represent a being that has a heavily polluted soul.

Unlike Hinduism, Buddhism discounts the notion that a human personality passes on to a new existence at death. According to the Buddhist view, at death the soul carries only the accumulated sins of past lifetimes; one's individual personality ceases to exist and is not retained in the next rebirth. Later followers of Hindu and Buddhist religious traditions softened the ancient notion of reincarnation by suggesting that ancestral spirits eventually go on to an afterlife in a spiritual "heaven" as a reward for a lifetime of moral and devoted service to a divine being and humanity.

The earliest form of Buddhism, called Theravada ("the teaching of the elders") strictly follows the Buddha's words, but later versions of the faith stray farther from the original teachings of the Buddha. Mahayana ("the great vehicle") Buddhism, which arose in the second century B.C.E., is more concerned with replicating the Buddha's experience of enlightenment and focuses less on close adherence to his words. Mahayana Buddhism found acceptance throughout China, Japan, Korea, and Vietnam, while Theravada Buddhism thrived mainly in India, Sri Lanka, and Southeast Asia. A third wave of Buddhism, Vajrayana, developed at Nalandia in India and spread to Tibet, Java, and China in the seventh century C.E. It emphasizes the power of rituals and sacred objects.

ISLAND CULTURES

As in most regions of Asia, Japan's earliest religious cults featured animistic beliefs, and these eventually evolved into the Shinto religion. Shinto is based on the worship of *kami,* or spirits, that are believed to inhabit all things in nature, both living and inanimate. Trees, bodies of water, and even stones have a kami; deceased humans also become kami and are to be honored by their descendants. By about the third century C.E., the Japanese imperial family began to claim descent from the Shinto sun goddess Amaterasu. After that time, the religion became a state cult of which the emperor was the ritual head.

Although the seas surrounding Japan effectively protected the islands from military invasion, they did not prevent the inflow of new religious ideas from mainland Asia. In about C.E. 538, Buddhist monks made their way to Japan, bringing their faith with them. Although the imperial court rapidly adopted the new faith, most Japanese still practiced Shinto or earlier animist religions. The court thus felt the need to reconcile the apparent differences between Shinto and Buddhism. In one explanation, the kami were considered to be supernatural beings who protect Buddhism and help spread its teachings. Other Japanese followers viewed kami as various manifestations of the Buddha.

Hinduism and Buddhism both spread across Asia from India, competing with and influencing one another for nearly 2,500 years. Although this temple in Uttar Pradesh, India is dedicated to the Hindu god Siva, its architecture shows that Buddhist influences and the shrine itself are sacred to followers of both faiths. (Martin Gray/National Geographic/Getty Images)

By this time, other Chinese creeds including Confucianism and Daoism had come to Japan, and worshippers found acceptance within Shinto. In the early eighth century C.E., existing Japanese myths and legends were compiled into accounts that introduced Daoist, Confucian, and Buddhist themes into Japanese religion. These works also were intended to support the emperor's claims to the throne, based on the imperial family's descent from the sun goddess, Amaterasu. Ultimately, Buddhist and Shinto principles were formally combined in *shinbutsu shugo,* a faith that was widely popular in Japan until the mid-1800s.

Australia and the Polynesian islands, even

TURNING POINT.

Indian Temples and Temple Worship

Indian temples are sacred spaces normally dedicated to the ancient gods Visnu or Siva or to one of their alternate forms, or personalities, known as *avatars*. After entering a temple, the worshipper prepares to embrace the divinity by meditating on the numerous statues, stone carvings, and murals (or wall paintings). These images are intended to help worshipers recall sacred stories that portray the various personalities associated with the divinity and prepare them to proceed on their individual pilgrimages. Temple worship includes prayer at several supplemental altars, culminating in entry to the innermost shrine of the temple, where the worshipper encounters the temple's most sacred icon of the divine.

Temple worship is in part *puja,* or reciprocal exchange between the worshipper and the divinity. The worshipper normally makes a material offering, such as money or food, which is presented to the icon of the god. The god in theory "consumes" the offering and is then thought to be spiritually present to receive the prayers of the worshipper.

It is at this moment that the second aspect of Indian temple worship takes place, in which the worshipper internalizes and temporarily becomes one with the divine presence. In preparation for this moment, the worshipper clears his or her mind of all external thoughts. The worshiper focuses exclusively on the aspects of the divinity as those characteristics are portrayed in the temple iconography and statuary—the depictions of the god's hands and legs, the items in the god's hands, the posture and facial expression—all of which are associated with well-known oral and written religious traditions. According to long-practiced ritual, the worshipper also may intone a chant or hymn, ring a bronze bell, light a candle or oil lamp, or burn incense to assure a successful prayer.

more remote and inaccessible than the islands of Japan, developed their own animistic religions that dominated local religious belief until the arrival of European settlers in the 1700s. Practitioners of Polynesian animism viewed sea creatures, birds, and the heavens to be the spiritual guides and protectors of the original inhabitants of the islands, people who migrated from Southeast Asia about 1500 B.C.E. Polynesian religious traditions also feature divine human figures personified by natural or heavenly objects.

In Australia, animist beliefs varied among the 400 or so different indigenous language groups. While no set of beliefs was universal to all of these groups, their religions did share some core similarities. As with other animist cults, all of the Australian beliefs were centered on nature. Many heroes of Australian myth are animals, such as the serpent, that are common to Australia. Human spirits are also considered tied to the earth and the natural world and are associated with specific places. Indigenous Australians all believed in a mythical past called "the Dreaming" or "Dreamtime." During this time, no clear differences existed between humans and animals, and some spirits were thought to be capable of alternating between human and animal form.

ASIAN RELIGION, 1000–1500 C.E.

By the second millennium C.E., Asian religious practice consisted of many layers of different beliefs and practices. In eastern Asia, Chinese religion embraced and blended aspects of Buddhism, Daoism, Confucianism, and traditional ancestral animism. Korean worshippers mixed their unique animistic religious heritage with Chinese Buddhism and Confucianism. Japanese believers practiced the Buddhist and Shinto religions, both of which influenced one another and also embraced elements of Confucianism. In the remote Pacific islands and the Australian archipelago, traditional animism was still the sole religion.

In northern India after C.E. 1000, Islam began to gain a foothold, evident in people's adopting a policy of tolerance toward local Hindu and Buddhist

MAJOR ASIAN RELIGIONS BEFORE C.E. 1500

Confucianism, Daoism, Shintoism, Hinduism, various forms of Buddhism, and traditional animistic religions all characterized the beliefs and practices of the ancient Asian and Pacific Island peoples. From about C.E. 600 to 1300, Buddhism was widely practiced throughout Asia, and Hinduism spread from India to Southeast Asia. After about 1300, some regions of Asia began to convert to Islam.

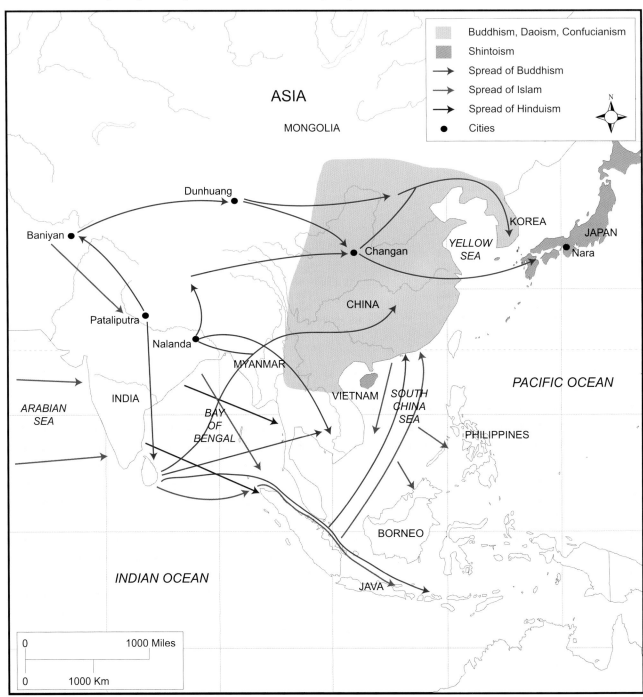

religious traditions. In this respect, Islam followed the pattern established by other religions, adapting to local conditions rather than imposing foreign beliefs by force. By C.E. 1200, Islam was making inroads into what is now Indonesia, and by C.E. 1500, it was becoming the most influential religion throughout most of the Indonesian islands. However, as in India, existing local religious traditions, including

Hinduism and Buddhism, remained strong. Although many local rulers adopted Islam as their official state religion, there is little evidence that Islamic influences displaced local cultural practices.

See also: Australia; Buddhism; China, Confucianism; Hinduism; India; Islam, Spread of; Japan; Korea; Shinto; Sri Lanka; Vietnam.

FURTHER READING

Bowker, John, ed. *World Religions: The Great Faiths Explored and Explained.* London and New York: DK, 1997.

Kitagawa, J.M., ed. *Religious Traditions of Asia.* New York: Macmillan, 1989.

Morgan, K. W. *Reaching for the Moon: Asian Religious Paths.* Chambersburg, PA: Anima, 1991.

Samurai *See* Japan; Society; Tools and Weapons.

Sanskrit *See* India; Language and Writing.

Shinto

Japanese animist religion dating from roughly 300 B.C.E. and based on local gods and the worship of nature. Shinto beliefs and practices have exercised a profound influence on Japan's culture, especially noted in the great reverence the Japanese accord nature.

Shinto, or "the way of the gods," reveres collective spirits, or *kami,* which are celebrated in traditional Japanese myth and ritual. A kami is the "spiritual essence" that in Shinto belief is associated with every natural object. All living creatures have a kami, as do specific places and objects of nature such as trees, rocks, bodies of water, and mountains. Upon death, all humans become kami as well. However, unlike the Western conception of divine beings, human kami are not superhuman or infallible; they coexist with humans and can experience human emotions and failings.

HISTORY AND DEVELOPMENT

Shinto developed as a collection of oral traditions that addresses the needs of humanity in this world—rather than being a guide to salvation in the afterlife. It had no single founder but evolved from the communal rites and symbolic expressions of ancient Japanese society. Kami were initially worshipped and presented with offerings at sites such as sacred rocks and outdoor altars. Since about the sixth century C.E., specific Shinto shrines became associated with local, individual kami. Among these was the shrine located at Izumo (C.E. 659), in western central Japan, honoring the deities of the Izumo family clan, and of Ise (C.E. 690), in eastern central Japan, honoring Amaterasu, the sun goddess, guardian deity of the Yamato imperial clan. Although Shinto does not rank the kami in any hierarchy, Amaterasu is one of the most widely worshipped kami because of her association with the emperor's family.

In the fifth and sixth centuries C.E., the Japanese imperial court adopted Buddhism and began to mix Buddhist and Shinto practices. It was at this time that Shinto first acquired its name, distinguishing it from Buddhism. Indeed, Shinto and Buddhism share a number of similarities. Neither religion believes in the existence of a supreme deity, and neither has a fixed set of doctrines that believers are expected to follow. Shinto is largely unconcerned with life after death. It stresses appreciation for life and living in harmony with the natural world rather than anticipating an afterlife. Similarly, Buddhism focuses on achieving a state of perfect peace and harmony with the universe during one's earthly existence.

The Japanese Shinto religion has its roots in traditional animistic beliefs involving nature and ancestor worship. Shinto shrines, such as this one on Japan's Honshu Island, feature a Torii, or gate, that symbolizes the barrier between the world of humans and the world of spirits, or *kami*. (Sylvain Grandadam/Stone/Getty Images)

In Shinto cosmology, the realm of the dead exists on the same plane as the human world that occupies the Japanese islands and the seas surrounding Japan. It also envisions three levels of gods existing above the earth. These beliefs were recorded in early Shinto works such as the *Kojiki* (*Record of Ancient Matters*, C.E. 712) and the *Nihon Shoki* (*The Chronicles of Japan*, C.E. 720), which identify certain kami as the guardian deities (*ujigami*) of each aristocratic Japanese clan. Japan's imperial Yamato clan, for example, derived its royal status from its privileged association with, and worship of, Amaterasu. The clan traced this association to Jimmu (ca. 711–585 B.C.E.), the legendary first Japanese emperor, who was said to have been directly descended from the goddess. According to the *Nihon Shoki*, Jimmu's grandfather, Ninigi, bestowed on his imperial successors the sword, mirror, and gem that became the sacred symbols of the emperor's authority.

Shinto became Japan's official state religion during the Meiji era (C.E. 1868–1912) and remained so through the end of World War II in 1945. Until this time, the Japanese worshipped their emperor as a god because of his divine bloodline. After Japan's defeat in World War II, Emperor Hirohito (1901–1989) publicly renounced his divine status. His successor, Emperor Akihito (r. 1989–), although no longer considered divine, remains the leading worshipper of the sun goddess on his society's behalf. The emperor worships at the sacred Ise Imperial Shrine on Japan's eastern coast, which celebrates the rising sun, thus, Japan is called the "Land of the Rising Sun."

RITUALS AND INFLUENCE

A Shinto shrine is usually simple and naturalistic in style, surrounded by tall trees or set in a mountain location. The shrines have water ponds, fountains, or streams, which are believed to cleanse the worshipper as well as the ritual site. Shinto shrines are framed by *torii,* simple open gateways to the sacred grounds. The focal center of a shrine is a sacred space framed by a large rope that symbolically holds the doors of the cave of the sun goddess open, preventing her from reentering and thus saving the world from eternal night. The shrine's altar may have a sacred object associated with the local kami, in which the kami may temporarily reside at the call of the worshiper.

Worship includes the clapping of hands or making other noise to summon the kami, which is followed by prayer and concludes with the offering of a small gift as a symbolic sacrifice. At some time during the year, a shrine will be the site of a community festival with a carnival-like atmosphere that celebrates the relationship between the community and the divine as the basis of continuing group success. Today, Shinto shrines remain the sites of personal appeals for divine assistance; community and patriotic celebrations; as well as traditional ritual places that mark certain life achievements.

Many Japanese secular cultural practices today trace their roots to Shinto belief. The importance Japanese place on observing proper forms of greeting or addressing others reflects the Shinto notion of *kotodama,* which asserts that words can have magical effects. The custom of removing one's shoes before entering a structure, and the use of wooden chopsticks as utensils, derive from Shinto's nature-oriented worldview.

See also: Buddhism; Japan; Religion.

FURTHER READING

Ellwood, Robert S., and Richard Pilgrim. *Japanese Religion: A Cultural Perspective.* Englewood Cliffs, NJ: Prentice-Hall, 1984.
Kasulis, Thomas P. *Shinto.* Honolulu: University of Hawaii Press, 2005.
Nelson, John K. *A Year in the Life of a Shinto Shrine.* Seattle: University of Washington Press, 1996.

Silk Road

Transcontinental caravan trade routes more than 5,000 miles (8,000 km) long that connected ancient eastern and western Eurasia beginning in the second century B.C.E. The Silk Road lay just north of the rugged Himalaya mountain range that separates India from China, central Asia, and southern Russia.

Westbound merchants on the route often began their journeys in China's northern capitals and traveled along a network of urban commercial centers in central Asia including Bukhara, Samarkand, and Tashkent in modern-day Uzbekistan. This portion of the route ended in northern Afghanistan, where the route split. One fork continued west to eastern Europe, another went south to India, while the main route went southwest through Persia (modern-day Iran) to Constantinople.

The portion of the route from China to central Asia developed first, by the second century B.C.E., in response to China's desire for central Asian jade. By 59 B.C.E., its extension to the West supplied the Roman elite with China's exquisite silk. The official opening of the route is attributed to the Han emperor Han Wudi (r. ca. 141–87 B.C.E.), who sent his envoy Zhang Qian and an army of 100 men to secure alliances with the central Asian Xiongnu and Yuezhi tribesmen (138–126 B.C.E.). Through the remainder of the Han dynasty (to C.E. 220), the tribesmen were well paid to keep the route open, but Han military outposts served to remind them who was in charge. When the Han dynasty fell, these tribesmen collected passage fees directly from the traders, as an alternative to seizing their goods.

Thereafter, the route was periodically secured when the lands at either end were governed by strong rulers in Persia and China.

The Silk Road reached its high point under the thirteenth-century Mongols, who had virtually conquered the entire territory from China to modern Turkey. Marco Polo, who traveled to China from Venice and back in the late thirteenth century, was one of many European merchants who benefited from Mongol stewardship of the Silk Road. In addition to bringing wealth to Europe, however, the Silk Road brought the Black Death, which spread from central Asian cities to Europe in the late 1340s.

The Silk Road was also an important avenue of cross-cultural exchange. Traders and travelers carried ideas and technology in both directions. It was the favored route of Buddhist pilgrims passing between China and India from the first millennium C.E., and of Christian and Muslim missionaries from the West who hoped to convert Asian populations in the second millennium. In the fifteenth century C.E., the volume of travelers on the route permanently declined. This was the result of several factors: the fall of the Mongol Yuan dynasty in China in 1368; the subsequent conversions to Islam among the post-Mongol hordes who controlled the overland passageway; and the opening of the ocean route between Western Europe and Asia in 1498.

See also: China; Golden Horde; Huns; Indian Ocean Trade; Islam, Spread of; Mongols; *Pax Sinica;* Spice Trade.

FURTHER READING

Boulnois, Luce. *Silk Road: Monks, Warriors, and Merchants.* Translated by Helen Loveday. New York: Norton (for Odyssey Publications, Hong Kong), 2006.

Wood, Frances. *The Silk Road: Two Thousand Years in the Heart of Asia.* Berkeley: University of California Press, 2004.

Slavery

Economic institution in which people are owned as property, must perform labor without compensation, and may be bought and sold at will. Different levels of servitude existed in ancient Asia. At one end of the scale were slaves who were wholly owned by another person and had no rights or personal freedom whatsoever. At the other end were several categories of bondsmen who enjoyed a measure of autonomy in their personal lives and occasionally rose to positions of power.

Both China and Japan distinguished among slaves, general bondsmen, and retainers. Bondsmen could serve as household domestic servants, agricultural laborers, and members of a military retinue. Technically, a Japanese *samurai,* or warrior, was a bonded client of his lord. In China, the eunuch corps, resident at the royal court and consisting of neutered males who were the military and bureaucratic bondsmen of the emperor, frequently wielded power in domestic politics.

A person might become a slave in several different ways. Criminals, especially those guilty of violent crimes, were enslaved as an alternative to execution. Prisoners of war often became the property of their conquerors. In some cases, societies fought wars to acquire slaves, especially in the largely underpopulated region of Southeast Asia, where additional manpower was essential to a society's well-being. There, war captives were usually placed in the military service of the conqueror, or resettled to develop previously uncultivated lands. Coastal Southeast Asia and southern Japan were well-known international slave trade marketplaces. Many of the humans sold there were captured by pirates in raids against shipping or agricultural communities in the China Sea.

Debt slavery was widespread in ancient Asia. Under this arrangement, an individual who could not repay borrowed money was obligated to perform services for the lender until the debt was repaid. It was not unusual for parents of starving children to sell their children into bondage to save them from certain death. The concubine contract, for example, was a form of debt bondage in which a woman or girl served as the sexual partner of a higher-status man, but did not become his wife. Transfers of entire families and their lands to wealthy patrons was a common survival strategy. Servitude could become **hereditary**, as an individual who owned a family might at some time transfer their services to someone else as a gift, or to repay a debt.

See also: China; Japan; Society.

FURTHER READING

Lala, Kishori Saran. *Muslim Slave System in Medieval India*. New Delhi, India: Aditya Prakashan, 1994.

Reid, Anthony, ed. *Slavery, Bondage and Dependency in Southeast Asia*. St. Lucia, Australia: University of Queensland Press, 1983.

Watson, Rubie, and Patricia Buckley Ebrey, eds. *Marriage and Inequality in Chinese Society*. Berkeley: University of California Press, 1991.

Society

Most ancient societies in Asia and the Pacific region were distinguished by social class groupings, or **hierarchies**, intended to impose order on often diverse and mobile populations. In Confucian China, for example, the social order was defined by a highly educated and cultured bureaucratic elite, who earned positions by passing examinations and advanced by meritorious service rather than by right of birth. Indian society, by contrast, was based in the **hereditary** Hindu caste system, which defined every person's social rank and the codes of acceptable behavior appropriate to it. Ancient societies in Japan, Korea, and Southeast Asia were also organized according to hereditary rank and privilege.

PREHISTORIC CHINA

Archeological sites in northern China's Yellow River basin provide evidence of settled agricultural communities in Asia dating from 4000 to 1900 B.C.E. They also demonstrate the origin of later Chinese societal patterns. Each of these village sites is associated with the cultivation of millet (dry rice) and grain and demonstrates long-term commitment to residence at a single site rather than periodic migration. Houses were grouped in family units, clustered around a larger house of a headman or family clan elder, with a common open space for a variety of community gatherings. Moats or pounded earthen walls surrounded the villages, with burial grounds located outside the walls. The common features of these distinctive settlements and the patterns of their pottery suggest communication among early village communities.

Such early Chinese housing sites collectively demonstrate the importance of family as the basic work unit and source of personal identity. Differences in individual burial sites at these villages indicate that the inhabitants considered adults to be more important than children, and distinguished males over females. Adult graves were elaborate and located outside the village walls in designated graveyards; children's graves were simple and nearby the residences inside the walls. Burial goods (pottery, weapons, animal bones) found in the gravesites of significant males demonstrate some degree of social **stratification** if not the emergence of a male leadership elite.

The prominence of defensive fortifications at early village sites suggests that villages came into conflict with hunting and gathering neighbors. **Seminomadic** bands, who had a less reliable

The Japanese Samurai Sword and the Javanese Kris

Weapons used in ancient Asia occasionally served both practical and ceremonial purposes. The Japanese *samurai* sword was one of the finest bladed weapons of any age, renowned for its strength and superior cutting ability, but also revered by owners as an integral part of their personal identity. A samurai wore both a long and a short sword, which he believed to be the "souls" of his warrior skills, and to which he gave individual names. This very personal association between warrior and weapon made it inappropriate to fight with the sword of a vanquished foe. The samurai believed that the soul of a sword could carry out retribution for the death of its original owner; even to possess the sword of a deceased samurai could be potentially fatal.

Like the samurai sword, the Javanese *kris* was a steel dagger that served as both weapon and spiritual object. The jagged-bladed kris was crafted by a blade smith, who was regarded to have magical powers that provided the blade with its "soul." Each kris blade was thought to have a life of its own. It was once considered a good idea for a new kris owner to sleep with the blade under his or her pillow. If the owner had a bad dream, the blade was considered unlucky and it was taken away; harmony, if not a spiritual bond, was essential between the owner and the kris. The spiritual power of the kris was so respected that some owners believe that carelessly pointing a kris at a person might cause that individual's death or bring other misfortune. To avoid this, the kris holder touched the tip of the blade to the ground to neutralize its negative potential.

source of food than did agricultural villagers, often raided **agrarian** settlements. The significance given to male burials and weapon artifacts found in many of the more elaborate grave sites suggests that the early societal elite played a significant role in defending the villages.

The importance of burial among these villages reflects a common concern with death and a basic sense of spirituality. Pottery remains in the burials are decorated with painted humans and animals, which are thought to symbolize early religious beliefs that acknowledged the importance of **animistic** and ancestral spirits.

SOUTHERN ASIA

South Asia's most spectacular early archeological sites are the remains of Indus Valley urban civilization (ca. 2500–1800 B.C.E.). The three most famous Indus civilization sites are Harappa in what is now the Pakistani Punjab, Mohenjo-Daro on the lower Indus river, and Kalibangan in modern Rajasthan. In addition, roughly 200 smaller town and village sites are scattered as far east as the Ganges and as far south as modern Bombay (or Mumbai). The civ-

ilization depended on the management of the annual floodwaters of the Indus River, produced by the melting snows of the Himalayas and the annual summer monsoons. Sophisticated water management allowed the society to cultivate substantial barley and wheat crops, and rice in its southern regions.

Indus Valley artifacts reflect standardization in the society's art forms. Its pottery and sculpted clay figurines include lifelike portrait statues of elite priests, as well as icons of fertility gods. A focus on order is also evident in urban architecture and city planning. City streets were laid out in an intersecting grid pattern, and the major thoroughfares had underground sewage systems. Residential districts composed of brick houses surrounded a public sector containing a few larger buildings, a ritual complex, a large public bath, granaries, and storehouses.

Historical interpretation and analysis suggests that Indus Valley society was organized as a **theocracy** led by an elite priesthood. Urban archeological sites are centered on a ritual complex that included municipal granaries, which stored surplus agricultural production from surrounding villages. In times of drought or famine, the priestly elite redistributed surplus grain among the population. The unpredictability of the local environment gave rise to cooperative social structures that made group survival possible.

Despite its accomplishments, Indus Valley civilization did not endure. For unknown reasons, its cities declined around 1800 B.C.E. Aryan migrants who entered India ca. 1600 B.C.E. found its population dispersed among productive but decentralized rural communities.

INDIAN CASTE SOCIETY

The Indian caste system had its origin in the hierarchical Aryan *varna* system, which dates to 1600 B.C.E. In this system, *Brahmin* priests and teachers occupied the highest caste, followed by *Ksatriya* warriors and rulers, then the *Vaisya* (a commercial and professional "middle class"), and finally, *Sudra* (laborers).

Early Indian codes of acceptable social conduct were collected in the *Dharmasastra* Hindu sacred texts, which reached their final written form in the fourth century C.E. In the *Dharmasastra*-based system, local caste hierarchy was determined by moral and behavioral purity, which was displayed in everyday human conduct. Individuals were expected as much as possible to engage in *dharma,* dutiful service to society. By contrast, *artha,* or service to oneself, brought diminished stature, except when it was appropriate to certain professions, such as among merchants. *Kama,* behavior that was self-indulgent, usually involving the conscious exploitation of others, was sinful and socially unacceptable.

FAMILY, SOCIAL STATUS, AND MARRIAGE IN INDIA

In early Indian society, male children reached full adulthood when they married and had children. Normally, only the birth of a male child could validate adulthood and thus confirm a marriage. Girls were married outside the family and became adult members of their husband's families upon giving birth to a male heir.

Marriages were generally arranged, consistent with the needs and abilities of the family to pay wedding expenses or dowries. Dowries were gifts of money and/or other valuables normally paid by the bride's family to that of the husband. The husband's family reasoned that it was doing the bride's family a favor in taking her off their hands, thus the need for a dowry. Unmarried daughters were a social embarrassment, indicating that something was seriously wrong with the girl or that the family could not afford to marry her.

Marriages were confirmations of a family's status in the community; they also fulfilled an obligation to the family's ancestors to marry appropriately. Ancestor spirits become malevolent ghosts when they were alienated by the offense of an especially inappropriate and socially demeaning marriage. Marriages would ideally take place between two families of similar social or caste stature.

The *Dharmasastra* code dictated that a marriage could take place between families within two levels of one another in the local caste hierarchy. If a family was upwardly mobile, due to its improved economic or other socially important factors, it was important to convince a family of higher stature to take a bride (or groom) from them. For example, Indian merchants (*Vaisyas*) were always desirable marriage partners for cash-short *Brahmin* or *Ksatriya* elites. Merchants were held in low esteem by society because of their self-centered economic activity (*artha*) but were attractive marriage partners because of their wealth and the fact that their children were usually cultured and educated. Victorious warriors also might be of low social esteem, but their positions of power made them attractive marriage partners.

SOCIALLY ACCEPTABLE BEHAVIOR IN CHINA

China's social system was defined by duty, as expressed in the concept of *li,* propriety, or proper conduct. This meant submission to the group. In Confucian theory, innate goodness among humanity arose from societal order. Order brought about success; the consequence of disorder was failure. The key to order was qualified leaders, who maintained order by setting good examples or by forcing individuals to behave in a manner appropriate to their society's code of conduct. Leadership was justified based on experience. Age qualified one to hold power because in theory elders had more life experience than did the young. Previous success in

Hindu society is divided into four classes (Varnas) from the ritually purest (*brahmin*) to the least pure (sudra) and are the basis of the Indian caste system. Brahmin, such as the man shown in this picture, are considered spiritual leaders and are expected to perform extensive prayers and purification rituals to benefit society. (Robert Nickelsberg/Getty Images)

judging right from wrong was thought to ensure that the older leader would appropriately guide the younger dependent to become a good person.

Males generally dominated rather than females. This was not completely because of Chinese **patriarchal** bias, but because in theory the males had a wider range of societal interactions, and thus more experience than did the house-bound female. Rank among male society was the consequence of holding a position of authority, such as being the head of a family, holding public office, or similar public leadership.

In the Chinese system, successful leadership was not based on authoritarianism but on discussions that ideally led to group consensus, implemented by the leader. In principle, participation in the decision-making process was healthy in that it brought differing opinions into the discussion. In addition, decisions in which everyone participated were more

likely to be implemented. If no consensus was reached, the leader dictated what he thought was in the best interests of the group. Once any group decision was reached, every group member was expected to act in a manner consistent with that decision.

CHINESE SOCIAL ORDER

In China, the traditional social system placed the scholar-gentry class at the top. These were land-holding families in which at least one member of each generation had passed the Confucian civil service exams. These annually administered examinations tested one's understanding of the classical Confucian texts. They featured written essays in which the candidate had to apply his knowledge to resolve specified problems he might encounter as a public servant. Passing these exams was a prerequisite for government office, as well as confirmation of a family's literacy. Only those who demonstrated literacy by passing the initial level of the exams could communicate directly with government. Thus, the literate were in a strong position to act as advocates on behalf of their dependents.

Below the scholar gentry in the Chinese social order were the peasants, considered loyal and settled dependent clients of the elite. **Artisans** were lower in rank: because their work was somewhat self-serving and they were potentially mobile, artisans were thought to be less likely to submit to the gentry's leadership. On the bottom of the social system were the merchants, whose interests were more focused on personal profit than on community service. They were the group least likely to follow the gentry's wishes, or to take on the acceptable lifestyle of the gentry. Social mobility might be achieved by marriage, or by passing the examinations, which were in theory open to all but in practice were limited to those who could afford to pay for their education.

THE WIDER ASIAN COMMUNITY

The Chinese social system was adopted in neighboring Korea, Japan, and Vietnam, with modifications relative to existing local cultural values. The Indian social system influenced societal development in Sri Lanka and Southeast Asia relative to notions of social behavior and ritual hierarchy but without the acceptance of the Indian caste system. Japan and several other Asian societies favored a household consisting of the nuclear family, in contrast to Indian and Chinese extended families, in which male relatives share a common household. In the Japanese nuclear family system, only one male in each generation succeeded his parents as head of the family household. Other males moved to homes on other family property or on frontier land that they would bring under cultivation.

In Southeast Asia, women traditionally had a higher degree of personal **autonomy** than was the case in the Chinese, Indian, and Japanese societies. This was in part the consequence of **matrilineal** and bilateral (equal value to both the maternal and paternal lines) family networks, in contrast to Indian, Chinese, and Japanese **patrilineal** systems.

See also: Archeological Discoveries; China; Confucianism; Hinduism; India; Japan; Korea.

FURTHER READING

Bellwood, Peter S. *First Farmers: The Origin of Agricultural Societies.* Malden, MA: Blackwell, 2005.

Bellwood, Peter S. *Prehistory of the Indo-Malaysian Archipelago.* Orlando, FL: Academic Press, 1985.

Ebrey, Patricia Buckley, and Peter N. Gregory, eds. *Religion and Society in Tang and Sung China.* Honolulu: University of Hawaii Press, 1993.

Inden, Ronald B. *Imagining India.* Cambridge, MA: Blackwell, 1990.

Spice Trade

Indian Ocean–based trade in spices, a system in existence by the first millennium B.C.E. Broadly, spices were rare items used in culinary, aromatic, and medicinal applications, with their medicinal value initially overshadowing their culinary use. Because virtually all spices were very expensive and imported in small quantities, only **aristocrats** could afford to buy them.

The most prized spices were pepper, ginger, cinnamon, turmeric, cardamom, cloves, nutmeg, and mace. The Spice Islands (in modern-day Indonesia), in Southeast Asia's eastern **archipelago**, were the source of the most valuable spices because cloves, nutmeg, and mace grew exclusively there. Cloves are the dried, unopened flower bud of an evergreen tree grown on five small islands in the Moluccas; nutmeg and mace are parts of the fruit of a rare evergreen tree native to the Banda Islands.

Borneo and Sumatra jungles were the source of benzoin and camphor barks, which were considered vital in preparations of Chinese medicines. Benzoin was also a demanded aromatic in Chinese and Indian religious ritual, as were aloewood and sandalwood from Southeast Asia and frankincense and myrrh from the Arabian Peninsula and eastern coast of Africa. India's southwestern Malabar Coast was considered the source of the best pepper as early as Roman times; northern Sumatra pepper was a less expensive alternative after about C.E. 1000.

These commodities made their way from their point of origin to Eastern and Western markets via the Indian Ocean trade routes. The Strait of Melaka, separating the Malay Peninsula from Sumatra, was a key passageway from Southeast Asia to the western marketplaces of India and the Middle East. The South China Sea was equally important in the transit of spices from Java to Vietnam, China, Japan, and Korea. An alternative route from the Spice Islands to China passed through the Sulu Sea by way of the Philippines.

As the trade developed in the first century B.C.E., Indonesian seamen monopolized direct access to the sources of spice; India-based and Middle Eastern mariners were the most common in the western Indian Ocean. By C.E. 800, Middle Eastern seamen were sailing all the way to China. Chinese navigators participated actively in the spice trade after C.E. 1100, depending on the Chinese government's restrictions on the navigators' maritime activities.

Traders bought deck and cargo space from a ship owner or captain. The timing of their travels depended on the seasonal monsoons, with winds blowing from southwest to northeast from roughly June through August and then reversing to blow from northeast to southwest from December through March. Captains found themselves regularly laying over in a port, where they might take on wives and raise families, until the next monsoon season allowed their return voyage. Because it took two to three years to make the complete east-west passage, traders would specialize in one sector of the route. For example, a merchant might trade only between the Middle East and India, India and Southeast Asia, or Indonesia and China. In most ports of trade, both populations and trading activities fluctuated widely, depending on the seasonal travels of the merchants.

Open marketplace competition was the norm in the early spice trade network. Ports of trade competed to provide the most agreeable conditions; favored ports offered the security, products (whether their own or acquired from secondary marketplaces), and provisions demanded by the traders.

See also: Indian Ocean Trade; Melaka; Monsoons.

FURTHER READING

Dulby, Andrew. *Dangerous Tastes: The Story of Spices.* Berkeley: University of California Press, 2002.

Reid, Anthony. *Southeast Asia in the Age of Commerce.* 2 vols. New Haven, CT: Yale University Press, 1990, 1995.

Sri Lanka

Island off the southeast coast of India that became the international center of Theravada Buddhist scholarship in the second millennium C.E. and, from the beginning of the first millennium, was a critical step in the maritime trade network that stretched from eastern Asia to the Middle East. Ancient Sri Lanka was the exclusive global source of cinnamon, and also supplied pearls and black pepper to international traders.

By 900 B.C.E., aboriginal groups called Veddas were living in small urban settlements centered on Anuradhapura in the northern Sri Lanka dry zone and growing dry rice, or millet. In the sixth century B.C.E., Indo-Aryan Sinhalese from northern India migrated to Sri Lanka. According to the Sri Lankan Buddhist chronicle called the *Mahavamsa,* the Sinhalese conquered the Anuradhapura region.

By 300 B.C.E., the Sinhalese had developed an elaborate irrigation system consisting of water tanks (reservoirs) and irrigation canals that enabled year-round cultivation in northern Sri Lanka. The remains of this early irrigation system are still impressive and once consisted of sophisticated valve pits (sluices) associated with massive dams and long-distance canals that crisscrossed northern Sri Lanka. In that same era, the Sinhalese converted to Theravada Buddhism, the oldest of the main Buddhist traditions. Buddhist monks and their monasteries partnered with Sri Lanka's Anuradhapura-based kings in the development of the critical irrigation systems. In C.E. 371, Anuradhapura became the home of a holy relic said to be the tooth of Siddhartha Gautama, the Buddha. The Buddha's Tooth Relic was smuggled to Sri Lanka from India at the initiative of the reigning king, and has since been the sacred symbol of political authority.

Anuradhapura, which became internationally famous for the massive *stupas* (dome-shaped towers that represented ancient earthen mounds used to cover relics of the Buddha) of its temples, remained the Sri Lankan capital city until C.E. 1000. At that time, invading Tamil Cola armies from southern India plundered the city and established a new capital at Polonnaruwa to the southeast. Sri Lankan forces retook the island in C.E.

1070, retaining Polonnaruwa as their capital. The Polonnaruwa-based state reached its height in the reign of Parakramabahu (r. C.E. 1153–1186), but by C.E. 1200 his realm had fragmented as southern Indian Tamils regained a foothold in Sri Lanka and began raiding their Sinhalese neighbors.

By the fifteenth century C.E., there were two new Sinhalese political centers, one at Kandy in the hills of central Sri Lanka (which remains the home of the Buddha's Tooth Relic) and the second at Kotte, inland from modern Colombo on the tropical southeastern coast, which was the center of Sri Lanka's international trade. Kotte eventually became the foothold from which the Portuguese extended their authority over the island after their arrival in C.E. 1505.

See also: Art and Architecture; Buddhism; India; Indian Ocean Trade.

FURTHER READING

DeSilva, K. M. *A History of Sri Lanka*. New York: Penguin Books, 2005.
Peebles, Patrick. *The History of Sri Lanka*. Westport, CT: Greenwood Press, 2006.

Sukhothai and Ayudhya

Centers of early Thai (Siamese) political development that eventually merged into a unified Ayudhya state (C.E. 1351–1767) that became the precursor of present-day Thailand. The territory brought under control by Ayudhya rulers in the late fourteenth and early fifteenth centuries C.E. remains roughly similar to the borders of the modern Thai nation.

EARLY HISTORY

Until C.E. 1238, the city of Sukhothai was part of the great Khmer Empire centered in what is now Cambodia. In that year, Thai chieftains Pho Khun Pha Muang and Pho Khun Bang Klang Hao declared their independence from the Khmer and established the Sukhothai realm in present-day northwestern Thailand. The rebellion marks the traditional founding of the Thai state. Sukhothai subsequently formed alliances with many smaller Thai states, such as the northern kingdom of Lanna,

that were also arising in opposition to Khmer rule. By the late thirteenth century C.E., Sukhothai had conquered the western portions of the Khmer Empire and become a regional power.

Ayudhya was founded in the early eleventh century C.E. on the western edge of the Khmer realm. Originally part of a Thai kingdom based in the city of Lopburi, Ayudhya became the capital in C.E. 1350, when an outbreak of smallpox in Lopburi forced king U Thong (Ramathibodi; r. 1351–1369) to move his court. By this time, the former Lopburi state had grown to challenge Sukhothai for political dominance over the Thai people. In the late fourteenth century, Ayudhya forced a declining Sukhothai to pay **tribute**. By the early fifteenth century C.E., the ruler of Ayudhya determined who sat on the Sukhothai throne. Ayudhya's King Trailok (Borommatrailokanat, r. 1448–1488) finally **annexed** the remnants of the Sukhothai kingdom in C.E. 1431.

POLITICAL CULTURE

Like the Sukhothai kings before them, the rulers of Ayudhya embraced Theravada Buddhism as the state religion. The aggressive and patronizing Theravada church, or *sangha,* evolved into a **hierarchical** network of monastic communities throughout the Thai realm that established close relations with the royal court. The ties between Thai **secular** and religious leaders were underscored by the construction of a central monastic and temple complex that was within the royal court. The Ayudhya state's political network, which depended on fragile personal alliances with small tributary kingdoms, was thus reinforced by the stable structure of the church.

By the C.E. 1460s, Ayudhya dominated the affairs of the upper Malay Peninsula. It shared in the regionwide prosperity that followed the establishment of the Melaka sultanate at the beginning of the fifteenth century. Ayudhya annexed the Tenasserim (1460s) and Tavoy (1488) regions on the northwestern Malay Peninsula, which provided it with direct access to the international trade of the Bay of Bengal and the Indian Ocean. The Ayudhya realm continued to prosper until raiding Burmese forces destroyed its capital in C.E. 1767.

See also: Buddhism; Indian Ocean Trade; Khmer Empire.

FURTHER READING

Lieberman, Victor. *Strange Parallels: Southeast Asia in Global Context, c. 800–1830.* Cambridge: Cambridge University Press, 2003.

Tarling, Nicholas, ed. *The Cambridge History of Southeast Asia.* Vol. 1. Cambridge, MA: Cambridge University Press, 1991.

Wyatt, David. *Thailand: A Short History.* New Haven, CT: Yale University Press, 1984.

Technology and Inventions

Asian scholars and inventors prior to C.E. 1500 far outstripped their European contemporaries in most areas of technological progress. Innovations that were pioneered in Asia often did not appear in the West until hundreds of years later.

AGRICULTURE AND INDUSTRY

The Chinese developed the ox-drawn plow in about 300 B.C.E. and followed this in the Han **era** (206 B.C.E.–C.E. 220) with a new collar that allowed draft animals to pull plows and wagons. The latter did not appear in Europe until some time after C.E. 500. The Chinese also invented the first wheelbarrow and were the first culture to resolve the problem of insect control; by C.E. 300, Chinese citrus growers in southern China were using "red tree ants" to protect their fruit from insects.

The Chinese invented a variety of sophisticated mechanical systems, including the first system of pulleys and winding gears to carry mined materials to the earth's surface. China boasted the first system of canal locks, the first gear system used for milling grain, and the first water-powered mills used for manufacturing. The Chinese talent for industrial innovation included the invention of coke, a key ingredient in iron smelting.

Gunpowder, not introduced to Europe until the late fourteenth century C.E., was invented in China during the Song era (C.E. 960–1279). At first, the Chinese used gunpowder for fireworks featured in ritual displays and public celebrations. They later applied the technology to produce the

TECHNOLOGY AND INVENTIONS

444 B.C.E. Chinese develop accurate solar calendar based on 365.5-day year

300 B.C.E. Chinese develop ox-drawn plow

206 B.C.E.–C.E. 220 Han-era Chinese invent improved collar for draft animals

C.E. 320–550 Indian scholars develop bonesetting, plastic surgery, administer the first inoculations

CA. C.E. 500 Indian mathematician Aryabhata develops theory of gravitation, asserts that Earth and the planets circle the Sun, calculates value

of *pi*, accurately measures length of the year and circumference of the earth

CA. C.E. 800–1000 Chinese Song dynasty pioneers new Indian Ocean shipbuilding and navigation technology

CA. C.E. 1000–1100 Chinese invent gunpowder

C.E. 1161 Chinese use explosives for the first time in warfare

CA. C.E. 1300 Printing press invented in Korea

CA. C.E. 1400 Chinese develop moveable type for printing press

---

first cannons, handguns, land mines, hand grenades, and rockets. The first recorded use of gunpowder in battle occurred in China in C.E. 1161.

ASTRONOMY, MATHEMATICS, AND MEDICINE

Chinese astronomers had developed an accurate calendar by 444 B.C.E., based on a year of 365.5 days. The Indian astronomer Aryabhata (C.E. 476–550) used his astronomical and mathematical calculations of the rotation of the earth to determine a year to be 365 days, 6 hours, 12 minutes, and 30 seconds (the precise value is 365 days and 6 hours). Aryabhata, whose studies were collected in his *Aryabhatiya* manuscript, made other significant discoveries. He was the first to explain the lunar and solar eclipses, he calculated *pi* at 3.1416, and he determined that the earth's circumference was 24,835 miles (39,970 km; just 0.2 percent off the precise distance). He was the first to develop a theory of gravity and he theorized that the earth and planets revolve around the sun—1,000 years before Nicolaus Copernicus (who knew of Aryabhata's prior studies) proposed the same theory in the West.

In addition to Aryabhata's calculation of *pi*, Indian mathematicians produced the Indian numbering system, called "Arabic" because Europeans imported it secondhand from the Middle East in the tenth century C.E. This system, universally used today, was much simpler and easier to use than the cumbersome system of Roman numerals used in Europe. Indians are also credited with developing the concept of zero, devising the decimal system, and calculating square roots and trigonometric functions.

Indian scholars based in Gupta-era hospitals (ca. C.E. 320–550) invented bonesetting and plastic surgery and administered the first inoculations, using an injection of cowpox serum to prevent smallpox. Chinese scholars developed their own precise anatomical knowledge and studied the principles of hygiene to promote longer life. The Chinese also studied pharmaceutical uses of plants and minerals. Chinese researchers were the first to write texts on forensic medicine and the first to propose that fingerprints might be used as a form of identification.

PRINTING

Scholars credit the Chinese with producing the first paper during the Han era, and with developing moveable type, which they were using by the fourteenth century C.E. By the tenth century C.E., Chinese could buy woodblock-printed copies of the Confucian and Buddhist classics, printed on bamboo

TURNING POINT

The Concept of Zero

Although Indian mathematicians had developed a decimal system that used zero as a number and placeholder by C.E. 600, the concept of zero is much older. Some scholars argue that the need for the mathematical zero arose in the Gupta era (C.E. 320–550) because of the introduction at that time of the Chinese abacus, a device for mathematical calculations. The abacus contained several columns, most strung with beads for counting, but one left empty; scholars who embrace this theory argue that zero provided a written symbol for the empty column. Others argue that the use of zero arose as a response to the need for more accurate written calculations.

The Indian mathematician Aryabhata (C.E. 476–550) used the number system that became known as "Arabic numerals," adding the word *kha* to differentiate numerical position, and his word would become the name for zero. In C.E. 628, the Indian mathematician Brahmagupta (C.E. 598–668) provided the rules for arithmetic involving zero and negative numbers. He explained that subtracting a number from itself resulted in zero; he also established that a number multiplied by zero was zero, and that mathematical calculations could produce both positive and negative numbers.

The earliest document to use zero is an inscription from Gwalior, south of Delhi, which dates to C.E. 876 and records the dimensions of a garden and the total production of flowers that it could be expected to produce. The inscription includes the numbers 270 and 50, written as they would be today, although the zero in both cases is smaller than the other numbers.

paper that had special additives to repulse insects. These were in high demand among those studying for the Confucian exams. The Chinese printed books, paper currency, and popular consumables, such as playing cards, almanacs, and calendars, in black or in color on printing presses, which the Koreans had previously invented around C.E. 1300.

Thanks to moveable type, by the early fourteenth

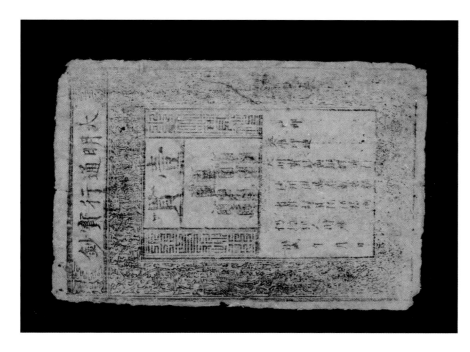

The Chinese Song dynasty (C.E. 960–1279) was the first state in the world to issue paper currency. By the time this Ming dynasty (C.E. 1368–1644) banknote was circulated in C.E. 1375, inflation had greatly eroded its value; the Ming ended the use of paper money in C.E. 1455. (HIP/Art Resource, NY)

THE SPREAD OF TECHNOLOGY

Many noteworthy achievements took place in mathematics, astronomy, medicine, chemistry, printing, and navigation took place in ancient Asia. Among the long list of inventions that were passed to the West were paper, the printing press, the seismograph, the magnetic compass, and the decimal system.

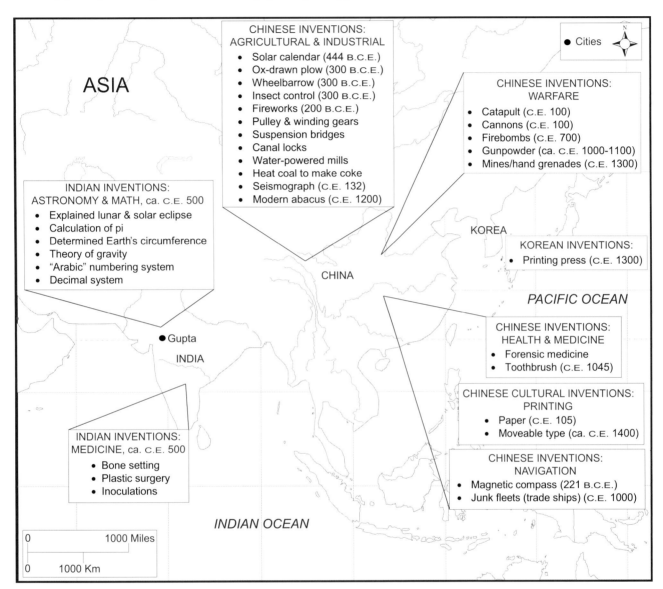

ASIA

CHINESE INVENTIONS: AGRICULTURAL & INDUSTRIAL
- Solar calendar (444 B.C.E.)
- Ox-drawn plow (300 B.C.E.)
- Wheelbarrow (300 B.C.E.)
- Insect control (300 B.C.E.)
- Fireworks (200 B.C.E.)
- Pulley & winding gears
- Suspension bridges
- Canal locks
- Water-powered mills
- Heat coal to make coke
- Seismograph (C.E. 132)
- Modern abacus (C.E. 1200)

• Cities

CHINESE INVENTIONS: WARFARE
- Catapult (C.E. 100)
- Cannons (C.E. 100)
- Firebombs (C.E. 700)
- Gunpowder (ca. C.E. 1000-1100)
- Mines/hand grenades (C.E. 1300)

INDIAN INVENTIONS: ASTRONOMY & MATH, ca. C.E. 500
- Explained lunar & solar eclipse
- Calculation of pi
- Determined Earth's circumference
- Theory of gravity
- "Arabic" numbering system
- Decimal system

KOREA

KOREAN INVENTIONS:
- Printing press (C.E. 1300)

CHINA

•Gupta

INDIA

PACIFIC OCEAN

CHINESE INVENTIONS: HEALTH & MEDICINE
- Forensic medicine
- Toothbrush (C.E. 1045)

CHINESE CULTURAL INVENTIONS: PRINTING
- Paper (C.E. 105)
- Moveable type (ca. C.E. 1400)

INDIAN INVENTIONS: MEDICINE, ca. C.E. 500
- Bone setting
- Plastic surgery
- Inoculations

CHINESE INVENTIONS: NAVIGATION
- Magnetic compass (221 B.C.E.)
- Junk fleets (trade ships) (C.E. 1000)

INDIAN OCEAN

| 0 | 1000 Miles |
| 0 | 1000 Km |

century C.E., a wide variety of printed books were available to the Chinese public. These included public records written in the formal Chinese language used by the government as well as inexpensive publications written in local languages. However, the large number of Chinese language characters (between 45,000 and 75,000) discouraged use of this early moveable type. One fourteenth-century C.E. gazetteer printed using this method needed 60,000 pieces of type and took two years to produce.

NAVIGATION

Asian navigation responded to the opportunities of the Indian Ocean trade routes. During the ninth and tenth centuries C.E., the Song **dynasty** sponsored efforts to help exploit these routes, such as the creation of detailed maps of routes, and the development of the magnetic compass to assist in navigation. This was also the era in which the Chinese began to develop the ship that would become known as the junk. By the late eleventh century C.E.,

The First Seismograph

In C.E. 132, Zhang Heng (C.E. 78–139), royal astronomer to the Chinese emperor, invented the world's first device to warn of earthquakes. Zhang's invention, which preceded the first such development in the West by more than 1,600 years, consisted of a cast bronze vase 6 feet (1.8 m) in diameter with dragons projecting from its sides in eight directions, their heads facing upward, each holding a ball in its mouth. Bronze frogs sat with their mouths open under each dragon. When the ground shook, a pendulum hanging inside the vase would swing in the direction in which the earthquake occurred. The pendulum moved a rod that would cause a dragon to release a ball into the waiting mouth of a frog, to show that an earthquake had occurred in the direction of the frog receiving the ball.

This was especially vital information in ancient China, which was subject to many devastating earthquakes. As a consequence of Zhang Heng's invention, the imperial government was able to provide more rapid assistance to earthquake victims in an age in which rapid communication was not available. Chinese legend relates that once the members of the court thought the device had failed when they felt nothing, only to find out from a messenger several days later that there had been an earthquake 400 miles (645 km) away.

Chinese commercial fleets were sailing as far as northern Sumatra, and by the mid-thirteenth century C.E. Chinese junks and traders were widely active in the entire Indian Ocean.

By C.E. 1500, the typical ship constructed in the ports of southern China and Southeast Asia had a carrying capacity of 350 to 500 tons (320 to 455 m tons). Some, such as those used by the Chinese commander Zheng He in his Indian Ocean voyages (C.E. 1405–1433), had a capacity of 1,000 tons (905 m tons). Many Asian ships were built without the use of iron, instead held together by wooden dowels inserted into the seams between the planks. Normally, these ships had multiple layers of hull planks (two to three layers were typical) so that if the outer layer was damaged, the inner layers would maintain the ship's buoyancy. A hybrid ship design, called *junco,* had planking that was fastened to the frame by iron nails, but which was also dowelled together by wooden pegs.

These "hybrid" vessels demonstrate the success of cross-cultural communication common in Asia in the pre-1500 era, when regular exchange of ideas and technology followed in the wake of trade. As Europeans made their way into Asia from the thirteenth century C.E. onward, they were surprised by the variety of Asian technology that was significantly ahead of their own. Accounts from these travelers captured the European public's imagination, and reinforced the popular belief that Asia was a far more civilized place that had much to teach the West.

See also: Agriculture; Society; Tools and Weapons; Zheng He.

FURTHER READING
Chow, Kai-Wing. *Publishing Culture and Power in Early Modern China.* Palo Alto, CA: Stanford University Press, 2004.
Needham, J. *Science in Traditional China.* Cambridge, MA: Harvard University Press, 1981.
Rahman, A. *Development of Philosophy, Science, and Technology in India and Neighboring Civilizations.* New Delhi: Oxford University Press, 1999.

Tools and Weapons

Early Asian civilizations advanced rapidly from the use of stone, wood, and bone tools to implements of bronze, iron, and steel. Highly organized early societies such as Zhou-era China (1122/1027–403 B.C.E.) developed innovative tools and weapons that allowed them to exploit the country's natural resources and defend it from invaders. By C.E. 1500, Asian tools and weapons included innovations such as looms and kilns that were critical to local productivity and gunpowder weaponry that was as advanced as that of the contemporary West.

EARLY CHINESE AGRICULTURAL IMPLEMENTS

The Banpo Village archeological site near modern-day Xian provides an example of early Asian agricultural tool culture (ca. 4000 B.C.E.), which depended on spadelike farm tools made of stone or bone. Other sites from this earliest era of settled agriculture also include millstones that were used for husking millet. The era from 770 to 476 B.C.E. marks the beginning of Chinese use of iron tools and beasts of burden to pull plows. Previously, humans pulled primitive plows made of wood, which limited farming to easily plowed areas. New iron plows pulled by cattle were able to plow deeper and thus opened previously uncultivated lands to agriculture. This same era produced better dam-building and water management techniques, as in the Dujiang Dam near modern-day Chengdu in the Sichuan Province and the Canal of the State of Zheng in the Shanxi Province, which supported the opening of new cultivated lands in northwestern China.

By the Han dynasty (206 B.C.E.–C.E. 220), iron tools were common, including pliers that are very similar to the same type of tool used today. Han-era metallurgy involved a bellows system made of leather and powered by humans to increase the temperature of an iron furnace. This produced a higher quality iron that was less likely to break under stress when plowing fields. One beneficiary was the triangular iron plowshare, which had a U-shaped board fixed to the rear of the plow to turn over and crush the earth.

Tang dynasty (C.E. 618–907) innovations included the curved-shaft plow and other new tools that further improved cultivation and brought about rapid growth in China's population. Paired with the breast harness, developed around 200 B.C.E., the new Tang plow allowed draft animals to breathe more easily while pulling heavier loads. The plow, which both crushed and plowed the soil, could turn both left and right, and even turn around easily. Another new Tang-era tool was the wheelbarrow, which could carry both people and cargo. Large self-powered bucket carriage waterwheels allowed the lifting of water over riverbanks into adjacent irrigation canals.

CHINESE INDUSTRIAL TOOL INNOVATIONS

During the Han dynasty, Chinese craftsmen produced the first metal calipers, made of bronze. This invention allowed much more precise measurement of small distances, enabling the development of more intricate innovations in metallurgy and craft production. Some of this new capacity to measure was applied to weaving technology. Although the Chinese had woven silk on locally produced looms since roughly 4000 B.C.E., in the Han era new twilled spinning wheels powered by foot peddles were the most advanced weaving apparatus in the world.

Yuan dynasty (C.E. 1279–1368) weavers modified the traditional spinning wheel into a new three-spindle cotton spinning frame. This increased the production of cotton yarn and supported a major increase in China's cotton production, both in terms of the growth of cotton as well as in the weaving of cotton cloth.

The Tang dynasty marked a significant increase

in the production of porcelain, which the West would later call "china," using new color glazes and more efficient kilns to fire the ceramics. Another new Tang dynasty "tool" was the brass mirror, which was a byproduct of new metallurgy developments using a mixture of silver and tin. Tang bronze mirrors came in a variety of shapes and sizes, and there were other mirrorlike implements, including one that was able to start a fire by reflecting the sun's rays.

WEAPONS

India's Aryan warriors introduced the chariot to Asia about 1600 B.C.E., and it had spread to China by 1100 B.C.E. The Aryans also introduced the shaft-hole axe, which was made of cast iron with an opening for the insertion of a wooden handle. By the twelfth century B.C.E., Chinese elite were being buried dressed in ceremonial bronze armor, which they would have worn in battle. By the Era of Warring States (403–222 B.C.E.), Asian warriors were increasingly using saddles and wooden stirrups more than chariots. The development of better metal technology in the Han dynasty (206 B.C.E.–C.E. 220) led to Asian cavalries

employing metal double stirrups. These allowed cavalrymen to better control their horses and provided a stable base from which they might shoot arrows at their opponents while on horseback.

Bows and arrows and spears were the chief armaments of the earliest Asian armies. Infantrymen fought with spears; unlike their early Roman legion contemporaries, they did not fight in close battle formations. Spearmen instead provided a forward defense for archers and crossbowmen standing behind them, shooting arrows or fire arrows at the enemy. The Han crossbow trigger mechanism was the best available in that age. Later, the Han would arm their cavalrymen with compound bows that used simple pulleys to draw or pull them back. The mace, besides being a symbol of authority, was also used as a weapon in battle, for jabbing or hurling and to break the helmets of enemies. Fireballs, missiles, and bombs, used to set fire to enemy camps, were special features of traditional Indian warfare.

Daggers were the so-called personal weapons of soldiers that were carried with them at all times, both on and off the battlefield. They were as much ceremonial weapons as they were fighting weapons, as demonstrated in their regular inclusion among the ritual items contained in the Chinese dynastic tombs. In terms of design and style, they were undoubtedly the most creative and colorful of all Asian weapons and rank with the Southeast Asian *kris* jagged daggers and Japanese *samurai* swords as uniquely Asian military artifacts.

Military strategy in the time of China's Song dynasty (C.E. 960–1279) focused on conquering and defending cities; thus, an extensive science of fortification and siegecraft developed. Use of rockets and other weapons employing gunpowder were common at this time. Following his conquest of China in C.E. 1276–1279, the victorious Mongol leader Genghis Khan, impressed with the technological advantages of the Song army, adopted Song battle technology, adding infantry and naval units to complement his efficient steppe cavalry tactics.

The Ming dynasty (C.E. 1368–1644) warriors made effective use of cannons and other firearms. They learned about firearm warfare from Vietnamese who opposed their brief occupation of Vietnam in the early fifteenth century C.E. Ming rulers subsequently hired Vietnamese instructors to teach Chinese soldiers at a new firearms training facility in Beijing. The Ming effectively used firearm warfare, combined with the rebuilt Great Wall, to defend China against steppe troops until the seventeenth century C.E.

The Song and Ming also developed effective battle fleets to engage in combat and patrol against pirates in the South China Sea. The Ming were able to make calculations about how many fighting forces were necessary, considering the weaponry necessary for battle success, and had the ability to deploy troops in smaller or larger numbers with the correct number of weapons. The West would not have similar battle efficiency until the eighteenth century C.E.

See also: Archeological Discoveries; China; Huns; India; Japan; Java; Mongols; Technology and Inventions.

FURTHER READING

Draeger, Donn F. *The Weapons and Fighting Arts of Indonesia*. Rutland, VT: Tuttle, 2001.

Friday, Karl F. *Samurai, Warfare, and the State in Early Medieval Japan*. New York: Routledge, 2004.

Graff, David A. *Medieval Chinese Warfare, 300–900*. New York: Routledge, 2002.

King, W. L. *Zen and the Way of the Sword*. New York: Oxford University Press, 1993.

Vietnam

Located on the southern border of China, country that has been a vital link between China and Southeast Asia since ancient times. The earliest Vietnamese rice culture developed in the Red River system of northern Vietnam and southern China and culminated in what is popularly called the Dongson culture (ca. 500 B.C.E.–C.E. 43). This culture, which was dominated by regional Sino-Vietnamese family clans, is known for its engraved bronze drums that were widely distributed through the South China Sea region.

A Chinese military victory in C.E. 43 established Vietnam as a government outpost under the Han dynasty (206 B.C.E.–C.E. 220). Chinese officials forced Vietnam's landholding elite to abandon their traditional matriarchal culture, which favored female leadership and inheritance, in favor of Chinese patriarchal family practices. Vietnam's Hanoi-centered civilization acquired a heavy overlay of Chinese culture, including Chinese written language and artistic, philosophical, and political forms.

A civilization that the Chinese called "Funan" emerged in the first century C.E. in the Mekong delta region of southern Vietnam. This civilization survived until the early sixth century C.E. Funan's development and eventual fall were tied to the activities of maritime traders who traveled between

India and China, making stopovers in Funan's ports. This trade reached its height after the fall of the Han dynasty in C.E. 220, but Funan's ports quickly declined after the route shifted south to the Strait of Melaka passage between Sumatra and the Malay Peninsula in the fifth century C.E.

By the sixth century C.E., the ports of the Cham civilization located along the central Vietnam coast (known collectively as Champa) took over Funan's position as the favored stopovers of merchants traveling between China and Java and the Strait of Malacca. The Cham realm included ports populated by multiethnic seagoing populations. Upstream rice farmers and highland tribesmen provided food and exotic jungle products to international traders. The Cham culture is noted for the impressive Hindu and Buddhist temples it built at Mi-son near modern-day Danang.

Northern Vietnam remained under Chinese sovereignty until the fall of the Tang dynasty (C.E. 907), when Vietnamese armies prevented the restoration of Chinese rule. Leaders of the newly independent Vietnam Ly state (C.E. 960–1225) partnered with China-trained Mahayana Buddhist monks to establish and administer new government institutions. Minor officials were chosen by examination for the first time in C.E. 1075, and a civil service training institute and an imperial academy were set up in C.E. 1076. In C.E. 1089, a fixed hierarchy of Buddhist and secular state officials was established, with nine degrees of civil and military scholar officials.

By the thirteenth century C.E., however, the Buddhist church had become a threat to Vietnamese secular leadership. Vietnam's Tran dynasty (C.E. 1225–1400), as well as the subsequent Le dynasty (C.E. 1428–1527), began to recruit newly trained Confucian scholars from among their Vietnamese landed aristocracy to replace Buddhist monks as state bureaucrats. Vietnam's emperors implemented their own version of the Chinese Confucian examination system. Unlike the Chinese exams, which were open to all qualified applicants, the Vietnamese system admitted only the sons of Vietnam's landed elite.

From the thirteenth to the fifteenth centuries C.E., the Vietnamese repelled repeated Chinese annexation attempts, as well as periodic raids by their Cham neighbors. The multiple wars between the Vietnamese and the Chams eventually resulted in the fall of Champa to victorious Vietnamese forces in C.E. 1471. The Vietnamese seized Champa's resources and carried off significant numbers of the Cham population as slaves to settle and develop new northern Vietnam rice lands. Shortly thereafter, in C.E. 1527, the Le state fragmented into regional courts ruled by rival factions of the royal family. As a result, Vietnam would lack effective central authority until 1800.

See also: China; Confucianism; Indian Ocean Trade; Khmer Empire; Mongols; Slavery.

FURTHER READING

Lieberman, Victor. *Strange Parallels: Southeast Asia in Global Context, c. 800–1830.* Cambridge: Cambridge University Press, 2003.
Taylor, Keith W. *The Birth of Vietnam.* Berkeley: University of California Press,

Zheng He (ca. C.E. 1371–1433)

Military commander and leader between C.E. 1405 and 1433 of seven major Chinese maritime expeditions into the Indian Ocean during the reign of the Ming dynasty (C.E. 1368–1644). Zheng He's expeditions asserted China's political, cultural, and commercial interests through Southeast Asia and beyond, to Arabia and the east coast of Africa.

Zheng He, from a Muslim family living in south China's Yunnan Province, was captured by Ming forces when he was 10 years old. He was trained to enter the Ming court's exclusive eunuch military guard. By the time he reached adulthood, he is said to have been 7 feet (2.1 m) tall and, with his booming voice, was a natural leader.

Zheng He rose to power as a military commander of the emperor Yongle (r. 1402–1424), who ordered Zheng He to build a fleet of ships to sail into the South China Sea region to project Chinese power there. His first voyage, which departed in C.E. 1405, consisted of 27,870 men (soldiers, scholars, scientists, and artisans) traveling on 317 ships, including supply ships and troop ships, some as large as 1,000 tons (910 m tons). After leaving the South China Sea region, Zheng He's fleet passed through the Strait of Melaka that separates the Malay Peninsula from Sumatra, and sailed west to Sri Lanka and to Calicut, on the southwestern India coast.

On this and subsequent voyages, the Ming fleet rarely intervened militarily in local affairs; the display of Zheng He's massive fleet of ships was sufficient to impress upon locals the power of the Chinese emperor. Zheng He's mission was to promote peace and to eliminate the regional piracy that threatened the flow of international luxury products (such as spices, rare woods, incense, ivory, and cotton) to China in exchange for China's silks, porcelain, and horses. He returned to the Ming court two years after his departure with diplomatic gifts, political hostages, and tribute collected from foreign rulers.

Zheng He was so successful that the emperor commissioned him to make six subsequent voyages. On his second (C.E. 1407–1409) and third voyages (C.E. 1409–1411), he returned to southern Asia, but on the fourth voyage (C.E. 1413–1415), he sailed beyond India to Hormuz (in Persia) on the Persian Gulf. On his fifth voyage (C.E. 1417–1419), he reached Aden on the Saudi Arabian Peninsula and several eastern African coast ports. Among the exotic commodities he brought back were two giraffes, which became the prized residents of a new court zoo at Beijing.

After the death of Emperor Yongle, the court of the new emperor, Xuande (r. 1425–1435), argued that Zheng He's voyages were overly expensive. Court officials also expressed concern that the voyages yielded advantages to the commercial classes, who might gain sufficient power to challenge the authority of the Confucian gentry. Also, in their view, China needed to shift its financial resources to build up its troop strength on its northern border to defend against a potential invasion from the steppes. After Zheng He's death in C.E. 1433, China's naval expeditions abruptly ended.

Today Zheng He is hailed by the Chinese. Because Zheng He was popularly deified after his death as a great hero of China's past, he is still portrayed in regional ancestral temple icons as a potential spirit who might be appealed to in hopes of resolving modern-day problems.

See also: China; Confucianism; Indian Ocean Trade; Melaka; *Pax Sinica*.

FURTHER READING

Levathes, Louise. *When China Ruled the Seas: The Treasure Fleet of the Dragon Throne, 1405–33.* New York: Simon and Schuster, 1994.

Ptak, Roderich. *China and the Asian Seas: Trade, Travel, and Visions of the Others (1400–1750).* Brookfield, VT: Ashgate, 1998.

Glossary

The following words and terms, including those in "The Historian's Tools," also appear in context in bold-face type throughout this volume.

The Historian's Tools
These terms and concepts are commonly used or referred to by historians and other researchers and writers to analyze the past.

cause-and-effect relationship A paradigm for understanding historical events where one result or condition is the direct consequence of a preceding event or condition

chronological thinking Developing a clear sense of historical time—past, present, and future

cultural history See history, cultural

economic history See history, economic

era A period of time usually marked by a characteristic circumstance or event

historical inquiry A methodical approach to historical understanding that involves asking a question, gathering information, exploring hypotheses, and establishing conclusions

historical interpretation and analysis An approach to studying history that involves applying a set of questions to a set of data in order to understand how things change over time

historical research An investigation into an era or event using primary sources (records made during the period in question) and secondary sources (information gathered after the period in question)

historical understanding Knowledge of a moment, person, event, or pattern in history that links that information to a larger context

history, cultural An analysis of history in terms of a people's culture, or way of life, including investigating patterns of human work and thought

history, economic An analysis of history in terms of the production, distribution, and consumption of goods

history, political An analysis of history in terms of the methods used to govern a group of people

history, social An analysis of history in terms of the personal relationships between people and groups

history of science and technology Study of the evolution of scientific discoveries and technological advancements

patterns of continuity and change A paradigm for understanding historical events in terms of institutions, culture, or other social behavior that either remain constant or show marked differences over time

periodization Dividing history into distinct eras

political history See history, political

radiocarbon dating A test for determining the approximate age of an object or artifact by measuring the number of carbon 14 atoms in that object

social history See history, social

Key Terms Found in A to Z Entries

absolutism The exercise of complete and unrestricted power by a ruler or government

agrarian Related to agriculture or farming

alluvial Associated with sediment deposited by rivers in flood plains or deltas

annex To incorporate or make part of

animism General belief that everything possesses a soul or a spirit

antiquity The ancient past, particularly referring to the history of the Western world before the fall of the Roman Empire in C.E. 476

archeologist A scientist who studies prehistoric people and their culture

archipelago A group of islands

aristocracy The nobility or ruling class in a society

aristocratic In a society, belonging to the nobility or the ruling class, whose wealth is generally based on land and whose power is passed on from one generation to another

artifact In archeology, any material object made by humans, especially a tool, weapon, or ornament; archeologists study artifacts of ancient cultures to try to learn more about them

artisan A skilled craftsperson or worker who practices a trade or handicraft

assimilate To conform or adjust to the customs or attitudes of a group or society

autonomous Independent; self-governing

Bronze Age Historical period marked by introduction of bronze for tools and weapons

celestial Relating to heaven or the divine

city-state A city and the area immediately around it

cosmology One's beliefs about the nature and structure of the universe

courtier Person who attends a sovereign at a royal court

deified Worshiped as a god

doctrine A set of principles presented for acceptance or belief, such as by a religious, political, or philosophical group

dynasty Succession of rulers, usually from several generations, from the same line or family

egalitarian Characterized by social equality

equinox Literally "equal night"; an astronomical term referring to the two days each year in which daylight and darkness are approximately equal; usually March 21 (spring equinox) and September 21 (autumnal equinox)

excavate To dig out of the earth; uncover

hereditary Passed from one generation to another

hierarchical Describing an organization, especially of persons, that ranks people by authority or importance; societies that are hierarchical have distinct social classes, some of which are considered to be superior to others

hierarchy Ranking by authority or importance

humanoid Creature possessing human characteristics

Ice Age An extended period of extremely low temperatures; there have been many ice ages in the history of the earth

icon A religious image or portrait

iconography The use of pictorial images to represent gods or divinities indigenous Native to a particular place

inscription Writing carved or engraved on a surface such as a coin, tablet, or stone monument

Iron Age Historical period, following the Bronze Age, and marked by the introduction of ironworking technology

maritime Relating to the ocean or ocean travel

matriarchal A type of society ruled by female leaders

matrilineal Tracing of descent through the mother

monarch A hereditary sovereign or ruler

monarchy Form of government in which power is in the hands of a hereditary ruler

monotheism Belief in a single deity

Neolithic Period Also known as the New Stone Age, an interval in human culture from about 10,000 to 3000 B.C.E., starting with the introduction of agriculture and ending with the introduction of the first metal implements and weapons

nomads People who travel seasonally to follow sources of food

pantheon All the gods of a particular people, or, a temple dedicated to all the gods of a particular people

pastoral Characterized by a rural life; peaceful, simple, and natural

patriarchal A type of society ruled by male leaders, where men typically possess sole religious, political, and domestic authority

patrilineal Tracing descent through the father

patron One who supports or sponsors a person or activity

pictograph A pictorial representation of a word or idea

polytheism Worship of a number of deities, often representations of natural forces, such as the rain or the wind

relief A type of sculpture in which partially raised figures project from a flat background, giving the appearance of dimension

Sanskrit Indo-European tongue that is the language of Indian religion and classical literature

secular Related to worldly things, as opposed to religion and a church

seminomadic People who travel seasonally to follow sources of food but also practice limited agriculture

shaman Human intermediary between the natural and supernatural worlds

solstice The longest (summer solstice, June 21) and shortest (winter solstice, December 21) days of the year

staple Basic or necessary item of food

stratification Division into different levels or orders based on rank

textiles Items made of cloth or fabric, or the fibers used to weave a fabric

theocracy Form of government in which power is held by a priestly class

tribute Payment from one nation or group to another as a sign of respect or to acknowledge submission

urbanization The growth and development of cities

vassal A person who owes loyalty or service to a more powerful individual in a social system or context

Selected Bibliography

Abu-Lughod, Janet. *Before European Hegemony: The World System 1250–1350*. New York: Oxford University Press, 1991.

Andaya, Barbara Watson, and Leonard Y. Andaya. *A History of Malaysia*. Honolulu: University of Hawaii Press, 2001.

"Asian History Timeline." http://www.asianinfo. org/asianinfo/history/history_timeline.htm. Accessed 31 May 2007.

"Asian Studies Resources." http://asia.rice.edu/ resources.cfm. Accessed 31 May 2007.

Attwood, Bain. *Telling the Truth About Aboriginal History*. Crows Nest, Australia: Allen and Unwin, 2005.

Basham, A.L. *Cultural History of India*. New York: Oxford University Press, 1999.

———. *The Wonder That Was India*. New York: Grove Press, 1959.

Belich, James. *Making Peoples: A History of New Zealanders from Polynesian Settlement to the End of the Nineteenth Century*. Honolulu: University of Hawaii Press, 1996.

Bellwood, Peter S. *Conquest of the Pacific: The Prehistory of Southeast Asia and Oceana*. Oxford: Oxford University Press, 1979.

———. *First Farmers: The Origins of Agricultural Societies*. Malden, MA: Blackwell, 2005.

———. *Polynesians: Prehistory of an Island People*. London: Thames and Hudson, 1987.

———. *Prehistory of the Indo-Malaysian Archipelago*. Orlando, FL: Academic Press, 1985.

Benton, Michael J., et al. *The Age of Dinosaurs in Russia and Mongolia*. Cambridge: Cambridge University Press, 2003.

Blainey, Geoffrey. *Triumph of the Nomads: A History of Aboriginal Australia*. Woodstock, NY: Overlook, 1976.

Blusse, Leonard, and Natalie Everts, eds. *The Formosan Encounter: Notes on Formosa's Aboriginal Society*. 2 vols. Taipei: Shung Ye Museum of Formosan Aborigines, 2000.

Boulnois, Luce. *Silk Road: Monks, Warriors, and Merchants*. Translated by Helen Loveday. New York: Norton (for Odyssey Publications, Hong Kong), 2006.

Bowker, John, ed. *World Religions: The Great Faiths Explored and Explained*. London and New York: DK, 1997.

Brook, Timothy. *The Chinese State in Ming Society*. New York: RoutledgeCurzon, 2005.

Chandler, David P. *A History of Cambodia*. Boulder, CO: Westview Press, 2000.

Chang, Chun-shu. *The Rise of the Chinese Empire: Frontier, Immigration, and Empire in Han China, 129 B.C.–A.D. 107*. Ann Arbor: University of Michigan Press, 2006.

Chapuis, Oscar. *A History of Vietnam: From Hong Bang to Tu Duc*. Westport, CT: Greenwood Press, 1995.

Chase, Kenneth. *Firearms: A Global History to 1700*. Cambridge: Cambridge University Press, 2003.

Chow, Kai-Wing. *Publishing Culture and Power in Early Modern China*. Palo Alto, CA: Stanford University Press, 2004.

Cleary, Thomas. *Practical Taoism*. Boston: Shambhala, 1996.

Coe, Michael D. *Angkor and the Khmer Civilization*. London: Thames and Hudson, 2005.

Cohn, Bernard S. *India: The Social Anthropology of a Civilization.* Englewood Cliffs, NJ: Prentice Hall, 1971.

Craven, Roy C. *Indian Art.* London: Thames and Hudson, 1997.

Creese, Helen. *Women of the Kakawin World: Marriage and Sexuality in the Indic Courts of Java and Bali.* Armonk, NY: Sharpe, 2004.

Curtin, Philip D. *Cross-Cultural Trade in World History.* Cambridge: Cambridge University Press, 1984.

Davis, Edward L. *Society and the Supernatural in Song China.* Honolulu: University of Hawaii Press, 2001.

De Bary, William Theodore, et al., eds. *Sources of Japanese Tradition.* Vol. 1. New York: Columbia University Press, 2001.

De Bary, William Theodore, and Irene Bloom, compilers. *Sources of Chinese Tradition.* 2nd ed. New York: Columbia University Press, 1999.

DeSilva, K.M. *A History of Sri Lanka.* New York: Penguin Books, 2005.

Di Cosmo, Nicola. *Ancient China and its Enemies: The Rise of Nomadic Power in East Asian History.* Cambridge: Cambridge University Press, 2004.

———. *Warfare in Inner Asian History: 500–1800.* Boston: Brill, 2001.

Draeger, Donn F. *The Weapons and Fighting Arts of Indonesia.* Rutland, VT: Tuttle, 2001.

Dulby, Andrew. *Dangerous Tastes: The Story of Spices.* Berkeley: University of California Press, 2002.

Duus, Peter. *Feudalism in Japan.* New York: McGraw Hill, 1993.

Eaton, Richard M., ed. *India's Islamic Tradition, 711–1750.* New Delhi, India: Oxford University Press, 2003.

Ebrey, Patricia Buckley. *China: A Cultural, Social, and Political History.* Boston: Houghton Mifflin, 2006.

———. *Confucian and Family Ritual in Imperial China.* Princeton, NJ: Princeton University Press, 1992.

Ebrey, Patricia Buckley, and Peter N. Gregory, eds. *Religion and Society in Tang and Sung China.* Honolulu: University of Hawaii Press, 1993.

Eckert, Carter J., et al. *Korea Old and New.* Cambridge, MA: Harvard University Press, 1990.

Edstrom, Bert. *Turning Points in Japanese History.* London: Routledge, 2002.

Ellwood, Robert S., and Richard Pilgrim. *Japanese Religion: A Cultural Perspective.* Englewood Cliffs, NJ: Prentice Hall, 1984.

Elman, B. *A Cultural History of Civil Examinations in Late Imperial China.* Berkeley: University of California Press, 2000.

Embree, Ainslee, ed. *Sources of Indian Tradition.* 2nd ed. New York: Columbia University Press, 1988.

Friday, Karl F. *Samurai, Warfare, and the State in Early Medieval Japan.* New York: Routledge, 2004.

Gilbert, Erik, and Jonathan Reynolds. *Trading Tastes, Commodities, and Cultural Exchange to 1750.* Upper Saddle River, NJ: Pearson Prentice Hall, 2006.

Gombrich, Richard F. *How Buddhism Began: The Conditioned Genesis of the Early Teachings.* London: Routledge, 2006.

Graff, David A. *Medieval Chinese Warfare, 300–900.* New York: Routledge, 2002.

Grousset, Rene. *The Empire of the Steppes: A History of Central Asia.* New Brunswick, NJ: Rutgers University Press, 1988.

Hall, Kenneth R. *Maritime Trade and State Development in Early Southeast Asia.* Honolulu: University of Hawaii Press, 1985.

Halpern, Charles. *Russia and the Golden Horde: The Mongol Impact on Medieval Russian History.* Bloomington: Indiana University Press, 1987.

Hardy, Grant, and Anne Behnke Kinney. *The Establishment of the Han Empire and Imperial China.* Westport, CT: Greenwood, 2005.

Higham, Charles. *Archeology of Mainland Southeast Asia.* Cambridge: Cambridge University Press, 1989.

———. *Civilization of Angkor.* Berkeley: University of California Press, 2002.

Hildinger, Erik. *Warriors of the Steppe: A Military History of Central Asia, 500 B.C. to A.D. 1700.* New York: DaCapo Press, 2001.

Holcombe, C. *The Genesis of East Asia, 221 B.C. to A.D. 907.* Honolulu: University of Hawaii Press, 2001.

Hooker, Virginia Matheson, *A Short History of Malaysia.* Sydney, Australia: Allen and Unwin, 2003.

Hucker, Charles O. *China's Imperial Past: An Introduction to Chinese History and Culture.* Palo Alto, CA: Stanford University Press, 1994.

Imamura, Keiji. *Prehistoric Japan: New Perspective on Insular East Asia.* Honolulu: University of Hawaii Press, 1996.

Inden, Ronald B. *Imagining India.* Cambridge, MA: Blackwell, 1990.

Irwin, Geoffrey. *The Prehistoric Exploration and Colonization of the Pacific.* Cambridge: Cambridge University Press, 1994.

Jackson, William. *Vijayanagara Voices: Exploring South Indian History and Hindu Literature.* Aldershot, UK: Ashgate, 2005.

Jansen, Marius B. *The Emergence of Meiji Japan.* Cambridge: Cambridge University Press, 2006.

———. *Warrior Rule in Japan.* Cambridge: Cambridge University Press, 2004.

"Japanese History Resources." http://www.snowcrest.net/jmike/japan.html. Accessed 8 Mar 2007.

Juneja, Monica. *Architecture in Medieval India: Forms, Contexts, Histories.* Andhra Pradesh, India: Orient Longman, 2001.

Kahn, Paul, and Francis Woodman. *Secret History of the Mongols. The Origin of Chingis Khan.* Boston: Cheng and Tsui, 1998.

Kasulis, Thomas P. *Shinto.* Honolulu: University of Hawaii Press, 2005.

Keay, John, *India: A History.* New York: Grove Press, 2000.

Kennedy, A.R., and G.L. Possehl, *Studies in the Archeology and Paleo-Anthropology of South Asia.* New Delhi, India: Oxford University Press, 1984.

Kim, D.K. *The History of Korea.* Westport, CT: Greenwood Press, 2005.

Kinney, Ann R. *Worshipping Siva and Buddha: The Temple Art of East Java.* Honolulu: University of Hawaii Press, 2003.

Kirkland, Russell. *Taoism: The Enduring Tradition.* London: Routledge, 2004.

Klostermeier, Klaus K. *A Survey of Hinduism.* 2nd ed. Albany: State University of New York Press, 1994.

Kohn, Livia. *Daoism and Chinese Culture.* Cambridge, MA: Three Pines Press, 2001.

Kulke, Hermann, and Dietmar Rothermund. *A History of India.* London: Routledge, 1998.

Kutcher, Norman. *Mourning in Late Imperial China: Filial Piety and the State.* Cambridge: Cambridge University Press, 1999.

Lee, Ki-Baik, et al. *A New History of Korea.* Cambridge, MA: Harvard University Press, 2005.

Lee, Peter H., Yongho Ch'oe, and Hugh H.W. Kang. *Sources of Korean Tradition.* New York: Columbia University Press, 1996.

Levathes, Louise. *When China Ruled the Seas: The Treasure Fleet of the Dragon Throne, 1405–33.* New York: Simon and Schuster, 1994.

Lieberman, Victor. *Strange Parallels: Southeast Asia in Global Context, c. 800–1830.* Cambridge: Cambridge University Press, 2003.

Lipner, J.J. *Hindus.* New York: Routledge, 1993.

Lopez, Donald S., Jr. *The Story of Buddhism: A Concise Guide to its History and Teachings.* New York: HarperCollins, 2001.

Ludden, David, ed. *Agricultural Production and South Asian History.* New York: Oxford University Press, 2005.

Mair, V., ed. *Columbia History of Chinese Literature.* New York: Columbia University Press, 2002.

Mann, S., and Y. Chang. *Under Confucian Eyes: Writings on Gender in Chinese History.* Berkeley: University of California Press, 2001.

Mason, Colin. *A Short History of Asia: Stone Age to 2000 A.D.* London: Palgrave Macmillan, 2000.

Mason, Penelope. *History of Japanese Art.* Upper Saddle River, NJ: Pearson Education, 2005.

McCurry, Steve. *Monsoon.* London: Thames and Hudson, 1997.

Michaels, Axel. *Hinduism.* Translated by Barbara Harshav. Princeton, NJ: Princeton University Press, 2003.

Miyazaki, Ichisada. *China's Examination Hell: Civil Service Exams of Imperial China.* Translated by Conrad Schirokauer. New Haven, CT: Yale University Press, 1981.

Morgan, K.W. *Reaching for the Moon: Asian Religious Paths.* Chambersburg, PA: Anima, 1991.

Morrison, Kathleen D., and Laura L. Junker, eds. *Forager-Traders in South and Southeast Asia.* Cambridge, MA: Cambridge University Press, 2002.

Morton, W. Scott, et al. *Japan: Its History and Culture.* New York: McGraw-Hill, 2004.

Mulvaney, John, and Johan Kamminga. *Prehistory of Australia.* Washington, DC: Smithsonian Institution Press, 1999.

Murphey, Rhoads. *A History of Asia.* 5th ed. New York: Longman, 2005.

Needham, J. *Science in Traditional China.* Cambridge, MA: Harvard University Press, 1981.

Nelson, John K. *A Year in the Life of a Shinto Shrine.* Seattle: University of Washington Press, 1996.

Nilakanta Sastri, K.A. *A History of South India.* Madras, India: Oxford University Press, 1972.

Nile, Richard. *Australian Aborigines.* New York: Steck-Vaughn, 1993.

Ortner, Jon, Ian W. Mabbett, et al. *Angkor: Celestial Temples of the Khmer.* New York: Abbeville Press, 2002.

Pai, H. *Constructing Korean Origins.* Cambridge, MA: Harvard University Press, 2000.

Peebles, Patrick. *The History of Sri Lanka.* Westport, CT: Greenwood Press, 2006.

Quanchi, Max, and Ron Adams. *Cultural Contact in the Pacific*. Cambridge: Cambridge University Press, 1993.

Rahman, A. *Development of Philosophy, Science, and Technology in India and Neighboring Civilizations*. New Delhi, India: Oxford University Press, 1999.

Ratchnevsky, Paul. *Genghis Khan: His Life and Legacy*. Translated and edited by Thomas Nivison Haining. Oxford: Basil Blackwell, 1992.

Ricklefs, M.C. *Mystic Synthesis in Java: A History of Islamization from the Fourteenth to the Early Nineteenth Centuries*. Norwalk, CT: EastBridge Press, 2006.

Risso, Patricia. *Merchants and Faith: Muslim Commerce and Culture in the Indian Ocean*. Boulder, CO: Westview Press, 1995.

Roberts, J.M. *Prehistory and the First Civilizations*. New York: Oxford University Press, 2002.

Robinson, R.H., and W.L. Johnson. *The Buddhist Religion*. Belmont, CA: Wadsworth, 1988.

Rossabi, Morris. *Khubilai Khan: His Life and Times*. Berkeley: University of California Press, 1988.

Saunders, J.J. *History of the Mongol Conquests*. Philadelphia: University of Pennsylvania Press, 2001.

Schirokauer, Conrad, David Lurie, and Suzanne Gay. *A Brief History of Japanese Civilization*. Boston: Wadsworth, 2005.

Schwartz, Benjamin I. *World of Thought in Ancient China*. Cambridge, MA: Harvard University Press, 1985.

Sen, Tansen. *Buddhism, Diplomacy, and Trade: The Realignment of Sino-Indian Relations, 600–1400*. Honolulu: University of Hawaii Press, 2003.

Skrine, Bennett, and Edward Denison Ross. *The Heart of Asia: A History of Russian Turkestan and the Central Asian Khanates from the Earliest Times*. Boston: Adamant, 2001.

Smith, Frederick M. *The Self Possessed: Deity and Spirit Possession in South Asian Literature and Civilization*. New York: Columbia University Press, 2006.

Smith, W. Ramsay. *Myths and Legends of the Australian Aborigines*. Mineola, NY: Dover, 2003.

Snellgrove, David. *Angkor: Before and After: Cultural History of the Khmers*. Boston: Weatherhill, 2004.

Soucek, Svatopluk. *A History of Inner Asia*. New York: Cambridge University Press, 2001.

Stanley-Baker, Joan. *Japanese Art*. London: Thames and Hudson, 2000.

Thompson, E.A. *The Huns*. Cambridge, MA: Blackwell, 1999.

Torday, Laszlo. *Mounted Archers: The Beginnings of Central Asian History*. Durham, NC: Durham Academic Press, 1998.

Van Bremen, Jan. *Asian Anthropology*. New York: Routledge, 2005.

Varley, H. Paul. *Japanese Culture*. Honolulu: University of Hawaii Press, 2000.

Wang, Bin. *The Asian Monsoon*. New York: Springer-Praxis, 2006.

Wolpert, Stanley. *A New History of India*. New York: Oxford University Press, 2005.

Wood, Frances. *The Silk Road: Two Thousand Years in the Heart of Asia*. Berkeley: University of California Press, 2004.

Wyatt, David. *Thailand: A Short History*. New Haven, CT: Yale University Press, 1984.

Yang, Xiaoneng. *New Perspectives on China's Past*. New Haven, CT: Yale University Press, 2004.

Index

Date Due

Ancient World Time Line

AFRICA	NEAR EAST AND SOUTHWEST ASIA
ca. 800 B.C.E. Egyptians use sundial	**ca. 700–500 B.C.E.** Prophet Zarathushtra founds Zoroastrian faith in Persia (modern-day Iran)
ca. 715–322 B.C.E. Late Period; Egypt suffers repeated attacks from Assyrians	**ca. 612–539 B.C.E.** Second Assyrian Empire ends; Neo-Babylonian Empire dominates Mesopotamia
ca. 700 B.C.E. Egyptians invent demotic	**ca. 586–538 B.C.E.** Babylonian Exile of the Jews
ca. 650 B.C.E. Kushites forced out of Egypt	**ca. 559–530 B.C.E.** Cyrus the Great unites Persians and founds first Persian Empire
ca. 575 B.C.E. Carthage, on North African coast, becomes center of Phoenician empire	**ca. 525 B.C.E.** Cambyses III adds Egypt to Persian Empire
ca. 525 B.C.E. Persia conquers Egypt	**ca. 500–479 B.C.E.** Persian Wars, pitting Persia against Greek city-states led by Athens; end in Greek victory
ca. 380–343 B.C.E. Egyptians overthrow Persian rule known as Thirtieth dynasty	**ca. 334–332 B.C.E.** Alexander the Great invades Persia
ca. 332 B.C.E. Alexandria founded by conqueror Alexander III, the Great	**ca. 330 B.C.E.** Alexander the Great defeats Persian king Darius III and declares himself king of Persia
ca. 332 B.C.E.– C.E.95 Greco-Roman Period; Egypt ruled by Greece until 30 B.C.E.	**ca. 323 B.C.E.** Seleuciud Empire begins and rules dwindling ancient Persia
ca. 323 B.C.E. Alexander III, the Great, dies	**ca. 165 B.C.E.** Revolt of the Maccabees establishes kingdom of Judah
ca. 264–146 B.C.E. Punic Wars between Carthage and Rome; Carthage defeated	**ca. 4 B.C.E.** Jesus of Nazareth born
ca. 218 B.C.E. Carthaginian Hannibal crosses Alps to attack Rome, beginning Second Punic War; defeats Rome 216 B.C.E.	**ca. C.E. 27** Jesus begins his ministry
ca. 203 B.C.E. Hannibal defeated; 183 B.C.E. Hannibal commits suicide to escape Romans	**ca. C.E. 30** Jesus crucified by Romans in Jerusalem
ca. 149 B.C.E. Romans attack Carthage, initiating Third Punic War	**C.E. 100–200** Christianity spreads throughout Judea and Asia Minor
ca. 31 B.C.E. Alexandria conquered by Roman forces after battle of Actium	**ca. C.E. 135** Romans expel Jews, the Diaspora
ca. 30 B.C.E. Death of Cleopatra, the last of the Ptolemaic rulers of Egypt	**ca. C.E. 622** Preaching Islam, Muhammad leaves Mecca for Yathrib, marking start of Islamic calendar
ca. C.E. 300 Last use of hieroglyphic writing; earliest known inscription written in Ge'ez, a language now used in Ethiopia	**ca. C.E. 632** Death of Muhammad; Arabian Peninsula under Islamic rule
ca. C.E. 324 Axum king Ezana makes Ethiopia first Christian state in world	**ca. C.E. 661–750** Umayyad Dynasty expands Arab territory throughout Southwest Asia into North Africa, India, and Iberia (modern-day Spain and Portugal)
ca. C.E. 350 Collapse of Kushite kingdom	**ca. C.E. 750–1258** Abbasid dynasty rules Islamic Empire
ca. C.E. 622 Romans reconquer Alexandria	**ca. C.E. 1100** Islam spreads to Indonesia
ca. C.E. 639 Arabs conquer Egypt	**ca. C.E. 1054** Great Schism; Christianity splits between Roman Catholic Church in the west and Greek Orthodox Church in the east
ca. C.E. 642 Arabs conquer Alexandria	
ca. C.E. 700 Ghana (once Awkar) emerges as great trading state; Arab merchants introduce Muslim beliefs to African states	
ca. C.E. 1000 Conflicts arise between Christians and Muslims	